ARAGON
ISSUES IN
PHILOSOPHY

PARAGON ISSUES IN PHILOSOPHY

FORTHCOMING TITLES

THE PARAGON ISSUES
IN PHILOSOPHY SERIES

At colleges and universities, interest in the traditional areas of philosophy remains strong. Many new currents flow within them, too, but some of these—the rise of cognitive science, for example, or feminist philosophy—went largely unnoticed in undergraduate philosophy courses until the end of the 1980s. The Paragon Issues in Philosophy Series responds to both perennial and newly influential concerns by bringing together a team of able philosophers to address the fundamental issues in philosophy today and to outline the state of contemporary discussion about them.

More than twenty volumes are scheduled; they are organized into three major categories. The first covers the standard topics—metaphysics, theory of knowledge, ethics, and political philosophy—stressing innovative developments in those disciplines. The second focuses on more specialized but still vital concerns in the philosophies of science, religion, history, sport, and other areas. The third category explores new work that relates philosophy and fields such as feminist criticism, medicine, economics, technology, and literature.

The level of writing is aimed at undergraduate students who have little previous experience studying philosophy. The books provide brief but accurate introductions that appraise the state of the art in their fields and show how the history of thought about their topics developed. Each volume is complete in itself but also complements others in the series.

Traumatic change characterizes these last years of the twentieth century: all of it involves philosophical issues. The editorial staff at Paragon House has worked with us to develop this series. We hope it will encourage the understanding needed in our times, which are as complicated and problematic as they are promising.

John K. Roth
Claremont McKenna College

Frederick Sontag
Pomona College

CRITICAL THEORY
AND
PHILOSOPHY

ALSO BY DAVID INGRAM

Habermas and the Dialectic of Reason,
1987

Critical Theory: The Essential Readings
(with Julia Simon-Ingram)
1990

DAVID INGRAM

LOYOLA UNIVERSITY OF CHICAGO
CHICAGO, ILLINOIS

CRITICAL THEORY AND PHILOSOPHY

PARAGON
ISSUES IN
PHILOSOPHY

PARAGON HOUSE · NEW YORK

FIRST EDITION, 1990

PUBLISHED IN THE UNITED STATES BY

PARAGON HOUSE
90 FIFTH AVENUE
NEW YORK, NY 10011

COPYRIGHT © 1990 BY PARAGON HOUSE

SERIES DESIGN BY KATHY KIKKERT

LIBRARY OF CONGRESS CATALOGING-IN-PUBLICATION DATA
INGRAM, DAVID, 1952–
    CRITICAL THEORY AND PHILOSOPHY / BY DAVID INGRAM. — 1ST ED.
        P.   CM.
    ISBN 1-55778-201-6
    1. CRITICAL THEORY.   I. TITLE.
    BD175.I54   1990
    142—DC20   90-30043
                                                         CIP

THE PAPER USED IN THIS PUBLICATION MEETS THE MINIMUM
REQUIREMENTS OF AMERICAN NATIONAL STANDARD FOR
INFORMATION SCIENCES—PERMANENCE OF PAPER FOR PRINTED
LIBRARY MATERIALS, ANSIZ39.48-1984.

MANUFACTURED IN THE UNITED STATES OF AMERICA

10 9 8 7 6 5 4 3 2 1

IN MEMORY OF
HERBERT MARCUSE AND ERICA SHEROVER-MARCUSE

*The function of education is to teach one
to think intensively and to think critically.*
—Dr. Martin Luther King, Jr.

CONTENTS

ACKNOWLEDGMENTS

I am deeply indebted to my colleagues in the administration and philosophy department for their kind support and interest in the project. Research for this project would not have been possible without a summer grant from Loyola. Thanks are also owed to Don Fehr of Paragon House and Fred Sontag and John Roth for their help in editing and preparing the manuscript, and to the anonymous readers who provided critical feedback during early revisions of the book. I am especially indebted to Herbert Marcuse and Erica Sherover-Marcuse for kindling my interest in critical theory. Their friendship and learned advice will not be forgotten. Above all, I am grateful to Julia Simon-Ingram for her careful readings of earlier drafts of the book. Her constructive criticism was a major ingredient in its revision. Last but not least, I would like to thank my students for making it all worthwhile.

PREFACE

Critical Theory and Philosophy is intended to provide an accessible introduction to some of the major figures and themes of the Frankfurt School. It is primarily directed toward undergraduate and graduate students who have little or no familiarity with the German philosophical tradition informing its heritage. At the same time, it presents a coherent argument that will no doubt be of interest to those already conversant with this tradition. Since it is virtually impossible to pick up any text by a critical theorist which does not refer to this tradition in either its use of technical terminology or its citation of specific sources, I have found it advisable to discuss it at great length. In general, more background on Kant, Hegel, Marx, and Weber has been provided here than would otherwise be necessary for a less elementary text.

Critical Theory and Philosophy satisfies two important needs. First, it provides the historical background necessary for understanding the specific social and political issues of concern to critical theorists. Accordingly, the book is structured in such a way as to give the reader some sense of the history of critical theory from its earliest inception in the writings of Kant, Hegel, and Marx to its most recent encounter with poststructuralism, postmodernism, and feminism. Second, it provides a logical sequence for relating specific social and political concerns to progressively deeper layers of philosophical reflection. A brief introduction provides a general framework for understanding critical theory as a unique form of social philosophy grounded in history and social science. The problems raised here concerning the relationship between theory and practice, the critique of ideology, the concept of reason, and the ideas of freedom, justice, and democracy are developed in later chapters. Chapters two through four discuss ideology and other symptoms of social malaise addressed by critical theorists. Concrete analyses of specific types of linguistic and social behavior are illustrated here by specific examples. Chapters five through seven relate these analyses to the methodological and philosophical underpinnings of critical theory. The final chapter and the postscript round out the discussion by evaluating the status of recent critical theory with respect to first-generation critical theory (looking back) and poststructuralism, postmodernism, and feminism (looking ahead). The issues treated here are more difficult and abstract, for they concern questions of method (causal explanation versus understanding of meaning) and questions of ultimate grounding (conceptual difficulties implicit in ideology critique, and the transcendental/contextual status of reason itself). The aim is to prepare the student in advance for these philosophical discussions by first examining specific social problems and then addressing the presuppositions underlying their possible conceptualization, explanation, and critical evaluation.

An introductory book of this nature has to be extremely selective in its choice of subject matter. For the sake of brevity, I have chosen to focus primarily on what are unquestionably the four major representatives of critical theory: Theodor Adorno, Max Horkheimer, Herbert Marcuse, and Jürgen Habermas. Here, too, I have restricted my discussion to major texts. My reason for doing so is pedagogical. The texts on which I have chosen to comment are those which are most representative of critical theory and, in some cases, most accessible to a general audience. The extensive inclusion of Marcuse's work on Freud and technology seemed appropriate since these texts are among critical theory's clearest contributions to these important topics. By contrast, less discussion was devoted to Adorno's work even though it represents what is arguably critical theory's most original and subtle analysis of rationality and philosophy. In this case, the difficulties his texts pose for even the most seasoned scholar recommended against a fuller treatment of his philosophy. On the other extreme, I have discussed Habermas's thought at great length. Aside from reflecting a personal bias, this decision can be justified on the grounds that his thought represents the ripest manifestation of the various tensions animating critical theory. His treatment of the theory/ practice problem as well as the dialectic of enlightenment harks back to his predecessors while looking ahead to contemporary challenges to critical theory posed by poststructuralism, postmodernism, and feminism.

Critical Theory and Philosophy thus provides an excellent accompaniment to those texts which would likely be taught at the undergraduate level. A companion anthology *Critical Theory: The Essential Readings*, also available from Paragon House, contains selections from many of the key works discussed in the book.

While I have sought throughout to emphasize the overall continuity of Adorno's, Horkheimer's, Marcuse's, and Habermas's respective philosophies with respect to subject matter and general orientation, I have also indicated their often considerable divergence from one another. The pedagogical aim of *Critical Theory and Philosophy* sometimes required simplifying these differences. In some cases, the desire to maintain narrative coherency required considerable flattening out of the dialectical tensions and, in some cases, deliberate contradictions, implicit within the corpus of a single writer. Whether simplification in these instances resulted in distorting the views being discussed is a matter that can be decided only by the informed reader. The danger of oversimplification is most obvious in the case of Adorno. Adorno's prose, especially his writing after 1950, is so dense and convoluted (not to mention deliberately paradoxical) as to make his thought virtually inaccessible to any newcomer to critical theory. Taking into account the almost impossible task of rendering his prose in readable English, it is not surprising that much of the subtlety and irony of his thought will be lost in an introductory survey of the sort undertaken here. For this reason, I strongly encourage the reader to supplement his or her reading of *Critical Theory and Philosophy* by referring to more detailed commentaries listed in the bibliographical sections located at the end of each chapter. In the final analysis, of course, commentaries are no substitute for reading the original texts.

Finally, while I have tried to provide concise definitions of technical terms in the main body of the text, the terms discussed are, in some cases, too overdetermined by the constellations of social phenomena to which they refer. For this reason, I have also included a glossary at the end of the book which provides further explanation of these terms. I have also appended short biographical profiles of the major figures discussed in the book.

INTRODUCTION

Critical theory offers a distinctive approach to understanding the social and political life of modern societies. Not all social and political theories are critical; in fact, most are not. In contrast to critical theory, their primary aim is to provide the truest description and explanation of social and political events. Scientists working in these fields collect factual data by means of observations and question-and-answer surveys. These are then used to classify the memberships and corresponding attitudes of particular groups. They also yield statistical information about general behavioral patterns and probabilities which can be used to explain why a given event was or is to be expected. This knowledge is valued by those who seek to control or influence the behavior of others. For by changing one variable in a social pattern (e.g., the amount of available currency in a society), one can alter other variables—the rates of inflation, interest, investment, and overall consumption.

CRITICAL THEORY AS SOCIAL PHILOSOPHY

Unlike descriptive and explanatory theories, critical theories are chiefly concerned with evaluating the justice and happiness of societies. In this respect they are more akin to philosophy than science. Philosophy, as it is traditionally conceived, involves reflecting on the essential meaning of life and the subordinate activities and terms under which it is carried on. The essential means the most basic, the most necessary, and/or the most universal features of some activity or thing. It is what defines something in its innermost identity, relating it to things that are like it and distinguishing it from things that are not. Although this defining activity is similar to the social and political scientist's penchant for constructing classifications, it involves considerably more than the mere description of reality; it prescribes a norm or ideal to which the activity or thing being defined must conform in order for it to be truly what it is. Therefore, the definitions sought by philosophers have a critical edge.

The following examples illustrate this difference. Take the concept *human being*. For physiologists, the attribution of humanity is a cut-and-dried matter. Either one possesses the requisite chromosomes or one does not. Lack of possession is not in itself cause for critical evaluation. For philosophers, on the contrary, humanity is more complicated. In everday parlance the word is closely related to evaluative terms such as "humane" and "inhumane." Philosophers may disagree about the peculiar attributes which make up humanity—rationality, ensoulment, consciousness of self, and possession of a meaningful world are some of the more popular ones that have been offered— but most would acknowledge its normative status. For them, humanity consists of *potentials* that *ought to be* realized. As potentials whose *ideal* fulfillment depends on human agency, humanity may be developed or stunted, affirmed or denied. Thus, one can criticize particular persons and the social and political institutions which "shape" them for frustrating or violating their basic humanity.

We can further illustrate this difference with respect to social and political philosophy proper. Social and political science cannot avoid using general classificatory concepts such as "democracy" or "socialism" in describing the actual workings of particular institutions. Scientific "objectivity" requires using these terms in ways that are "value neutral." Nevertheless, most social and political scientists agree that it is virtually impossible to eliminate all evaluation from the descriptive use of classificatory concepts. What counts as democracy or socialism will depend on what features are preselected as "essential." Is freedom of speech the most essential feature of democracy, popular elections of officials, or multiparty competition for positions of power? Is government-managed economy, the provision of social-welfare services, or popular democratic control over the production and distribution of goods the defining feature of socialism?

Notwithstanding the role that subjective preferences and values play in defining the essential features of classificatory concepts like these, social and political scientists insist that their application of such concepts is intended solely for descriptive purposes—to highlight certain aspects of complex social phenomena over others. For most social and political scientists, the mere fact that popular elections exist in which some officials are chosen, some political opposition sanctioned, and some freedom of speech tolerated, suffices to establish the democratic nature of a regime.

The same, however, does not apply in social and political philosophy.

For philosophers, "democracy" is an evaluative term whose essential meaning refers to certain ideal conditions and institutions. "Democracy" in this sense means roughly, "rule by the people for the people." This latter notion needs philosophical clarification. Do we mean an ideal state of affairs in which: (a) the general good of all or most people is likely to be produced (rule *for* the people); (b) everyone has an equal chance to contribute input (rule *by* the people); or both (a) and (b)? Many people would include both (a) and (b) in their ideal of democracy. And most who would reject (a) would at least accept (b). Taking (b) as a necessary condition for democracy, it is apparent that even a polity which institutionalizes free and open elections in an exemplary manner may yet be judged undemocratic on philosophical grounds if it permits great disparities in wealth, education, and opportunity that deny many an equal voice in shaping public opinion.

To sum up, critical theory is like other forms of social and political philosophy in that it reflects on the basic meaning of social and political life in order to discover universal standards of evaluation. Its primary aim is not the discovery of statistical patterns enabling the prediction and technical control of social and political processes but the proferring of critical enlightenment regarding the justness and goodness of social and political institutions. Yet critical theory also distinguishes itself from social and political philosophy in being ruthlessly realistic and critical about its *own* philosophical assumptions.

CRITICAL THEORY AS SOCIAL SCIENCE

This takes us to the key problem underlying critical theory—its problematic relationship to philosophy. By its very nature philosophy is idealistic; this means it abstracts from, or goes beyond, the actual limitations of reality in prescribing ideal goals which ought to be attained. Such idealism can be problematic for two reasons. First, it tends to be utopian in its demand for perfection. But how can persons be expected to take seriously goals which are so ideal as to be impossible of any practical implementation? Suppose we say that an ideal democracy must satisfy conditions of perfect justice in which everyone has an equal say in all decision making affecting them. Such a goal could be implemented only by greatly reducing the vastness and complexity of modern societies. All hierarchies based on technical expertise would have to be eliminated, as well as those based on wealth, social standing, and natural circumstance. For each person the network of social relations would have to be reduced to a minimum, so that he or she would be guaranteed a direct say in all decisions affecting him or her. Life would be simple—but difficult—

under such radically egalitarian conditions. Indeed, one wonders whether democracy would even make sense in a world in which persons' overall literacy and scope for political action is subordinated to the narrow task of making a living. Under these conditions the need for democratic resolution of conflict would decline in proportion to the increasing superfluousness of legal, judicial, and executive institutions generally.

This takes us to the second difficulty besetting philosophical idealism. Perhaps, to use the above example, the ideal of democracy cannot be construed in so utopian a manner as to undermine itself. In that case, it will have to accommodate itself to the real conditions underlying the possibility of political life generally. Let's assume that perfectly equal and universal democratic input may not be desirable because it conflicts with other human ideals, such as the achievement of happiness and the progressive enhancement of human intelligence and freedom. Let's assume further that happiness and progress depend upon technological and cultural specialization requiring ever vaster and more complicated forms of society. Is there an ideal of democracy that would be compatible with the sorts of inequalities and privileges required by such a society? How much equality and democracy should we strive for given these unavoidable limitations? Should it be more or less than what our society currently permits?

I mention the above example because critical theorists are deeply concerned about the way in which modern societies have restricted democracy in the interest of promoting material security and technological progress. They would say that true happiness and progress cannot be equated with material security and technological advance but requires more, not less, democracy. Yet what entitles them to say this? More basic still, on the basis of what sorts of considerations can we or anyone else know what conduces to human happiness and freedom?

Philosophical idealism attempts to answer this question by providing a theory of human nature that purports to be universally valid for all time. But what is human nature? And how can specific ideals of happiness be gleaned from it? It is hard to imagine how philosophy could answer the first question without observing and understanding the actual behavior of human beings in different societies. Observation and understanding, in fact, reveal certain features common to all forms of human life. These include sociality and the use of symbolic systems for communication. Unfortunately, these very general "facts" about human nature do not tell us very much about what makes human beings happy and free. Indeed, might we not have greater success in this endeavor by turning our attention to the differences among particular human life-styles? If you ask an Australian aborigine what makes him happy and fulfills his nature you will get one kind of answer. If you ask a successful businesswoman in America the same question you will get another.

We seemed to have reached an impasse with philosophical idealism. In order for it to avoid the charge of utopian irrelevancy it must address evident facts about reality. But evident facts about reality discourage the notion that there is any one universal activity that preeminently fulfills human beings. Social and political philosophy that tries to be relevant to reality is thus forced to question its own idealism. Can we be sure that democracy—whatever it is—is the most just political system? If it is the most just, is it also the most humane, the one that most fulfills human aspirations for freedom, progress, and happiness? Or must we abandon philosophical speculations such as these in favor of the more modest task of simply describing and explaining the irreducible plurality of social formations and their respective modes of human fulfillment?

Social philosophy that accomodates itself too much to social reality achieves a kind of practical and theoretical relevancy that renders it irrelevant as a form of critical enlightenment. For no amount of knowledge regarding the way things are in our world will tell us how they ought to be. It seems that critical theory is caught in a dilemma. Either it remains faithful to its philosophical heritage, in which case it runs the risk of becoming lost in utopian speculation. Or it tries to be truthful to human nature as it really appears, in which case it ceases to be critical.

This paradox, known as the theory/practice problem, constitutes the chief dilemma addressed by critical theory. Critical theory is critical of both the utopian idealism of social and political philosophy and the uncritical realism of social and political science. Social and political theory ought not be so far removed from actual practice as to be useless. Yet it ought not limit itself to describing the regular patterns of existing social practice for fear of becoming an uncritical tool in the service of government officials and public-opinion manipulators bent on maintaining the status quo. Somehow social theory must combine social philosophy and social science, social idealism and social realism, theory and practice, without assimilating one to the other.

THE THEORY/PRACTICE PROBLEM
AND THE CHALLENGE OF IDEOLOGY

Thus, the interdisciplinary synthesis of social science and social philosophy is the distinctive trademark of critical social theory. It is also its problem. How can one claim to discover universal norms of justice and happiness in light of the ever unique and changing patterns of concrete historical life revealed by social science? Indeed, how does one combine transcendent moral reflection and prescription with this-worldly understanding, description, explanation, and prediction?

I noted above that critical social theory cannot avoid addressing the philosophical problem of justice and happiness. This is a philosophical problem because the mere fact that people in a given society happen to think that their social relations are just and mutually fulfilling does not necessarily make them so. Slaves can be taught to accept slavery as the most just and fulfilling system for people "like themselves" who are "by nature inferior in intelligence, weak and dependent." Likewise, business executives no less than ordinary criminals can deceive themselves into thinking that the acquisition of power and wealth is all that matters in achieving true happiness. In short, people can *rationalize* existing injustice and unhappiness by convincing themselves that it is the natural thing that all human beings—or, at least, all human beings of a certain rank—ought to want.

From a philosophical point of view, commonly shared assumptions about what constitutes justice and happiness must be viewed with suspicion as potentially *ideological*. Those opinions, cultural values, practices, and institutions are ideological ones, which appear to be generally true or valid for all persons but are not. Accepted out of ignorance or sheer force of habit, these opinions, values, etc. may reflect nothing more than the interests of an elite few who benefit—or think they benefit—from the social relations that constrain their acceptance.

The principal aim of critical theory is to expose such ideologies for what they are. In order to do this, however, it must show that the ideals of happiness and justice—appealed to by the ideology in question—are in some sense false or irrational. In that case, critical theory will have to possess true knowledge of these ideals. But this, as we have seen, is problematic. Ideals, which so totally transcend reality, are practically impossible. Being neither true nor rational they are themselves ideological. Therefore, the trick for critical theory is to show how true ideals of justice and happiness are somehow implicit in the ideological opinions and practices that constitute social reality.

This is not the appropriate place to discuss how critical theorists propose to derive ideals of justice and happiness from social realities that mask injustice and unhappiness. Most, if not all, critical theorists appeal to general theories of historical development which purport to rank the religious and metaphysical beliefs, cultural artifacts, and social practices of particular societies in accordance with standards of rationality. Beliefs, value systems, cultural representations, and practices that exhibit a greater degree of rationality will thus be judged less ideological—or truer—than those which exhibit a lesser degree. But, one might ask, how do we discover the standards of rationality in terms of which ideologies are to be evaluated?

THE PROBLEM OF RATIONALITY

Resolution of the theory/practice problem hinges on the question of rationality. Critical theory aims at enlightening people regarding their rational interests in creating a just and happy society. But what is meant by "rationality?"

For critical theorists the problem of rationality is problematic. For one thing "rationality" is both descriptive and evaluative in the same way that "humanity" and "democracy" are. Like these other concepts, its true ideal meaning must take into account actual social reality. "Rationality" is the general term we use to describe certain ways of thinking and behaving which have emerged in the course of human history and have insinuated themselves into institutions such as science, jurisprudence, government, and public morality. However, it is also a term we use to evaluate these ways of thinking and behaving. Consequently, it points beyond actual thinking and behaving toward ideal potentials that can be more or less realized.

According to critical theorists the emergence of rational modes of thinking and conduct accelerates with the advent of modern capitalism. Beginning in the late Renaissance and continuing through the eighteenth century—a period known as the Enlightenment—rational forms of thinking and conduct began to take hold in science, jurisprudence, government, and public morality. Standards of logical consistency and deductive reasoning that had existed since antiquity began to play a more important role in the codification of laws and the construction of scientific and philosophical theories. Modes of economic and political conduct based on a scientific calculation of probable effects enabled capitalist enterprises and governments to acquire wealth and power efficiently. Last, but not least, reason began to replace religion as the chief guide to public morality. Persons were now encouraged to justify their conduct in terms of universally valid principles whose primary value resided in rational consistency and utility. Thus, along with rationality came greater individual responsibility and freedom for differentiating between right and wrong. The emphasis on greater moral autonomy, in turn, lent impetus to political reforms which ensured individual rights and democratic self-determination.

Although the different sorts of rationality mentioned above—logical, calculating, and moral—are entwined with one another, they are also, critical theorists maintain, irreducibly distinct. This proves problematic in light of the internal dynamics of capitalist and bureaucratic socialist societies. For, according to critical theorists, these societies inevitably end up encouraging the growth of logical and calculating forms of thinking and conduct at the expense of the moral. The more scientific and technological efficiency is stressed, the less egalitarian—and hence the less democratic—social relations become. Paradoxically, it appears that the very institutions and social forces, which lend rationality concrete shape, also distort and undermine it. Modern societies appear to be one-sidedly rational, stressing only the scientific and technological in which success, not rightness and justice, function as over-arching values.

SCIENCE AND TECHNOLOGY AS IDEOLOGY

It was mentioned above that critical theory appeals to ideal standards of moral rationality pertaining to justice and happiness in evaluating the ideological content of beliefs and practices. Like all ideals, these standards cannot tran-scend social reality so far that they become purely utopian; otherwise they, too, would degenerate into falsehood and ideology. As social science, critical theory must ground its standards in social reality. But what if that social reality embodies rationality in a one-sided—and to that extent, irrational—way? What happens when science and technology cease being one legitimate type of reason and become the sole mode of rational thinking and practice? Today, many philosophers would argue that the rightness of moral choices and values cannot be rationally determined. If moral decision is relegated to the sphere of arbitrary (private) preference, then only science and technology, logical and calculating thought, can lay claim to universal reason. But in a society in which the rightness of basic goals and values is assumed to be beyond rational assessment social practice itself—however scientifically en-lightened it may be—becomes irrational. When science and technology ex-clusively dominate social life they themselves become ideological.

The paradox of critical theory is that, in some sense, it is a part of the very society it wishes to criticize. The *crisis* that it exposes in modern society— the contradiction between scientific and moral rationality—is its own. Critical theory has renounced its claim to being pure moral philosophy and has taken on the burden of scientific verification. At the same time, however, it cannot but contradict its own scientific identity in the name of a higher reason. This is especially so when science and technology have become ideological. For this reason, critical theorists are faced with the necessary task of engaging in philosophical reflections that are historically responsible. Just how this is to be accomplished is itself problematic. Where does one locate moral reason if not in science or religion? Are there forms of modern culture (e.g., art), which might provide rational insight? Or, perhaps, we should turn to aspects of culture that are more or less historically invariant, such as linguistic communication.

THE PROBLEM OF FREEDOM, HAPPINESS, AND DEMOCRACY

Critical theorists are keenly sensitive to the tensions inherent in the conceptions of justice and happiness that have taken shape in modern "rational" society. More specifically, their work can be seen as attempts to spell out the implications—of this crisis in moral reason—for individuals living in advanced capitalist societies.

It was noted above that the coincidence of justice and happiness is a matter of some dispute. Part of the reason for this is that each of these terms can be defined in ways that are mutually antagonistic. Take justice, for instance. One predominant strand in our conception of justice emphasizes a notion of deserts based on individual achievement. Persons are entitled to what they earn through their own labor. Since reason dictates that we pursue our self-preservation in the most efficient way possible, it follows that we *should* be allowed to pursue our interests freely, so long as it doesn't prevent others from doing likewise. The freedom corresponding to this notion of justice also implies a certain concept of legal and moral right. One is assumed to possess a property right in one's own body and in the legitimately acquired fruits of one's labor. This concept of right procures a *negative* freedom because it prohibits others from interfering with one's property (broadly defined). It does not, however, procure a *positive* freedom, or access to resources necessary for utilizing one's freedom. It only permits persons to acquire property and interact with one another freely, so that neither the possession of property nor the means for influencing public policy are guaranteed.

It is clear that a society which institutionalized only this entitlement conception of justice would develop a capitalist economy in which the state would do little more than guarantee a minimal degree of law and order. Given inequalities in natural endowments and inherited advantages, such a society would tolerate very high levels of social inequality. The other strand in our conception of justice runs contrary to this view. If the aim of the state is to secure the well-being of its citizens—whether this be protection of private property or the provision of public works—it is rational that it somehow reflect the interests of its citizens. This is best achieved by instituting procedures of democratic electoral representation in which all have an equal chance to fully participate. In order for democracy to be fair, all persons would have to possess roughly equal educational and financial resources and opportunities for lobbying representatives and shaping public opinion. The right to democratic participation would thus entail positive access to healthcare, education, and income. Operating with this notion of justice, the state would be obligated to redistribute the wealth acquired independently by individuals, thereby restricting their right to private property. Further democratization might entail socializing the means of production, so that workers and consumers have a say in what they produce and how they produce.

The conflict between democratic self-determination and the individual freedom described above is one of the central concerns of critical theorists. They are especially interested in the way in which this conflict operates in the modern welfare state. The modern welfare state can be understood as a kind of compromise solution to the above dilemma. Yet, like many compromise solutions, it ends up undermining—so critical theorists maintain—what it is supposed to preserve. Modern capitalism, they claim, is detrimental to both negative and positive freedom, individual autonomy, and collective self-determination.

Critical theorists do not recommend a return to the unregulated capitalism of the nineteenth century. They realize that the modern welfare state arose in response to contradictions implicit within this type of capitalism. In particular, they contend that the idea of freedom, understood as the right to private property, and the idea of justice, understood as a contractual entitlement, results in forms of social inequality and domination that exploit and enslave the greater mass of wage laborers. In this system, individual freedom, now reduced to the selfish pursuit of profit, ends up undermining itself. For the seemingly rational and calculated pursuit of personal gain by competing entrepreneurs produces global effects that result in recurrent economic crises. Unregulated capitalism thus appears as an irrational and anarchistic system of production in which the individual's freedom is continually frustrated by economic laws operating beyond his or her rational control.

By assuming rational control over the economy the modern welfare state attempts to mitigate some of the factors responsible for business cycles, thereby warding off economic collapse and class war. This strategy succeeds, critical theorists argue, only to the extent that individual freedom and democracy are curtailed. The price for the state's success in mitigating the most blatant forms of exploitation and inequality through redistribution of wealth and social-welfare policy is government interference in the lives of citizens. While education and family life come increasingly under the direction of the state, production and consumption remain largely under the control of big business. Thanks to the techniques of mass marketing, the personal preferences that presumably define one's individuality become mass preferences that can be manipulated by either the state or big business. Thus, big business and state bureaucracy converge to form a technological apparatus that verges on the totalitarian in its ubiquitous control over everyday life.

Critical theorists generally agree that the modern welfare state has lulled people into abdicating moral responsibility for the direction of society by plying them with material goods. Absorbed in their private lives, people are only too willing to let bureaucrats and powerful businessmen do their thinking for them. Indeed, in the absence of such apathy it is unlikely that big government and big business would be able to make controversial decisions without inciting public outcries from disadvantaged groups. Despite this gloomy picture, critical theorists are far from conceding that the modern welfare state has successfully patched over the cracks of injustice with general happiness.

Happiness, like freedom and justice, is a vague notion. With the advent of modern society it is hard to imagine a state of happiness that doesn't involve progress in the achievement of material well-being. Yet, as critical theorists point out, our modern notion of happiness is closely tied to notions of dignity and self-respect that refer back to justice. How can we feel confirmed in our freedom and dignity without being recognized as such by others who feel the same way about themselves? Individual happiness would appear to be related to a notion of communal solidarity founded on justice for all. But communal solidarity is just as problematic as individual autonomy. No one would want a form of communal solidarity that was imposed by the state—even if such solidarity happened to reflect the democratic will of the vast majority of citizens. For if liberalism has taught us anything, it is that the tyranny of a democratic majority can be just as "totalitarian" in its suppression of individuality and freedom as that of a state-imposed dictatorship.

This takes us to the final problem addressed by critical theory: What must a just society be like in order for individuals to affirm their autonomy in relations of solidarity? How must a democratic society be structured so as to approximate a felicitous balance of material well-being, negative individual freedom, communal identity, and equality? And who will be the new wave of revolutionaries that will bring this change about? If neither current forms of capitalism nor current forms of socialism satisfy our rational expectations for justice and happiness, are there any practical alternatives that will?

The preceding introduction touches on the most basic problems of critical theory. Left out of the discussion are issues concerning the domination of nature and the exclusion of women's perspectives on the nature of reason, justice, and happiness. These will be dealt with later on in the book. However, none of the issues addressed by critical theory can be adequately grasped until we have a better understanding of the diverse philosophical, sociological, psychological, economic, and historical contexts in which they emerged. With this in mind let us turn to critical theory's most original, philosophical root—the German Enlightenment from Kant through Marx.

ONE

THE PHILOSOPHICAL ROOTS OF CRITICAL THEORY

In 1937, the journal of the Frankfurt-based Institute For Social Research published a programmatic essay by its chief editor and director, Max Horkheimer, entitled "Traditional and Critical Theory."[1] From that moment on *critical theory* has designated a school of thought—known by many as simply the Frankfurt School—whose ranks have included such prominent figures as Theodor W. Adorno, Herbert Marcuse, and Jürgen Habermas.

No introductory text can possibly do justice to the enormous complexity, subtlety, and diversity of critical theory. It has been variously characterized as a radical social theory (or sociology), a sophisticated form of cultural criticism, combining Freudian and Marxist ideas, and a utopian brand of philosophical speculation deeply rooted in Jewish and German idealism. For their own part, critical theorists saw themselves as responding to the historical events of their day. These were the changing composition and direction of the European labor movement, the evolution of Soviet communism and Western capitalism, the decline of patriarchy in the nuclear family, the psychosocial dynamics underlying authoritarian, anti-Semitic, and Fascist tendencies, and the rising potential for totalitarian "mind control" in the mass production and consumption of "culture."

We will have more to say about the history of critical theory below. Before doing so, it is necessary to examine the theory's philosophical roots. It is no coincidence that Horkheimer explicitly appealed to the critical philosophy of Immanuel Kant (1724–1804) and the critique of political economy developed by Karl Marx (1818–1883). Taken together, these traditions of critical thought have defined the main tasks of the school to this day: to critique scientific knowledge and rationality from the standpoint of a social theory proffering "moral" enlightenment and to critique capitalist society as a crisis-laden system frustrating human freedom and fulfillment. Because the theme of enlightenment is so central to their critical endeavors, let us take a moment to examine it in the context of the philosophical movement from which it first emerged.

KNOWLEDGE AND POLITICS IN
THE AGE OF ENLIGHTENMENT

The critical theories of Kant and Marx have their source in the eighteenth-century philosophical movement known as the Enlightenment. The movement was fueled by faith in the power of reason to propel scientific and moral progress leading to political emancipation. The connection between enlightenment and emancipation was certainly not a new idea. In the *Republic*, written over two thousand years before the Enlightenment, Plato had attributed the same power to philosophy. The famous section entitled the "Allegory of the Cave" illustrates the practical, liberating effects of philosophical knowledge. Prior to enlightenment people are bound to the prejudices and illusory appearances of their society in much the same way that slaves chained to the bottom of a cave since birth are bound to the deceptive shadows of things projected on the wall before them. Since the slaves have no other experience to compare to their own they assume that they are free and that they possess true knowledge of the things themselves.

Plato points out how difficult it would be to tear these slaves away from their illusions. They would most likely resist anyone trying to lead them out of the cave into the light of day. Such enlightenment would be painful to eyes accustomed only to darkness. Those who managed to escape would think twice about returning. Having achieved true enlightenment regarding justice and happiness they would seem hopelessly utopian and "out of place" in the world below. At best, they would be ignored as dreamers; at worst, they would be killed as subversives. Those who succeeded in getting heard would have to compromise their views considerably.

The only other alternative countenanced by Plato is one in which the enlighteners, having somehow gotten the upper hand, force the unenlightened to be free. Here we see the dangers of a philosophical idealism which simply cuts through the theory/practice problem. The real world of everyday practice will be made to conform to the ideals of theory, even if this means revolutionizing it from the ground up. Plato doesn't hesitate to draw the necessary conclusions: all but the very young will be banished from his ideal republic; those who remain will undergo a rigorous reeducation. Of course, this presupposes that the philosopher-educators, having superior insight, are in no need of education from those below, a view which even Karl Marx would reject. Plato himself understood how difficult—indeed, impossible—it would be to implement utopian ideas in an imperfect and ever-changing world. Being absolutely timeless and immutable, ideal principles of justice will inevitably be corrupted or compromised by the very realities to which they are applied; and the educators who apply and interpret them will always remain subject to the vicissitudes of changing circumstances.

It would be wrong to read the *Republic* as a gloss on the futility of philosophical idealism. What it tells us about philosophy and enlightenment, generally, is that the ideal demands of transcendent moral reason which emancipate us from the bonds of a false social reality have to make their peace with that reality. This is something that the advocates of enlightenment in the eighteenth century understood full well. For unlike Plato, they were generally more optimistic about the capacity of average people to reason about right and wrong. Enlightenment would cease being the privileged insight of philosophers, and the educated would themselves become educators, once the masses took advantage of their own innate faculty of reason and common sense.

The eighteenth-century Enlightenment is distinguished from earlier philosophical movements—Plato's included—in its overtly political character. Also new is the emphasis on subjective consciousness as the ground of all knowledge and moral right. René Descartes (1596–1649) is considered by many to be the first to expound this idea. Descartes argued that, by relying on one's own innate reason, one could achieve metaphysical knowledge of God, soul, and the true nature of things. Descartes's emphasis on pure reason rather than sense perception as the true path to knowledge is reminiscent of Plato's doctrine of transcendent ideas. Both were directed against the dogmatic prejudices of religious learning and traditional custom. Yet Descartes's rationalism endows each and every individual with the capacity to turn inward and discover the truth within himself.

Descartes's philosophy propelled the Enlightenment in two seemingly incompatible directions. On the one hand, it encouraged the view that the essence of the self resided in a use of reason, which transcended limitations of time and space. In this view, persons were accorded a transcendent freedom unlimited by the immediate testimony of the senses. On the other hand, it lent impetus to the development of a mechanistic science of physical nature. In this view, persons were regarded as composite physical-mental beings whose corporeal nature was governed by causal laws beyond their control. This tension—between philosophical idealism and scientific materialism, freedom and determinism—runs through the entire history of the Enlightenment and later becomes the focal point around which the critical theories of Kant and Marx turn.

Other philosophers, influenced by Descartes's attempt to ground knowledge in the individual subject, emphasized sensory observation as the true ground of knowledge. Thus, they were inclined to emphasize a more mechanistic and materialistic view of human nature. Yet they, too, ended up according the individual a certain moral and cognitive priority. Persons were encouraged to rely on the testimony of their own observations of reality rather than on the dogmatic authority of the Church. The individual acting on his own could achieve true knowledge of nature's laws, especially the laws of human nature. Not surprisingly, these were interpreted in a way that conformed to the individualistic spirit of the age. If knowledge—so central to the natural instinct for self-preservation—was to be obtained only through the free exercise of one's own mental faculties, one *ought* to be free to pursue it and any other resources deemed necessary for self-preservation without interference from Church and state.

What tempered this self-centered individualism was the belief that nature endowed humanity with certain social inclinations that dictated peaceful cohabitation within lawful bounds. Hence, there emerged the notion of a natural law that entailed certain individual rights. These rights were originally formulated as basic property rights. The notion of a "natural" property right was used by John Locke (1632–1704) and others to justify constitutionally limited government. According to Locke, the legitimate authority of the state rests on the consent of the governed. The state is to be thought of as the real or imagined result of a voluntary contract among persons seeking to protect their property. It follows that, if the state were to violate its compact with the people, they would have the right to overthrow it.

Locke's justification of revolution inspired both the English Revolution of 1689 and the American Revolution of 1776. However, the revolutionary side of Locke's theory was tempered somewhat by his conservative belief that social and political institutions should conform to persons' "natural" acquisitiveness. In short, his observations told him that social inequalities were both necessary and natural, and that it would be unwise to permit all but a few— the wealthy and educated portion of the adult male population—to have a say in government.

The revolutionary implications of Locke's "social contract" theory of the state would be developed in more radical directions by the rationalistic and idealistic philosophies which closed the eighteenth century. John Locke was no democrat. Yet his idea—of consent as a condition of legitimate government—led Jean-Jacques Rousseau (1712–1778) to advocate a model of democracy having radically egalitarian implications. According to Rousseau, persons are obligated to obey only those laws which represent the true rational interests of everyone—what he called the General Will. On his reading of the social contract, each person would be required to vote directly on all legislative matters. Moreover, to ensure that the General Will is given impartial expression, all partisan interest groups would be curtailed as well as all social inequalities preventing persons from exercising their own independent judgement.

Rousseau's democratic egalitarianism helped flame the republican idealism that led to the French Revolution of 1789. His rationalism prevented him from being content with human beings as Locke had observed them. Whereas Locke had stressed the materialistic, individualistic, and acquisitive side of the Enlightenment, Rousseau stressed the more idealistic, communitarian, and democratic ideas. Yet, in doing so, he acknowledged the existence of both sides. In fact, he was the first to appreciate the tensions implicit in the enlightenment that would later preoccupy critical theorists. On the one hand, he observed that the development of the arts and sciences creates new needs and new forms of privilege. As specialization occurs, social relations become more complex; private property and wage labor become more generalized; persons lose their natural freedom and come under the servitude of others. In exchange for the traditional emotional bonds—that once united them—they subject themselves to the laws of the market. Social inequality, acquisitive individualism, and inauthenticity become ever more prevalent. On the other hand, he conceded that enlightenment also brings into play an awareness of a common humanity, or General Will, which guarantees one's moral freedom.

This last aspect is later developed by Kant, who was greatly influenced by Rousseau. Although he was not an advocate of democracy as such, Kant believed in the principle of government by popular consent. More importantly, he went beyond the idea of democratic self-determination in claiming for reason a more exalted role—that of universal legislator for reality as such. In endowing the subject with so much power over reality, Kant developed a notion of freedom that was more revolutionary than any other preceding it. At the same time, however, it remained burdened by the idealistic heritage of Platonic philosophy. For Kant, each person in theory is a free, rational agent who inhabits an ideal community of equality and reciprocity. However, in their daily practice they are governed by irrational selfish inclinations that lead them to dominate one another.

Kant tried to solve his theory/practice problem by suggesting that the conflictual dynamics of selfish inclination would providentially lead to intellectual progress culminating in a lawful regime. His appeal to the rational purposefulness of human history proved to be decisive for his followers, who felt that the transcendent side of his idealism needed to be grounded in concrete historical reality. By solving this problem, they felt that they could also solve the problem of enlightenment—the unification of individual freedom and communal solidarity, reason as a material instrument of self-preservation and reason as transcendent moral law. In Marx this train of thought culminates in the transformation of philosophy into critical social science, the birth of critical theory proper.

KANT AND THE CRITIQUE OF OBJECTIVISM

Kant's *Critique of Pure Reason* (1781) was written in response to a "rationality crisis" inherent in the Enlightenment. The crisis was originally rooted in a disagreement between rationalists and empiricists over the proper foundations of knowledge. Both schools of thought believed that in order for knowledge to be justified, it had to be founded on truths whose *certainty* could be *directly intuited*. The rationalists held that such truths were intuited by pure reason unaided by sensory experience. In his *Meditations on First Philosophy* (1641), Descartes had argued that nothing attested to by his senses—even the very existence of his own body and the surrounding world—was certain, since it was logically possible that he could be dreaming. Worse yet, he could be deceived by an evil deity into falsely believing that a world existed outside his mind. He observed, however, that he could not doubt his own existence *as a thinking thing*. Using this foundational belief as a test case for all legitimate knowledge, he then proceeded to show that he knew other things with certainty as well. These were the truths of mathematics, geometry, and—above all—the existence of a perfect God who would not deceive him into believing there was an external world if there wasn't one. Having thus established a metaphysical warrant for believing in the existence of pure spatial substance, Descartes felt that he had discovered the foundation for science he was looking for. More importantly, he felt that he had shown why mechanistic science was no threat to the freedom and immortality of the soul. For how could one possibly doubt the fact that the very act of thinking—which confirmed one's existence—was logically distinct from physical extension? If thoughts and ideas do not possess physical extension, how can they be subject to its causal mechanism?

The empiricists, by contrast, contested the possibility of founding scientific knowledge on pure reason. Their most sophisticated and radical representative, David Hume, maintained that truths of reason consisted of "relations of ideas" which, though certain, were not informative. Such statements as "2 + 2 = 4," "Either it will rain or it will not rain," and "All bachelors are unmarried" are necessarily true *by definition of the very terms* (*ideas*) *contained in the statements*. Knowing that "unmarried" is necessarily contained in the idea of "bachelor" does not, however, extend our knowledge about bachelors; it does not even tell us whether such things as bachelors exist or not. Beliefs regarding the existence of things and their properties—what Hume called "matters of fact"—are truly informative. Therefore, he concluded that they must have their source in sense experience, not reason.

At this juncture the skeptical implications of empiricism make their appearance. Hume accepts Descartes's contention that sense experience cannot provide certain grounds for our belief in an external world of objects. The most any individual is entitled to say with certainty is that he or she presently has such and such a sense impression. Indeed, our sense impressions are all radically different from one another. Not only is a visual sensation logically distinct from a tactile sensation, but the visual sensation I had a moment ago is temporally distinct from the one I have now. Thus, I am not entitled to affirm the existence of any unitary, continuous event, be it an object (as the unified substrate of distinct properties outside the mind) or a self (as the unified substrate of distinct sensations inside the mind).

Kant's *Critique of Pure Reason* attempts to resolve the crisis of knowledge by combining rationalism and empiricism in a manner that avoids dogmatic metaphysics and radical skepticism. The empiricists, he notes, were correct in denying that reason could provide informative knowledge about the world in the absence of sensory experience. Metaphysical beliefs about God, soul, and the totality of things unobserved can be topics of moral speculation and articles of *faith*, but cannot rightly claim to be true or false. Nevertheless, the rationalists were correct to point out that the possibility for judging a cluster of discrete sensory properties as belonging to one and the same temporally perduring object *necessarily presupposes* a rational intuition (or judgment) of unity.

Descartes illustrated the irreducibility of objective knowledge to sensation with his famous example of the melting wax. If we still judge the wax to be the same thing after *all* its sensory properties have changed, this is less because we *see* (sense) it to be so than because we *infer* (reason) it to be so. Hume had denied the rationality of such inferences. They were not logical inferences based on relations of ideas, but appeared to be grounded in matters of fact. That is, they rest on the *expectation* that events of a certain sort that had always been conjoined in past experience *must* continue to be conjoined in the future. However, such expectation of *causal regularity, necessary connectedness* or invariance, inhering in *factually contingent* bundles of discrete sensation was, he believed, patently absurd. For it was neither *logically* necessary that the future conform to the past (viz., the denial of the causal principle does not issue in a logical contradiction), nor was it factually so, since sense experience at most testifies to what *is* (or has been) the case, not what *must* be the case.

Despite the apparent irrationality of causal inferences—for Hume they were nothing more than imaginary associations produced by blind force of habit or custom—Hume conceded that no conceivable experience of objects (and no intuition of self) would be possible without them. Indeed, he himself often took a less skeptical, naturalistic view of human knowledge and action in his moral philosophy. There, as in his theory of knowledge, he emphasized the role that custom and habit play in irrationally shaping human conduct. However, unlike his theory of knowledge, moral custom takes on the causal force of social and natural "passions." Because he believed that reason was handmaiden to passion, he could hardly subscribe to Descartes's belief in transcendent moral freedom.

As we shall see below, Kant was as much disturbed by Hume's denial of human freedom as he was by his denial of causal necessity. Hume's objection to a rational belief in causal necessity, Kant argued, rests on a one-sided view of reason. Both rationalists and empiricists mistakenly presuppose that reason is but a *passive* faculty of logical *analysis*, which retrospectively *discovers* necessary relations among *pregiven ideas*. However, if we assume that reason *actively constitutes* our experience from the very beginning by bringing it under necessary relations (the logical forms of judgment existing in the mind *prior* to experience), we can explain the possibility of any experience whatsoever. It might be helpful to think of the mind as a computer. The former *synthesizes* sensory data into complex mental representations of causally ordered events like a preprogrammed computer processes raw data. For Kant, only if we assume that the logical program of the mind actively pieces together discrete sensory input in the form of a *unified* spatio-temporal manifold, can we explain how permanent objects standing over against the fleeting impressions of the sensing subject could have been represented in the first place.

Indeed, the passive association of discrete sense data into complex representations of objects noted by Hume already *presupposes* a *necessary unity of consciousness*. I could not associate the contents of my experience unless past, present, and future mental states were *rationally* intuited as all belonging to *me*. It is in this manner—by introducing a *transcendental*, or *productive*, notion of reason—that Kant resolved the crisis of knowledge.

How does Kant's resolution of the crisis of knowledge enable him to resolve the other crisis of the Enlightenment—the crisis between transcendent moral reason and worldly scientific reason, freedom and causal necessity? We noted above that in Kant's view, the fixed world of objects, with all of its lawlike necessity and resistance to human purpose, is in some sense a product of the spontaneous activity of subjects possessing, as it were, the same transcendental "program." This notion is one that has played a profound role in German philosophy down to the present day. It is also the main idea connecting critical theory's interest in problems of knowledge with its deep concern for social emancipation. Now rationalism and empiricism both share with everyday "common sense" the assumption that our thoughts and experiences are mirror reflections, or copies—more or less accurate—of a world existing independently of our minds. This *objectivistic* way of viewing things, Kant argued, not only fails to explain the necessary unity of our knowledge, but it implicitly denies the radical freedom and responsibility of the moral agent. For belief in the passivity of the knowing subject is closely related to belief in the passivity of the acting subject.

Once we reverse our commonsense assumptions about the priority of the object over the knowing subject, we realize that the causal necessity imposed on our world is something that our minds *produce* rather than passively mirror. Then, Kant reasoned, we are in a position to regard ourselves as truly free. From the cognitive point of view of sense experience we must *perceive* ourselves as causally predetermined "bodies in motion." But causal necessity is only something the mind imposes on sensation and does not apply to the world independently of our efforts to perceive it. We can at least imagine that, from a God's eye point of view, the world known independently of sensory and causal conditions might appear as an immaterial realm of purely rational beings. Therefore, it is possible that we might be *free*. Indeed, we must *think* of ourselves as free in order to establish the possibility for our own moral responsibility.

It is here that Kant rehabilitates pure reason. What reason loses as a faculty of metaphysical knowledge it gains back as a faculty of universal moral commands. As Kant puts it in the *Critique of Practical Reason* (1788), it follows from the *rational* "fact" of human freedom that persons are the ultimate sources of valuation. As such, they are themselves supreme values or "ends in themselves," worthy of absolute respect and dignity.[2] Thus, we must never treat others merely as means for the attainment of our ends. We are obliged within reasonable limits to provide them with whatever means are necessary to further their own (moral) ends—independence and self-determination. Since we are required to regard the interests of each of these ultimate ends as possessing merit equal to our own, reason forbids making any exceptions on our behalf. What Kant calls the *categorical imperative* commands that we act only on those general maxims of behavior, which we could will to be a universal law. These apply equally—and without exception—to all persons. Indeed, we are acting responsibly only to the extent that we rationally choose to conduct our lives in accordance with commands our own sovereign reason dictates to us. Thus, to the extent that we allow external authority, bodily desire, or unconscious prejudice to causally influence our behavior, we are neither fully free nor fully moral.

It would be difficult to assess the many ways in which Kant's critical philosophy influenced the Frankfurt School. Certainly, the value of individual freedom must be accorded a privileged place in their thought. Along with this is the idea of a universal community in which exploitation, privilege, and domination are abolished. Nor must we forget Kant's *revolutionary* contribution in criticizing the tendency to objectify the natural and social world, or treat it as an object independent of and opposed to the productive capacity of the subject. Such objectivistic thinking resigns us to the cynical acceptance of the manner of life predetermined by the existing conditions of our environment.

Still, critical theorists find many aspects of Kant's thought to be unacceptable. His reduction of knowledge to the discovery and confirmation of particular causal laws does not leave much room for a "scientific" theory of society aiming at critical enlightenment. Indeed, it perpetuates the notion that society, no less than nature, is a causally predetermined, law-governed mechanism. The shortcomings of Kant's rigid dualism between knowledge and morality (between what *is* and what *ought to be*) is likewise reflected in the dualistic conception of human nature he inherited from Descartes. Depending on one's point of view, that of sensory cognition (science) or of pure reason (moral philosophy), this was conceived to be either causally conditioned by natural and historical forces or purely transcendent and free. Such a notion seems to militate against the idea that freedom is a force affecting historical changes within human nature itself. It also ignores the obvious fact that reason is not an unchanging faculty innate in every individual, but is itself the *product* of a long history of *social* development.

HEGEL'S HISTORICAL DIALECTIC

It was Kant's descendants in the German philosophical tradition, especially Hegel and Marx, who appreciated the historical nature of reason. Kant himself had proposed a philosophy of history in which he viewed nature nonmechanistically, as a purposive force bringing about political institutions conducive to moral development. However, his overly individualistic and transcendent view of reason prevented him from seeing reason as itself "practically" shaped by these very same institutions. Unlike Hegel and Marx, he never saw the need to transform critical philosophy into critical social theory.

Georg Wilhelm Friedrich Hegel (1770–1831) is the most important transitional figure linking Kant's critical philosophy and Marx's critical social theory. His major contribution to critical thought consists of his claim that reason is an *objective historical force*—which must be conceived dynamically or developmentally. The history of humanity, he believed, could be understood as the progressive unfolding of rational ideas that were already implicit in the relatively primitive social, political, and cultural institutions of antiquity. On this reading, rationality is not reducible to logical or transcendental operations innate within each person's soul. Rather, the very identity of the personal self arises, Hegel argues, only within the practical context of labor and social interaction.

Kant had argued that the identity of the self, as a continuous subject of fleeting sensation, is necessarily related to the identity of the object as a permanent substrate of discrete, changing qualities. The key term in this relationship is *reflection*. The continuous experience of an objective world of causally ordered events *reflects* or mirrors the unifying activity of the subject.

Reflecting activity is essential to reason. A *reflective* person is one who reasons about life. He or she *turns away from* life's distractions, ceases to be absorbed in the immediacy of daily tasks, and *turns inward*. This "turning inward" is a "reflecting back" to the subject. Life, objectively experienced, reflects back upon itself as life subjectively internalized. Internalized experience is experience that has been *critically analyzed, thoughtfully interpreted*, and *meaningfully unified*. Reflection thus implies *reversal*. I, as subject, make of myself an object of thought; life externally lived becomes life internally contemplated.

Reflection is normally understood as voluntary mental activity directed toward a preexisting subject or object. Reflection makes *explicit* (rationally articulates) what is *implicit* or already there. Kant, however, significantly alters the meaning of reflection by interpreting it as an involuntary, unconscious activity that *produces* the *identity* (unity) of subject and object. At the same time, he still conceives it in purely *psychological* terms, as an *immediate mental* reflex of the *isolated* subject. Hegel is more radical. He wants to *combine* both senses of reflection mentioned above (as freely making explicit what is implicit and as producing identity). Furthermore, he wants to show how psychological reflection itself "reflects" an activity that goes on *outside* of the mind. Reflection, he will argue, is something that occurs in *labor* and *social interaction*. In *embodied* activity of this sort the self *externalizes* (or expresses) itself in something wholly other than itself, material nature and society. It then contemplates itself in this "other."

In a famous section from the *Phenomenology of Spirit* (1807) Hegel shows how rational identity and freedom—the twin goals of enlightenment—are won only in the course of a long struggle involving the progressive mastery of nature and the elimination of social domination. The section, entitled "Self-Consciousness," begins with the insight that all *desire* is driven by a lack of self-certainty (self-knowledge). The Cartesian need to be in possession of oneself, to acquire a sense of one's own absolute freedom, can be satisfied only through possession of another, who objectively confirms what one feels only subjectively. This is typically achieved at the expense of the other's independence. My need to be affirmed as free and independent is initially satisfied by dominating the other. For the other, to whom I attribute the same need for total recognition animating my own behavior—Hegel alludes to the economic domination of lord over servant—is also a threat to my independence. However, such domination invariably fails to achieve its goal. Here, *recognition* that is not freely given by one of equal rank and status does not satisfy. In the final analysis, it is the servant who gains a sense of freedom and self in working for the lord. For by expressing one's inner subjectivity in one's work—literally, objectifying oneself in a resistant matter—one gains a sense of independence and mastery with respect to nature. But one also recognizes and thus confirms one's own identity and freedom in the stability and permanence of the product.

The kind of reflective identity that Hegel is establishing here—between self, other, and nature—is *dialectical*. In the *Critique of Pure Reason*, Kant had observed that the inherent logic of rational reflection led to the posing of metaphysical questions about the *totality* of conditions (the unconditioned). Such questions, Kant argued, could not be answered without implicating reason in a fundamental *contradiction* or *transcendental dialectic*. There are, for example, no answers to the question, "Does the universe have a beginning?" which aren't absurd or self-contradictory. If I answer that the universe has an absolute beginning, then I've postulated the idea of a first cause (i.e., a part of the universe that is itself uncaused or lacking sufficient reason). Likewise, if I answer that the universe has no beginning (or is uncaused), then I contradict the fundamental principle of reasoning itself, namely, that nothing happens without a cause.

Kant tried to eliminate the dialectical tendencies inherent in reason by limiting the *cognitive* employment of such rational categories as causality to particular observable events within space and time. Hegel found this to be an arbitrary denial of rational reflection. It undermined the very possibility of gaining transcendental insight into the *total preconditions* for cognition as such. He, therefore, sought to resurrect the speculative—or metaphysical—deployment of philosophical reflection as a process of discovering a purely rational knowledge of the whole (the Absolute Idea). To do so, however, involves accepting dialectic (contradiction) as a positive "moment" in the attainment of such knowledge.

In a dialectical relationship, one term in the relationship presupposes and contains the opposing term as a necessary condition of its own identity. This relationship, Hegel claims, is both logical and historical. Laboring activity, for example, not only reveals but also transforms the identity of the self. It makes explicit in the object produced what was previously implicit in the form of vague feeling; in this instance, the unreflected and more or less unconscious identity of the laborer. But it also brings about a change in self-understanding. Deepened insight gives rise to *new needs*, requiring for their satisfaction the invention of new modes of labor. These, in turn, reconstitute the identity of the subject. Indeed, the dialectical interdependence of self and nature in instrumental activity is itself productive of higher stages of rationality and freedom. Labor not only reveals a rational *potential* to be progressively realized, but contributes to its very shaping. This leads to a potentially freer, more civilized, more complex, and yet more needful humanity.

Thus, dialectical rationality implies a unity of opposites, whose necessity is apparent from the very beginning, but only in a very undeveloped and imperfect sense. The unity of human subjectivity and natural objectivity, constitutive of free rational agency, designates a potential realizable in history. "Reconciliation" with nature comes with mastering it. Literally, it comes by imposing one's identity on it and assimilating it to one's needs through technology and science. Reconciliation with others proceeds on a different plane. It requires the establishment of legal, moral, economic, and political institutions guaranteeing universal equality and freedom. So long as domination exists, recognition will at most be limited and imperfect. No one will be truly free, not even the masters, because their own freedom and sense of self will be continually challenged by the will of oppressed people.

Progress in morality and ethics occurs primarily in the production of cultural ideas, not in the production of material necessities. The struggle for recognition, as mentioned earlier, designates a social activity whereby individuals come to realize that their very identity as free subjects depends on social recognition. Yet, it is primarily at the level of culture that this Enlightenment dilemma—the mediation of individual freedom and communal morality—is resolved. Hegel calls cultural life Absolute Spirit, by which he means art, religion, and philosophy. It is at this level, he argues, that a people or nation articulates its *ideal* self-image or self-concept. More specifically, this self-concept expresses the level of freedom which this people or nation feels it has ideally attained. The ideal is prior to the real insofar as it lends the real total unity, meaning, legitimacy and purpose. In short, it lends "truth" to existing economic, social, and political relations.

Yet, the relationship between the ideal and the real is more complicated and dialectical than this priority would suggest. The ideal is itself objectively "realized" or concretely defined by existing relations and so is nothing apart from the real. However, it also transcends the real. The ideal is *other* than the real, because it is more rational and perfect than it. When the dialectical implications of the cultural ideal are made explicit by philosophers and religious leaders, a *rationality crisis* occurs—of the sort mentioned above with respect to the Enlightenment. The "truth" of existing institutions is called into question and either stagnation or revolution occurs. In the latter case, an attempt is made to bring existing reality into harmony with the ideal.

However, this attempt at overcoming the contradiction between reality (apparent manifestation of truth) and ideality (the truth in its essence) by producing a new identity, merely perpetuates the dialectic. Since transformation of existing social reality necessarily brings with it *reinterpretation* and transformation of the cultural ideal, a new contradiction appears, albeit at a more *advanced* level. The "truth" of the previous social formation is preserved, but possibilities for freedom that were hitherto suppressed by the former contradiction are now revealed in all their dialectical complexity.

We see here how Hegel resolves the Enlightenment's opposition between moral rationality (freedom) and scientific rationality (determinism). Neither view is held to be absolutely true. Or rather, each of these types of reason are shown to be complementary aspects of a higher, philosophical form of reason that has achieved final insight regarding the Idea. Philosophy shows us that freedom without causal necessity is meaningless—both conceptually and factually. A will that was determined by nothing would be arbitrary and without direction. If the willing self were only pure spontaneity it would lack the desire, experience, and bodily habits necessary in order to act. Factually, scientific knowledge of causal necessity enables the subject to gain mastery over nature, thereby achieving freedom from nature. Causal necessity without freedom would also be meaningless. For it is only by freely intervening in our world that we "constitute" it as orderly, thereby enabling the "discovery" of lawful patterns.

To sum up: Hegel maintained that world history reflects the progressive unfolding of reason and freedom along a course that has been predetermined from the outset. Although the Idea of reason is subject to the vicissitudes of history, its successive interpretations by the great systems of philosophy are ultimately determined by its own *internal* logic. This logic is characterized by three principal "moments." First, there is a stage of latency or *immediacy* in which the Idea as inner potential has not yet taken definite shape in actual institutions. Plato's purely philosophical intuition concerning the relationship between knowledge, freedom, and happiness exemplifies this moment. Next, there is a stage of *mediation*, or *externalization*, whereby the Idea as movement of self-opposition achieves definite articulation in cultural, social, economic, and political institutions. The Enlightenment's actualization of Plato's intuition in the conflicting institutions of mechanistic science and moral law would exemplify this stage. Lastly, there is a stage of *reconciliation* in which the *objectified* character of the institutionally embodied Idea is surpassed. Philosophically comprehended, we now realize that the causal world—which science constructs in opposition to our moral world—is somehow an inextricable part of that moral world. Both worlds now appear as what they essentially are—the product of "our" common subjectivity or Spirit.

The objectification characteristic of the second stage is initially experienced as a loss of self to an object which the self itself has created. Here the object produced takes on a life of its own, *alien and opposed* to the freedom of the self. In Christianity, for example, the rational perfectability implicit in humanity as a whole is projected outward in the form of an all-powerful transcendent deity in comparison to which we feel limited, unfree, and worthless. The Enlightenment succeeded in eliminating the radical transcendence of reason by secularizing the divine principle. Reason is now understood as a faculty within each individual. However, a new split, between transcendent moral reason and this-worldly scientific reason is reproduced within the individual. Our universal nature as free and moral beings is opposed by our materialistic nature as self-centered, causally predetermined individuals. This contradiction, between our "externalized" essence and our internal self-understanding, Hegel believes, is a necessary stage in the development of individual moral conscience. It sets universal reason (the Holy Spirit within each of us) against the particularity of our own selfish inclinations and cultural prejudices. Nevertheless, moral and religious alienation must be overcome in order for us to achieve complete freedom and happiness.

The potential for such overcoming, of course, is already implicit in the rational necessity of divine Incarnation. For Hegel, the reign of freedom began when the individualism and universalism implicit in Protestant Christianity—set in motion by the Enlightenment—was actualized (institutionally embodied) in the legal constitution of the modern state. However, it is only the philosopher, Hegel adds, who achieves complete freedom and self-fulfillment. Only persons like himself who have rethought the historical phenomenology are reconciled to God, nature, and state. They see the progressive stages of enlightenment as these have unfolded within the dialectic of human experience. For it is the totalizing perspective, opened up by philosophical reflection, that first reveals such objectifications to be what they are in truth. They are nothing less than ideal *products* of the combined cognitive and moral activity of the human spirit.

Hegel's most important contribution to critical theory consists in conceiving reason as institutionalized social practice and living dialectic. The cognitive as well as moral concepts by which we impose meaningful order on ourselves and on our world are intertwined in the *totality* of our "way of life." In everyday life one cannot rigorously distinguish facts from values, what is the case from what ought to be the case. Our moral ideals are instantiated in the institutions and practices in which they are factually embedded. These institutions and practices, in turn, circumscribe our traffic with the world and determine the way we perceive it. Kant's "abstract" distinction between science and morality, natural necessity and human freedom, historical change and universal reason is *analytically* correct. But this reproduction of the Enlightenment's own unresolved contradiction fails to do justice to the *dialectical* unity and dynamic tension informing the *whole* of our historical experience.

A true understanding of society presupposes a *comprehensive dialectical* grasp of the *totality of relationships*, both intensive and extensive, logical and historical, that sustain its unity even while threatening its *dis*unity. This idea is one of the guiding principles of critical theory. Beneath the "abstract" mathematical world of static proportions and externally related causal events there lies a deeper subjectivity, or spiritual life, possessing its own dynamic rationale. The rationalist and empiricist objectivism characteristic of modern natural and behavioral science gives us access only to the *appearances*. These are the superficial statistical "laws" governing events taken in isolation from the totality of living relations constitutive of their *essential* meaning, unity, and purpose. The dialectical approach characteristic of philosophical reflection, by contrast, integrates the partial—and to that extent, false—perspectives of analytic reason into a complete organic system. It does so without thereby concealing the potential for conflict buried within that system.

Significantly, it was precisely over the issue of systemic completeness that Marx and later critical theorists broke ranks with Hegel.[3] Hegel had argued that the basic contours of rational life were in the process of being finally established in Europe's liberal monarchies.[4] Not surprisingly, the notion that the dialectic of reason was coming to an end struck Hegel's more radical followers (known as Young, or Left Hegelians) as highly undialectical. Likewise, many of them found irony in Hegel's belief in the "cunning of reason" as determining the destiny of Western civilization. In Hegel's reading, free, rational insight, into the emancipatory potential inherent in the historical process, is denied to the actual makers of history. Such insight is limited to the retrospective reflection of the philosopher. For them, the general course of a history all but completed is necessarily regarded as the inevitable outcome of an impersonal logic. Thus, reason and freedom make their appearance at the conclusion of a history whose actual meaning, at least as far as the participants are concerned, is one of unreason and unfreedom.

Again, many Left Hegelians argued that Hegel's idea of the rational state contained serious "unresolved" contradictions that were incompatible with universal freedom. In his early writings, the young Marx pointed out that Hegel's attempt to "reconcile" civil society and state fails. Civil society designates the system of private property wherein persons pursue their own particular interests. The state, by contrast, designates the ethical order of shared customs and laws instantiating the general good of all. Hegel believed that civil society and state, particular and universal interests, could be "mediated" by larger corporate bodies, such as professional and business associations, as well as by an impartial bureaucracy. Such mediation is bound to fail, Marx claims, since each of these groups will put their own corporate or class interest ahead of the public good.[5]

Furthermore, the "negative" freedom afforded by abstract property rights and civil liberties is rational only up to a point. The universal freedom and equality of everyone to pursue their private interest unhindered by others also results in mutual exclusion, alienation, and social conflict. Formal equality under the law stipulates that each is *permitted* to exercise a freedom consonant with the right of others to do the same. This is compatible with great material inequality, so that the rights to property, public opinion, and free speech of those who possess wealth far exceeds *in actual power* the rights of those who don't. Although Marx criticized Hegel for not acknowledging the inherent rationality of direct universal suffrage, he realized that formal democracy— under conditions of great social inequality—was but a pretext for the wealthy to extend their class domination under the rational guise of advancing the common interest.

Finally, in a manner reminiscent of Kant's moral teachings, Marx criticized the system of private property as an unfree system of mutual exploitation and egoism in which individuals are reduced to mere means in the pursuit of profit. Hegel, too, had expressed deep concern over the brutal exploitation and impoverishment of the working class in the nineteenth century. But, like most thinkers of his period, he did not think that persons lacking property or education should be allowed to elect representatives to governing bodies. Instead, he adopted the paternalistic and (from a Marxian perspective) naive view that business and professional organizations would voluntarily take care of their workers. He thought that the state would intervene, when necessary, to guarantee their humane treatment.

For Marx, on the contrary, a system that denied any voice in governance to the vast majority of its citizens—while subjecting them to exploitation and poverty—was neither rational nor free. Indeed, how *could* it be if the human powers externalized in the process of production and consumption took on a life of their own? This is especially true if production is hostile and alien to the very producers whose development these powers were supposed to advance. In the final analysis, the conflicts between individual and society, freedom and necessity, ideality and materiality, which Hegel inherited from the Enlightenment were incapable of being resolved philosophically. Thus, Marx, who was the first to regard these conflicts as real and unavoidable tensions within capitalism itself, called for the practical—and that meant, social, economic, and political—completion of the Enlightenment legacy through revolutionary action.

MARX'S CRITIQUE OF POLITICAL ECONOMY

Marx radicalized the critique of reason, as undertaken by Kant and Hegel, by showing how ideas were themselves *ideological* manifestations of real socioeconomic forces. In particular, he showed that they reflected a politically charged, class-based content. In effect, this amounted to transforming philosophy into social science, *idealistic* critique of *knowledge* into *materialistic* critique of *political economy*.

Although Marx was profoundly influenced by the master-servant dialectic expounded by Hegel, he objected to the way in which Hegel elevated ideal philosophical activity (cultural production) above material labor (scientific and economic production) as the primary vehicle of historical progress.[6] By emphasizing the ideal over the material, Hegel could "delude" himself into thinking that, at least from the vantage point of pure philosophical reason, the contradictions between the individual and society, freedom and natural necessity, had been overcome. For Hegel, workers and capitalists might be mortal enemies in the workplace, but are otherwise reconciled by common membership in the ideal communities of Church and state. For Marx, on the contrary, these "ideal communities" lack a basis in real everyday life: the life of work and consumption. They are mere ideologies or *illusory legitimations* of the status quo. They mask real inequality and domination behind the veneer of rational (i.e., necessary and universal) laws ostensibly designed to advance the interests of all persons equally and impartially.[7]

Marx described his own materialist approach to history as standing Hegel's dialectic "rightside up."[8] It is not ideas and philosophical reflection that determine the course of history, but the forces and relations of material production. *Productive forces* include labor, its instruments, and organization. *Productive relations* designate forms of ownership that regulate access to the means of production and the distribution of wealth. Together these forces and relations constitute a definite *mode of production*. Modes of production can be ranked on an evolutionary scale, depending on how much they advance the emancipation and realization of human powers. They begin with the communal mode of production, characteristic of primitive societies and advance through ancient (slave), feudal, capitalist, socialist, and communist modes of production. The mode of production thus comprises "the real foundation on which rises a legal and political superstructure and to which correspond definite forms of social consciousness . . . (and) conditions the social, political, and intellectual life processes in general."[9]

Marx's critique of philosophical idealism does not signal a wholesale abandonment of critical theory. Philosophical ideas are still accorded an important role in guiding practice. Thus, it would be wrong to assume that for Marx the economic "base" causally conditions the social, legal-political, and cultural-ideological "superstructure" unilaterally. As Marx repeatedly points out, the state's monopoly over education (ideological indoctrination) and coercive violence (law and order) is vital to the maintenance of the economic system. He also notes that the predominance of economy over culture and polity fully obtains only under capitalism. However, the motor of historical progress ultimately resides within the economy. In a nutshell, Marx's theory of *historical materialism* maintains that progressive advances in the ideological sphere—above all in religion, morality, and law—reflect deeper advances in the economic and political spheres. The ascendance of new social and economic classes gives rise to new forms of government which, in turn, reflect advances in the mode of production.

Advances in the mode of production are *necessitated* by unresolved contradictions between the forces and relations of production. Sometimes Marx attributes the contradiction to the development of productive forces beyond the regulative capacity of productive relations. This happened when the development of new agricultural techniques, in conjunction with the rise of large-scale manufacturing, forced (or drew) peasants off the land. The old feudal economic obligations binding lord and serf were thereby undermined. However, one could just as easily characterize the contradiction as involving a "fettering" of the development of productive forces by productive relations. Thus, the craft mode of textile production organized around the feudal guild, with its restrictive wage and price setting, its hostility toward more mechanized and segmented labor practices, etc. could be seen as frustrating the emergence of more competitive, cost-effective factory production needed to clothe a growing—and increasingly impoverished—urban work force.

The contradiction between a more rational, capitalistic organization of production and distribution and the less-rational system of feudal privileges and restrictions, Marx argued, was reflected "upward" in the form of a political class struggle. The aristocracy defended the unlimited right of monarchic rule. The bourgeoisie pressed for representative (if not democratic) forms of constitutionally limited government. These political differences were further articulated in opposed religious and philosophical ideologies. The feudal defense of hierarchy and privilege—the divine right of kings to unlimited dominion—found cognate expression in the exclusive, divinely appointed, authority of priests to administer sacraments in communal ritual. It was also reflected in the paternalistic obligation to ensure that even the poorest subjects were provided for (noblesse oblige). By contrast, the bourgeois defense of formal equality, individual freedom, and the constitutional separation of powers (the system of checks and balances), was reflected upward in the competitive achievement ideology of Protestantism. It manifested itself in the hostility toward centralized religious authority, the need for the lone believer to confirm his or her faith (and therewith, salvation) through accumulating the blessings of industry, and in the unbrotherly belief in predestination—the salvation of the elect few, the damnation of the many.

If Hegel regarded the bourgeois state as the apex of institutionalized rationality in which reconciliation is achieved, Marx saw it as an ideological illusion concealing a profound contradiction. For him it was a system of "rationalized" social production producing irrational, antisocial consequences. Capitalism, Marx believed, contains the greatest emancipatory potential—as evidenced in its ideology of individual freedom, equality, and democratic self-determination. But it is embodied in the most perverse (i.e., the most unfree and undemocratic), system of alienation and exploitation.

Alienation, exploitation, and fetishism are catch phrases in Marx's description of the principal ways in which the system of capitalism comes to dominate and oppress the very subjects whose essential humanity it incorporates. The most detailed critique of alienation is contained in the *Economic and Philosophic Manuscripts* of 1844. There Marx observed that under capitalism, workers are alienated from their products, their labor, others, and, ultimately, from themselves. The premise underlying this four-pronged critique derives from Hegel's notion that *self-expressive* labor is the principal vehicle for realizing the free creativity and rational sociality, the individuality and universality, of the human subject.[10] First of all, workers under capitalism no longer identify with the products they produce. Contrast, for example, the pride that craftsmen take in producing a complete individual artifact from scratch with the indifference of, say, a bolt-tightener on an automobile assembly line, a clerk-typist, or a miner, who seldom see their individuality expressed in the final product.[11] Second, and more serious, workers no longer control their own laboring activity. Working conditions are dictated to the worker by management, and these conditions—often involving simple repetitive movements determined in advance by the mechanical rhythm of machinery—are both mentally and physically debilitating.

As the intelligence and skill of workers are diminished, their potential to respond freely, rationally, and creatively to their nonworking environment is greatly reduced. The dehumanization of workers impacts upon their relations with others. The fragmentation of the labor process destroys a sense of cooperation. Indeed, competition among workers for scarce jobs, promotion opportunities, and long-term security often breeds mistrust and competitiveness. Those who feel their own self-worth diminished through failure to succeed on the job are likely to project these negative feelings onto friends and family as well. This explains the high incidence of violence among the most marginalized sectors of the working class.

Finally, workers under capitalism are alienated from their own humanity and subjectivity. Workers are not regarded as moral ends whose humanity and freedom is of the highest value. Rather, they are treated as mere means for the production of profit. Their "worth" consists entirely of the market value of their labor. Workers come to see themselves as just another commodity, another piece of machinery, another *object* whose value depreciates or appreciates over time, depending on something that is entirely beyond their control—the vicissitudes of supply and demand. It is not surprising, therefore, that the pursuit of money replaces the pursuit of excellence. For, as Marx points out, what's important under capitalism is not the kind of person you are (loving, sensitive, caring) but how much capital you possess. All endowments can be purchased and all deficiencies compensated for with enough money. Thus, far from engaging in the sorts of creative pursuits that lend themselves to the enhancement of their *individuality*, workers end up performing undistinguished tasks and leading undistinguished lives. The simple uniformity of their workaday routines is reflected in the simple uniformity of their daily existence as passive consumers of standardized products.

This last form of alienation is directly related to Marx's theory of exploitation and commodity fetishism. As in the case of his theory of alienation, the key to understanding exploitation and commodity fetishism resides in the perverse transformation of the combined laboring power of living subjects into an objective force (capital). Standing over and against them is a hostile destiny to which they must submit. Operating under the quasi-natural, *objective* laws of the market, the mechanism of exchange determines the flow and value of all commodities, human and nonhuman alike.

Marx introduces the notion of exploitation in conjunction with the inability of bourgeois political economists to explain surplus value (profit) in accordance with their assumption that market transactions are just (i.e., involve a free exchange of equal values).[12] If one assumes that commodities of equal value are freely exchanged (e.g., that the labor of the worker is freely exchanged for its equivalent value in wages), then how is it that capitalists accumulate such a disproportionate share of society's wealth in comparison to workers? Marx's answer harks back to John Locke's theory that labor is the principal source of value. He underscores the disproportion between labor power, understood as *exchange value*, or commodity, and labor power understood as *use value*, or living productivity. Under capitalism, the exchange value of labor power is equivalent to the food, clothing, and shelter requisite for maintaining and reproducing workers and their families under historically variable conditions of basic subsistence. As use value, however, labor power is capable of generating more value—food, clothing, etc.—than is required for subsistence. The disproportionate value between labor power as commodity and labor power as living productivity is registered in the difference between workers' daily wages and their daily productivity. This difference gets pocketed by the capitalist in the form of profit.

Despite the appearance of justice, Marx argues, the wage contract is coercive and exploitative. It is exploitative because only a portion of the working day is spent by workers producing the value requisite for their own subsistence. The rest is spent working—without remuneration—for the capitalist. It is coercive because, under fairly constant conditions of marginal unemployment, workers have little choice but to either accept the contracts that are offered them or "starve" (i.e., fall below society's minimal standard of subsistence).

For Marx, the problem of unemployment is endemic to capitalist exploitation. It also illustrates how the "fetishistic" nature of the market is reflected in recurrent crises (business cycles) over which the combined producers have no control. Here, the negative freedom and individualism touted by the Enlightenment turns against itself.

In the third volume of *Capital*, Marx argued that business cycles caused by overproduction are ultimately rooted in the increasing accumulation of capital in the hands of fewer and fewer capitalists. This is compounded by chronic unemployment and depressed wages. These latter symptoms ultimately diminish investment opportunity and force the scaling back of production. Thus, we see a general tendency within capitalism for profit rates to decrease as production becomes more capital-intensive.

The tendency for the fall in the rate of profit is directly related to the labor theory of value. Marx believed that fixed capital—the machinery, technology, and raw materials expended in the production process—does not add value to the product produced. It only transfers past value. "Dead" labor is congealed in the machinery and raw resources. All things being equal, the less "living" labor that is utilized in the production process, the less opportunity provided for exploitation and generation of surplus value. Marx expressed this reduction in terms of the following equation, which defines profitability as the ratio of surplus value to total capital outlay. Since the rate of profit P is equal to the ratio of surplus value S over constant capital C plus variable capital (wages) V—or $P = S/C + V$—the greater the percentage spent on C relative to V the lower the rate of P. The falling rate of P is explained by the fact that S will proportionally decline in relation to increases of C. This decline can be offset only by proportionally increasing the rate of exploitation (S/V). That is, you must lower wages relative to constant rates of productivity or increase productivity relative to constant rates of remuneration.

Marx observed that the laws of competition force each individual capitalist to increase the amount of capital spent on machinery and technology relative to the amount spent on labor. Given the limits of the workday and of subsistence wage rates, capitalists can only expand their markets by underselling their competitors. That is, they must produce more value for less total expenditure through the introduction of labor-saving technology. Where the introduction of such technology enhances the production of surplus value, by enabling workers to produce the same amount of goods in a shorter period of time, the cost of a single item produced can be depreciated without necessarily lowering the profit obtained from total sales. Here we have a case in which an *increase* of C might also result in an *increase* of S, so long as the labor cost V, of the items necessary to maintain the worker, is proportionally *decreased* relative to the decrease in the cost of producing commodities generally.

There is an *initial* profitability in technological innovation. More efficient production results in cheaper products, lower wages, and greater exploitation (surplus value). Thus, it is unclear how a fall in the rate of profit could come about. Yet Marx noted that the initial advantage gained by an innovative capitalist, or sector of the economy, is nullified once the rest of the competition "catches up." Given the accelerated pace at which machinery is rendered obsolete and replaced under ever more intense conditions of competition, expenditures in constant capital will increasingly become too costly. That is, the machinery will fail to recover its original cost through higher productivity by the time it is "prematurely" depreciated.

Thus, Marx believed that the introduction of labor-saving technology would eventually produce disfunctional side effects. Not the least of these is the accelerated destruction of uncompetitive industries and the replacement of workers by machinery, culminating in increased unemployment and declining wages. The resulting decline in consumption would then cause a crisis of overproduction. The decreased demand would depress prices and lower the rate of profit. An alternative scenario envisaged by Marx ties the falling rate of profit to increased wage demands. Increases in productivity would raise the cost of maintaining living standards commensurate with workers' heightened *expectations*. It would also raise the cost of reproducing an ever more sophisticated, educated, skilled labor force needed for handling new technology.

Marx was certainly not unaware of other tendencies which might counteract the falling rate of profit. But he believed that the fundamental contradiction between production for private profit and production for social consumption would inevitably result in economic collapse or long-term stagnation.[13] In a system such as this, market forces take on an irrational life of their own, regardless of the rational calculations of individual workers and capitalists in "free" pursuit of their private aims. It's as if the role of master and servant were reversed. The "masters," or would-be rational producers, are reduced to passive objects. They become mere appendages and victims of a system they have fetishized—or endowed with a stubborn will of its own—and which has become resistant to their needs.

THE PHILOSOPHICAL HERITAGE
OF CRITICAL THEORY: AN OVERVIEW

Let us briefly recapitulate the ground we have covered so far. The driving force behind the philosophical genesis of critical theory can be traced back to several key problems revolving around the relationship between theory and practice. During the Enlightenment this problem took the following form: How does one reconcile the idealistic and largely ethical heritage of philosophical reason with the materialistic heritage of scientific reason? To put it another way, how does one reconcile the democratic and communitarian thrust of a moral reason emphasizing universal equality with the individualistic and acquisitive thrust of a scientific reason emphasizing self-preservation? Or again, how does one reconcile the notion of transcendent freedom with natural and historical causation?

Kant attempted to solve the contradiction inherent in Enlightenment rationality philosophically, by means of a critique of reason itself. Reason, he argued, is not merely a passive faculty of analysis. It is also an active faculty of synthesis. Transcendental reason is not wholly transcendent; it is not independent of and cut off from reality. Rather, it is directly productive of reality, including the mechanistic world of material objects.

Kant's transcendental idealism enabled him to affirm the radical freedom of the rational subject against the objectivism of empirical science. However, the price he paid for endowing humanity with radical freedom was a new metaphysical dualism separating moral from scientific reason and ideal from material reality. Once again, a gap was introduced between moral theory and everyday practice.

Hegel sought to bridge the gap by integrating philosophy and history—a strategy which Kant himself had anticipated in his writings on history. Reason, he argued, was not a transcendent subjective faculty, but consisted of real objective institutions whose development had been propelled by contradictions inherent in the ideas they embodied. These contradictions—between freedom and necessity, communality and individuality, philosophy and science, Spirit and nature—were precisely those that achieved their fullest expression during the Enlightenment. Regarding his own philosophy as the culmination of Enlightenment thought, Hegel believed that the contradictions inherent in reason had, in fact, been more or less resolved in the constitutional monarchy of early nineteenth-century Prussia. The reconciliation of individual freedom and ethical community, he believed, was now a fact to be contemplated, not a task to be accomplished.

The conservative implications of Hegel's philosophy, however, still seemed to contradict social reality. For Marx, at any rate, the fulfillment of the emancipatory aims of the Enlightenment remained a task that could not be dismissed philosophically. The contradictions besetting the Enlightenment reflect contradictions inherent in capitalism itself. In capitalism, the contradictions between individual and community, freedom and necessity, morality and science all boil down to the principle of private property. Production is social but consumption is private. Private entrepreneurs are scientific in calculating the profitability of their enterprises, but the cumulative impact of their decisions results in an irrational anarchy of overproduction. Freedom to buy and sell is circumscribed by the law of supply and demand. One's individuality as proprietor demands alienation of those social powers which truly individuate.

Marx takes what appears to be the decisive step in resolving the theory/ practice problem. The critique of reason must move beyond philosophy and become the scientific critique of political economy. The overcoming of objectivism and the realization of enlightenment can only be achieved politically, by abolishing capitalism. In communism, individual freedom and democratic community will be joined together by true justice and happiness.

In the next chapter we will see how Marx envisaged the political struggle for emancipation. It was an optimistic forecast. Workers would achieve rational insight into their world historical destiny and establish a humane socialist state. That this did not happen, critical theorists argued, was primarily due to two factors, both of which were absent in Marx's thought: state intervention in the economy and deep psychological undercurrents resisting enlightenment. It is the latter problem, illuminated by Sigmund Freud (1856–1939), which led them to appreciate the intransigence of ideological modes of thought and behavior.

All this raises new philosophical questions. What role does philosophy continue to play in the aftermath of Marx's critique of Hegel? If Hegel blunted the revolutionary force of moral reason by assimilating it to existing social reality, must we then turn to a more transcendent notion of reason? Are there agencies within existing social reality that embody this rationality? Or, does the heritage of the Enlightenment ultimately present us with an unsolvable set of contradictions pitting individual against society, science against morality, negative freedom versus positive freedom? These are just some of the questions we will explore in the chapters to come.

NOTES

1. M. Horkheimer, "Traditional and Critical Theory," *Critical Theory* (New York: Herder and Herder, 1972), 188–243. Selections of this essay are reprinted in *Critical Theory: The Essential Readings*, ed. David Ingram and Julia Simon-Ingram (Paragon House: New York, 1991). Hereafter *CTER*.

2. According to Kant, moral reason compels us to *think* we are free, even though we can never *know*—that is, empirically demonstrate or theoretically prove—this to be the case.

3. There was great disagreement among members of the Frankfurt School as to Hegel's positive contribution to critical theory. Contrast, for example, Marcuse's highly appreciative reading of the Hegelian legacy in *Reason and Revolution: Hegel and the Rise of Social Theory* (New York: Oxford University Press, 1941) with Adorno's penetrating critique of the same in *Negative Dialectics* (New York: Seabury Press,

1973). For a concise statement of Adorno's views abut philosophy in general and Hegelian dialectics in particular, see his essay "Why Philosophy?" reprinted in *CTER*.

4. Hegel's chief work on political philosophy (1821) was translated into English by T.M. Knox under the title *Hegel's Philosophy of Right* (Oxford: Oxford University Press, 1952).

5. See the following works by Marx (all written in 1843): *Critique of Hegel's Philosophy of Right, On the Jewish Question*, and *Toward a Critique of Hegel's Philosophy of Right*.

6. Marx discusses the importance of Hegel's analysis of labor in his *Economic and Philosophic Manuscripts* of 1844.

7. For Marx's critique of German Idealism and its ideological functioning see *The Holy Family* (1845) and *The German Ideology* (1845), both of which were coauthored by Friedrich Engels.

8. Karl Marx, Afterword to the Second German Edition, *Capital* (1873).

9. Karl Marx, *Preface to a Critique of Political Economy* (New York: International Publishers, 1968), p. 182. Originally published in German in 1859.

10. The concept of human nature as instantiating an awareness of universal freedom and sociality also owes a great deal to Ludwig Feuerbach's humanism.

11. For a more recent analysis of alienation, see Harry Braverman, *Labor and Monopoly Capitalism* (New York: Monthly Review Press, 1974). Of the members of the Frankfurt School, it was Herbert Marcuse who repeatedly stressed the importance of the *Economic and Philosophic Manuscripts* for providing a humanistic ground for critical theory. See, for example, "The Foundation of Historical Materialism" (1932) translated from the original German and republished in H. Marcuse, *Studies in Critical Philosophy* (Boston: Beacon Press, 1973), pp. 1–48; and "Philosophy and Critical Theory" (1937) reprinted in *CTER*.

12. See Marx's discussion of the general formula for capital in volume one of *Capital*.

13. The falling rate of profit can be offset by transferring assets abroad or to regions (the Southern states) where unions are weak and labor costs are low, or by acquiring government subsidies, tax breaks (depletion and depreciation allowances) and research funds. Of course, the tax revenues required for such government expenditures must themselves be drawn largely from business profits, thus once again offsetting whatever advantage might have been gained through government intervention. See Manuel Castells, *The Economic Crisis and American Society* (Princeton: Princeton University Press, 1980), pp. 102–23.

SELECTED BIBLIOGRAPHY

Descartes, René. *Meditations on First Philosophy*. In *The Philosophical Works of Descartes*. Translated by E.S. Haldane and G.R.T. Ross. Cambridge, 1911.

Hume, David. *An Inquiry Concerning Human Understanding*. In *David Hume. On Human Nature and the Understanding*. New York, 1962.

Hegel, Georg Wilhelm Friedrich. *The Phenomenology of Spirit*. Trans. A.V. Miller. Oxford, 1977.

———*Hegel's Philosophy of Right*. Trans. T.M. Knox. Oxford, 1973.

Kant, Immanuel. *Critique of Pure Reason*. Trans. Norman Kemp Smith. New York, 1965.

———*Critique of Practical Reason*. Trans. Lewis White Beck. New York, 1976.

Marx, Karl. *Capital: A Critical Analysis of Capitalist Production*. Trans. S. Moore and E. Aveling. New York, 1973. 3 volumes.

———*Karl Marx: Selected Writings*. Ed. David McLellan. Oxford, 1977.

Commentaries: A few of the more accessible introductions to the thought of Kant, Hegel, and Marx may be found in the following: Stephan Körner *Kant* (Oxford: Penguin, 1960); Charles Taylor, *Hegel* (Cambridge, 1977); Erich Fromm, *Marx's Concept of Man* (New York, 1961); David McLellan, *The Thought of Karl Marx* (London, 1971).

Works by Critical Theorists on Kant, Hegel, and Marx: The most accessible studies by critical theorists on classical German thought are the following: Jürgen Habermas, *Knowledge and Human Interests* (Boston, 1971); *Theory and Practice* (Boston, 1973); Herbert Marcuse, *Reason and Revolution: Hegel and the Rise of Social Theory* (Oxford, 1941); and "The Foundation of Historical Materialism," in *Studies in Critical Philosophy* (Boston, 1973).

TWO

FROM THEORY TO PRACTICE: FREUD AND THE PROBLEM OF IDEOLOGY

In the preceding chapter I sought to show how critical theory arose out of the philosophical movement known as the Enlightenment. This movement attempted to implement politically the Platonic idea that knowledge emancipates. Knowledge is here understood in a practical sense, incorporating both the scientific discovery of technically useful causal laws and the philosophical disclosure of moral principles. Together, these forms of practical knowledge were supposed to spearhead progress in the attainment of freedom, justice, and happiness.

The advocates of enlightenment felt optimistic about prospects for rational progress because they believed that moral theory was not a utopian undertaking cut off from everyday practice. It was assumed that each individual possessed the requisite mental faculties—reason and common sense—by which insight into universal truths could be attained. However, the optimistic belief that the theory/practice problem would be inevitably resolved in the course of time foundered on a basic tension between science and philosophy. Despite the seamless manner in which these two were often equated at the beginning of the eighteenth century, it became clear by the end of that century that science and philosophy were not so easily reconcilable, after all. For Kant, at least, moral philosophy presupposed the existence of a purely rational form of freedom that transcended the mechanistic, spatio-temporal world of science. Indeed, he found it necessary to limit critically the valid use of scientific rationality to explain the possibility of moral freedom.

Kant's dualistic philosophy, which categorically distinguished the rational from the empirical self, showed just how little the theory/practice problem had been resolved. He and his followers in the German philosophical tradition therefore turned to history to explain how a state of natural unfreedom and individual self-interest could bring about a truly free, rational, and moral community. Hegel appealed to a dialectical conception of reason to show that the inherent contradictions in the Enlightenment—that had prevented it from being fully realized—had finally been resolved in the modern state. Marx, on the contrary, felt that Hegel's resolution of the theory/practice problem was premature. Sounding more like Kant, he maintained that the completion of enlightenment was a task that had to be accomplished in practice, not in theory.

Criticizing the one-sided idealism of philosophical rationalism, Marx argued that real freedom could be brought about only by radically changing the material (economic) conditions of life. Capitalism is the penultimate expression, not the resolution, of what Hegel had diagnosed as the unresolved contradiction of the Enlightenment: the opposition between subject and object, individual and society, freedom and nature. Alienation and objectivism do not refer merely to the philosophically unenlightened state of the modern psyche. The dehumanization and loss of freedom experienced by producers is directly correlated with market systems that possess a life of their own, beyond the rational control of the producers themselves.

It is with Marx that objectivism ceases to be a problem of knowledge or metaphysics and becomes a political problem. The problem is one of relating social theory to revolutionary practice. Marx agrees with Hegel that the subjective conditions for gaining true insight are largely dependent on objective sociohistorical factors. Under capitalism these factors directly contribute to alienation, objectivistic illusion (commodity fetishism), and ideological falsification. Therefore, the question arises about how persons living in capitalist societies can achieve the theoretical insight necessary for rationally changing their society. We are confronted here with a vicious circle: Rational insight is a prerequisite for enlightened revolution, but revolution would appear to be a prerequisite for rational insight.

Marx tried to solve this problem by citing the dialectical relationship between the rising *class consciousness* of workers—a class whose emancipatory interests he regarded as universally valid for all persons—and the breakdown of the capitalist system. Later critical theorists, however, saw that this dialectic could be mitigated through state intervention in the economy. With economic collapse by no means assured, the objective conditions leading to heightened class consciousness appeared to be lacking.

It was at this point where critical theorists saw the need to recover the philosophical idealism of Hegel and Kant that had been largely—though never entirely—suppressed in Marx's own critique of political economy. Followers of Marx tended to take their lead from his longtime friend and collaborator, Friedrich Engels, who emphasized the "scientific" aspect of socialist thought.

By collapsing theory into a narrowly conceived scientific practice, they ended up severely compromising the critical thrust of Marxist thought. Marxism became increasingly identified with a predictive economic theory that had no need for raising political consciousness.

Orthodox Marxists like Karl Kautsky and V.I. Lenin believed that the "inexorable laws" of capitalism would inevitably lead to economic collapse and, with it, the spontaneous unification of a proletariat conscious of its class interests. On this interpretation, the role of theory is limited to articulating this inevitably to the proletariat. Because workers lack scientific insight regarding their own destiny, they must be guided along by the intellectual vanguard which composes the leadership of the Communist party. *Revisionist* Marxists like Eduard Bernstein broke with the economic determinism of the orthodox camp in arguing that the formation of class consciousness depended on political organization. However, they also held a "scientistic" view of Marxism which left little room for critique. If the economic status of workers is one of division, so that their interests are spread over many conflicting roles—that of citizen, consumer, and so on—then a purely descriptive theory is inadequate to argue that any one of these interests is morally superior to any other. Therefore, to the extent that capitalism itself becomes humane and democratic, workers may come to accept social-welfare reform and not revolution as best satisfying their true needs.

Critical theorists rejected both of these "scientistic" versions of Marxism as insufficiently critical, arguing that a philosophically enlightened social theory could adduce universal moral standards from historical practice. Because of the role that nationalist and other sectarian ideologies play in shaping political consciousness, they realized that one could not directly appeal to the actual preferences of workers or any other social class, in determining what their true interests are. Like Hegel, they were inclined to regard cultural artifacts—especially those of art and philosophy—as best revealing the true interests and ideal norms underlying the just and happy society. However, in conformity with Marx's critique of ideology, they understood the need to mediate philosophical insight with social science. In this respect, Marx's analysis of capitalism was deemed to be necessary but not sufficient. What was needed was a psychological science explaining the natural and social dynamics of consciousness as such. Their discovery of Freudian psychoanalysis filled this gap by enabling them to appreciate the *instinctual* dynamics underlying ideological *false consciousness*. By returning Marxism to its original philosophical base in German idealism and by linking this base to Freudian psychology, critical theorists hoped to resolve the theory/practice problem in ways that would open the door to a scientifically responsible form of moral criticism. Thus, the peculiar interdisciplinary social philosophy known as critical theory, was born.

THE FAILED REVOLUTION: THE REVISION OF MARX BY CRITICAL THEORY

Although Marx believed that crises were endemic to capitalism, he noted that the transition to an emancipated Communist society would have to pass through an intermediate stage of socialism. This would require the attainment of a socialist class consciousness on the part of workers, as well as economic collapse. Industrialization polarizes society into a vast mass of workers on one side and a diminishing number of capitalists on the other. It also forces the former to overcome their mutual competitiveness and alienation from one another in uniting in an organized political struggle to defend their common interests. These interests include not only the maintenance of wage scales, but also the maintenance of a collective, democratic association.[1]

As Marx notes, it is the union that galvanizes workers' awareness of their own unique role in history: as bearers of a universal human interest. This involves nothing less than the abolition of class society and political/economic domination. Marx believed that others, too, would join the struggle, once it became apparent that capitalism no longer represented a progressive force in history.

Today many would agree that private property and the pursuit of profit have become "fetters" obstructing the resolution of the world's most serious problems. These include the increasing disparity in living conditions between wealthy and poor nations, the unrelenting consumption of nonrenewable energy sources, and the continuing pollution of the globe accompanied by the depletion of the ozone layer, the potential dangers of the "greenhouse effect." There is also the persistence of urban crime and poverty, which is increasingly skewed in terms of race and gender.

Contrary to Marx's thinking, however, awareness of these problems has not resulted in the revolutionary overthrow of the capitalist system. Hence the question: How did Marx conceive the transition from capitalism to socialism and communism? To begin with, Marx noted that countries such as England had already made considerable strides in labor reform and in extending democratic rights to workers. He believed they might succeed in effecting a peaceful transition to socialism. Elsewhere, where the bourgeoisie would very likely resist any popular movement aimed at democratic reform, the only alternative remaining would be the resort to violence. This is often precipitated, Marx notes, by the counterrevolutionary forces of those who have been deposed. In any case, the new socialist state would further develop the forces of production inherited from the previous regime.

Unfortunately, the few occasions, in which Marx writes about the political structure of the new regime, are rather vague. The "dictatorship of the proletariat" mentioned in *The Communist Manifesto* (1848) implies a form of class rule that may seem incompatible with broad-based democracy. But as Marx indicates in his comments on the Paris Commune of 1871 (*The Civil War in France*), such a state would be democratic. However, it would not permit multiparty competition for elective offices. A bourgeois party representing the interests of deposed capitalists would probably not be allowed. But it would be "democratic" in the sense of permitting nearly universal participation in workers' councils, election of representatives to higher administrative offices, and so on.

We should note, in passing, that Marx's own tendency to focus on the economic to the exclusion of the political and cultural led him to underestimate the importance of the individualistic legacy of the Enlightenment. Marx criticized bourgeois individualism as antisocial and egoistic. Consequently, his failure to appreciate the value of negative freedom and pluralism for sustaining true democratic socialism probably contributed, at least indirectly, to the failure of future Communist movements to develop along fully democratic lines. We shall return to this problem below. Before we do so, we must first examine his conception of emancipated society in greater detail.

Marx believed that production would be centrally managed by the socialist state. However, it is unclear how far this would extend. Interestingly, Marx remarks in his *Critique of the Gotha Program* (1875), that for the first time ever the bourgeois principle of right—that one receives what one has earned—is fully respected. Of course, given substantive inequalities between persons' natural endowments, a bourgeois distributive justice will result in corresponding disparities in income. Yet income—in the form of labor certificates received from the state—would be redeemable only for consumable goods, not stocks or bonds. Thus, social inequality would not result in political inequality.

As class antagonisms fade away, productivity is heightened, and the overall condition of humanity is elevated, the socialist state apparatus will, in the words of Friedrich Engels, "wither away." In its place will arise a stateless Communist society, in which persons receive what they need regardless of the labor expended. Clearly, Marx envisaged a radical change in the quality of life under communism. Not only would persons become truly peaceable and cooperative, but the working day would itself be organized in accordance with the more aesthetic and democratic principles of job rotation and worker management. This would reduce the working day to a minimum, so that individuals would be able to devote most of their time and energy to developing themselves intellectually, physically, and aesthetically.

Marx's conception of Communist society can be seen as fleshing out the social preconditions that would have to obtain in order for Kant's Kingdom of Ends and Hegel's reconciliation of universal and particular to be realized. These moral ideas—of autonomy and reconciliation—inform the emancipatory aspirations of later critical theorists as well. Yet, despite their acceptance of the "moral" goals animating Marx's quest for social justice, they remained skeptical about the theoretical and historical underpinnings of his thought. Such skepticism regarding the prospects for emancipation was especially confirmed by the events following the Russian Revolution of 1917.

The principal leaders of the Russian Revolution, Vladimir Ilyich Lenin (1870–1924) and Leon Trotsky (1877–1940), were inspired by Marxist thought. However, they realized that the conditions, which prevailed in czarist Russia early in the twentieth century, were not those which Marx envisioned as ripe for revolution. First, Russia, in 1917, had not yet achieved the level of industrial development which Marx had thought necessary for socialism. Second, class relations had not matured to the point where industrial workers constituted a majority of the population. Because many workers and peasants had not achieved a revolutionary, *socialist* class consciousness, Lenin felt that the intellectual elite of the Communist party would have to lead the revolution from above.[2] It is this line of reasoning that led the Communists to exclude less revolutionary socialist parties from any effective power-sharing. The need to centralize authority, enforce Party discipline, and limit democratic worker control over industrial production was further justified in the name of defending the new regime against counterrevolutionary violence. Yet the end of the civil war did not bring greater democracy in its wake.

Although the democratic centralism embodied in the organization of the Party was much more exclusive and bureaucratic than anything Marx had envisioned, it did allow for some economic freedom and worker democracy. This was no longer the case after Joseph Stalin (1879–1953) came to power in 1925. Stalin abolished the New Economic Policy (1921–28), which had allowed free enterprise in the agricultural sector and the leasing of nationalized and state-owned businesses to individuals and groups. He was also instrumental in destroying the remaining vestiges of worker democracy.

It is in light of these bureaucratic tendencies that the Frankfurt School's critique of Marxist-Leninism and Stalinism must be assessed. An early economist of the Frankfurt School, Friedrich Pollock, was the first to criticize bureaucratic tendencies in the USSR. He took issue with the authoritarian expropriation of large peasant holdings as well as the forcible industrialization of the economy, which Stalin had initiated in the late twenties. By 1936, both Marcuse and Horkheimer had made it clear that socialization of the means of production must be accompanied by "freedom and happiness in the social relations among men" (Marcuse). This implied the development of "essential elements in real democracy and partnership" (Horkheimer). Thus, they agreed that the mere change in property relations did not constitute a bonafide socialist revolution in the Marxist sense.[3]

The above comments were made during a period in which the European labor movement had become seriously splintered and susceptible to the allure of reformism—or worse, fascism. In 1919, the new German Social Democratic government had cooperated with the most reactionary elements of the military in brutally suppressing a workers' revolt in Bavaria. Having failed to resolve the country's economic problems and achieve the support of its working-class base, the government fell fourteen years later (in 1933) to the National Socialists, led by Adolf Hitler.

The same year, 1933, also marked the beginning of the Frankfurt School's eventual resettlement in New York under the auspices of Columbia University. In that year, the chairman of the German Free Trade Unions had offered to cooperate with the National Socialists. Earlier studies by the Frankfurt School had already shown that only 15 percent of those workers affiliated with the German Social Democratic party (SPD) and the German Communist party (KPD) possessed a revolutionary class consciousness. Authoritarian patterns of dogmatic indoctrination were especially prevalent in the KPD, whose members were largely unemployed and uneducated.[4]

The lack of class consciousness among the workers posed a serious problem for critical theorists. Marxism had always emphasized the close relationship between critical theory and revolutionary practice. The role of the former was to articulate the emancipatory aspirations of the most advanced sectors of the working class while giving this class the historical and theoretical tools necessary to act them out. Thus, the revolutionary fervor of the German and Hungarian proletariat following the Russian Revolution of 1917 found expression in a critical theory whose outlook was anything but pessimistic. The most optimistic assessment of labor militancy was presented by the Hungarian Communist Georg Lukács, whose *History and Class Consciousness* (1923) was enthusiastically received by first-generation critical theorists. This study marked a significant turn from an overly scientific Marxism obsessed with economic prediction toward a more idealistic Marxism oriented to ideology critique. Bearing a striking resemblance to the as-yet unpublished *Economic and Philosophic Manuscripts* of the young Marx, about which I spoke earlier,

History and Class Consciousness drew a strong parallel between economic alienation under capitalism and natural science as a kind of alienated; or objectifying, knowledge.

Lukács argued that the location of the proletariat at the point of production ostensibly enables it to penetrate beyond the *reified* (or objectified) veneer of economically fetishized, scientifically "naturalized" *appearances*. Capitalist society, he observed, appears as a mechanical concatenation of commodified forces governed by "natural" cycles and laws. To the proletariat, however, capitalism is directly experienced in its essential contradiction, as living, transformative labor.

Lukács was convinced that the prospective practice of the proletariat, rather than the retrospective contemplation of the philosopher, provides privileged access to the meaning of history; however his conviction was soon belied by actual historical events. Subsequently, one detects in the Frankfurt School's theoretical writings of the late thirties a return to a more Hegelian emphasis on the superior, "detached" understanding of the philosopher vis-à-vis potential revolutionary practice. For them, bourgeois art and philosophy, not the unreflective consciousness of the proletariat, provides a better clue to understanding the universal goals of human history. However, despite their appreciation of the importance of philosophical idealism in grounding critical practice, they could not deny its ideological function in legitimating the status quo. Consequently, they would seek to integrate this aspect of their research with economic, political, and psychological analyses.

Before turning to their all-important reception of Freudian psychology, let us briefly examine their economic and political research. A principal cause for the proletariat's failure to achieve a critical knowledge of its universal interests, they argued, was the increasing involvement of the state in managing the economy. Prior to Friedrich Pollock's controversial essay, "State Capitalism: Its Possibilities and Limitations" (1941), the school more or less took for granted Marx's assertion that capitalism could not simultaneously provide high employment, sustain economic growth, coordinate production, and continue along the path of technological progress. Pollock argued, however, that the state had largely replaced the market as the chief mechanism for coordinating production and distribution in major industries.[5] The state disrupts the law of supply and demand by permitting the formation of noncompetitive monopolies, fixing prices and wages, controlling credit, banking, and monetary flow, subsidizing industry and research. It also underwrites development, guaranteeing constant consumption through social security savings, unemployment compensation, and social-welfare policies.

Although profit still provides an incentive for efficient investment, owners of stock are increasingly deprived of any effective voice in the management of their businesses. This function devolves upon professional administrators working in close conjunction with government planning agencies. The state now assumes major risks in insuring banking institutions and major industries. It also takes an active role in negotiating wage settlements in key sectors of the economy, especially in defense-related industries. Ultimately this results in a two-tiered economy. On the one hand, there is a public, or monopoly sector in which organized labor is permitted relatively high wage scales in exchange for passive compliance with industrial policy. On the other hand, there is a quasi-private service sector, in which unorganized workers compete for low-paying jobs.

Pollock believed that the economic contradictions analyzed by Marx had finally been resolved by state intervention. This view opposed Marx's revolutionary optimism. Moreover, Pollock was inclined to think that state capitalism was incompatible with any kind of political activism. In his reading, economic contradictions are now displaced onto the state, in the form of political struggles among competing elites. Yet such struggles are largely suppressed, due to government pressure to "close ranks" for the sake of national security. National security is a major concern of capitalist governments, since the need to expand economic markets in search of cheap labor and raw resources inevitably generates political conflicts abroad.

Furthermore, government investments in military hardware can stimulate economic growth without competing with private industries for consumer markets and generating excess consumer goods. Given the interdependence of the economy, the state, and an expansionist foreign policy requiring restrictions of freedom in the name of national security, Pollock's prognosis of capitalism's fate was understandably less optimistic than Marx's. The post-liberal state capitalism that Pollock observed in the United States would, he thought, eventually evolve into the totalitarian state capitalism exemplified in Nazi Germany and Stalinist Russia.

Not all the members of the school agreed with Pollock's analysis of post-liberal capitalism. Franz Neumann and Otto Kirchheimer argued instead that increased state ownership, centralization, and planning were not incompatible with private capitalism based on market mechanisms.[6] Neither the totalitarian Fascist state nor the democratic social-welfare state completely controls the economy, they argued. The need to strike political compromises between organized labor and the various sectors of industry will tend to weaken centralized planning. Therefore, the very notion of state capitalism remains contradictory. Capitalism is not transcended in these regimes as it is in the USSR. This is true even when its contradictions *are* displaced upward, from the economic to the political system.

As we shall see, Adorno, Horkheimer, and Marcuse were largely sympathetic to Pollock's diagnosis. But later critical theorists, Habermas and Claus Offe, have adopted a position that is closer to that held by Neumann and Kirchheimer.[7] Even after it became apparent that, at least in the near future, the United States would not evolve into the kind of totalitarian regimes characteristic of bureaucratic socialism and fascism, those influenced by Pollock continued to doubt the resilience of its liberal democratic institutions. The United States may not be overtly totalitarian—that much they granted— yet it was so, implicitly. This is due to its imposition of a kind of *ideological* hegemony. Indeed, they would eventually come to believe that late capitalism's assimilation of all groups and classes to the same consumer mind-set all but extinguished the dying embers of independent intellectual resistance.[8]

FROM MARX TO FREUD: POLITICAL ECONOMY TO IDEOLOGY CRITIQUE

By emphasizing the importance of ideology in maintaining post-liberal capitalism the Frankfurt School was deviating from the vulgar economic determinism of "orthodox" Marxism. Such determinism tended to subordinate the political and cultural superstructure—for them, the main repository of critical consciousness—to the economic infrastructure. It did this in a way that left little room for revolutionary initiative. Capitalism would inevitably give way to socialism. This would occur either through protracted reform or sudden collapse. Workers' consciousness would simply follow suit. Now, however, it had become apparent to the school that the inevitable collapse of capitalism could be forestalled indefinitely through state planning and—most importantly—dissemination of ideology.

What Marx meant by "ideology" is any doctrine or belief that supports or justifies the economic and political domination of one class over another. In *The German Ideology* (1845), ideologies are identified as illusions, or "false consciousness." They generally take the form of abstract ideas (e.g., God, the people, the state, the general will, human nature, inalienable right, etc.), which prescribe universal and/or otherwise unchanging and eternal norms. Although such ideas claim to be valid with respect to real historical relations, they are far removed from, and thus are distorted reflections of, such relations.

However, much critical theorists found Marx's analysis of ideology useful, they could not accept its scientistic bias against philosophical idealism. Philosophical ideas, they maintained, were not false simply because they transcended—and therefore failed to adequately reflect—real historical relations. On the contrary, they were inclined to agree with Hegel that the "truth" of these ideas consisted precisely in their transcendence of a "false" or imperfect social reality. Obviously, the criterion of truth to which they appealed was not correspondence with factual historical reality, but correspondence with essential humanity and its goals of universal justice and happiness. At the same time, however, they agreed with Marx that transcendence of social reality lent philosophical ideas an ideological cast. To the extent that these ideas anticipate purely utopian states of affairs they are impossible of realization and, therefore, "false." Moreover, their being false in precisely this sense also renders them functional for ideology. As for being utopian, there is never a question that social reality could, or even should, correspond to them, just as there is no question that they could, or should, correspond to the needs and interests of social reality. Lacking any content that might prove critical of social reality, they end up legitimating that reality.

Critical theorists, therefore, understood the necessity of developing an approach to ideology critique that would somehow preserve the truth of cultural ideas, while exposing their ideological veneer. This required mediating cultural understanding with historical explanation. Somehow, one would have to show how the universal content implicit in cultural tradition could be: (a) extracted from the particular mode of expression characteristic of its historical manifestation; and (b) correlated with real historical interests. The latter would involve comparing the general goals of humanity with real historical possibilities for implementation. The actual level of economic development would obviously be the key in determining the extent to which justice, equality, and happiness might be attained. Equally important would be facts about human psychology.

Psychology would not only provide information regarding necessary stages of human development, but it might also suggest preferred or optimal stages of human development. On one hand, it would enable the determination of real historical interests against the background of natural, instinctual dynamics. These insights could be played off an understanding of cultural tradition and an explanation of economic processes to determine nonutopian ideals of freedom, justice, and happiness. On the other hand, they could be used to explain the psychological dynamics underlying the indisputable attraction of authoritarian patterns of thinking and behaving, which block attempts at critical enlightenment.

Although Marx had understood the significance of ideology in reproducing the system, he had no inkling of the subtle psychological dynamics informing its tenacious hold on the masses. In order to remedy this deficiency, the school turned to Freud. His studies on mass-psychology and the role of authority in the development of ego-identity proved invaluable in diagnosing the breakdown of the nuclear family and corresponding extinction of individual moral autonomy.

Freud is best known for his discovery of the role of the unconscious. It is the repository of publicly censored wish fantasies centered around instinctual life. It is also decisive in shaping human behavior. Basically, Freud believed that the most powerful instincts were sexual in nature and had, as their primary aim, immediate gratification (the Pleasure Principle). While growing up, the child learns that he or she must *repress* these instincts in order to conform to the survival needs of society. Such needs are reflected in the conventional expectations of parents and other authority figures (the Reality Principle). Indeed, it is principally through the development of reason as a conscious mechanism of self-control that something like an *ego*, as distinct from an unconscious *id*, emerges.

The ego is the psychic agency responsible for assuring *self*-preservation vis-à-vis the constraints of reality. The *superego* is that part of it which represents society's interest in maintaining social order. It is basically equivalent to moral conscience. But Freud, deviating from Kant, traces its origin to an act of repression. On one hand, the child internalizes the punitive aggression inflicted by his or her parents. That is, he or she learns to punish himself/herself mentally so as to avoid physical punishment by them. On the other hand, the child introjects his or her own feelings of aggression toward them. This is because he or she experiences guilt as a result of both loving and hating them. In both instances, natural instincts—sexual and aggressive—are repressed.

The most important stage in the development of a superego occurs when the *male* child enters the Oedipal phase of development. He must learn to repress sexual feelings directed toward his mother and aggressive feelings directed toward his father. It should be noted that, for Freud, the dynamics of female maturation are so fundamentally different as to preclude the full development of a moral conscience!

Given the overwhelming sense of guilt experienced by persons of high moral repute, Freud speculated that the roots of the superego lie deep in the archaeology of the unconscious. It is the repository of primal memories of violent deeds committed at the dawn of human civilization (the Primal Horde hypothesis). Freud himself believed that the repression of instincts was necessary for civilization. Yet, he acknowledged that it was a mixed blessing. In *Civilization and Its Discontents* (1930), he pointed out that the buildup of repressed erotic and aggressive energy must eventually find a release. This can take the form either of neurotic symptoms or psychotic behavior.

More darkly, he indicated that "the return of the repressed" found increasing expression in *social* psychosis. Among the examples he mentions are anti-Semitism and fascism. At the same time, he warned of the organic interlocking of sexuality and aggression. By 1930, Freud was convinced that the erotic instinct, furthering life and social bonding, coincided with a regressive death instinct inclined toward cessation of pain. This convergence, he believed, was also responsible for sadomasochistic behavior.

We shall have occasion to discuss Freud's theory of the instincts in much greater detail in chapter five. For our present purposes, it suffices to note the manner in which he was originally received by the Frankfurt School during the thirties. Erich Fromm was the first member of the school to appreciate the importance of Freudian theory for ideology critique. His essay, "Method and Function of Analytic Social Psychology" (1932), showed that the biologism of Freudian theory was not as opposed to Marxist historicism as one might think.[9] Fromm criticized the ahistorical dimension of Freud's developmental theory. In particular, he pointed out that the Oedipal complex posited by Freud as a universal phase of development would not arise in matriarchal societies. He also noted that the dynamics of instinctual development and repression were, in Freud's own reading, historically conditioned by economic factors. Properly understood, instinctual impulses impose "natural limits" on a process of historical adaptation. These limits are, in turn, modified by progress in historical adaptation.

For Freud, all work involves some repression of instinctual energy, but the amount varies depending upon the development of productive forces and relations. In *Civilization and its Discontents*, he observed that the more creative and fulfilling the work, the less repressive it was. He also observed that, in class societies, workers are required to carry a greater burden of the responsibility for reproducing the economic life of society than other persons. Thus, they are forced to repress more of their instinctual energy.

Fromm was mostly interested in how Freud's theory could be used to explain the ideological attachment of workers to a system that demands of them so much "surplus," or socially unnecessary, repression. Marx and Engels had already pointed out how religion induces the oppressed to accept their lot as deserved suffering, or as suffering to be compensated for in a life hereafter. They did not, however, realize that the "religious reflex" had its source in unconscious instinct. For Fromm, ideologies are similar to what Freud called *rationalizations*. They are *substitute gratifications*, which enable us to rationalize away real repression by satisfying our social, emancipatory desires in the realm of fantasy. A prime example is the image of a blissful afterlife. Without such rationalizations, life for the vast majority of oppressed people would be intolerable.

Marx and Engels doubtless appreciated this fact. Yet they were unaware of the subterranean forces sustaining class domination. Something other than a "religious reflex" was needed to explain why German workers were drawn to the authoritarianism and virulent anti-Semitism of National Socialism. For an explanation of this phenomenon, the members of the school turned to Freud's *Group Psychology and the Analysis of the Ego* (1922). As in some of his earlier writings, Freud noted that there exists an archaic memory of a primal horde predating civilization. The primal horde was ruled by a single patriarch who monopolized sexual relations with his wives and daughters. This image still exerts a strong attraction, since unlimited power and gratification is subconsciously desired by all. Indeed, admiration of such patriarchal authority is reinforced by residual feelings of guilt stemming from the primal patriarch's violent overthrow.

The desire to identify with the father, Freud notes, is strong in both boys and girls (who experience "penis envy"). Viewed positively, it provides a basis for developing a strong sense of moral autonomy. This development presupposes the healthy resolution of the Oedipal conflict. The Oedipal conflict is experienced as a conflict between the male child's low self-esteem and his fearful admiration of his father. Yet, this need not conclude with the healthy assimilation of the patriarchal "ego ideal" into the child's personality. Admiration of the father is often weakened among children whose families are on welfare. Lack of admiration for one's father can then issue in personality disorders. The narcissistic adolescent who possesses a weak ego may try to compensate for this deficiency by projecting himself onto a "strong" leader. According to Fromm, this explains why workers accept domination by others who, being more successful and independent than they, are viewed as surrogate fathers to be respected and obeyed.

Adorno's essay, "Freudian Theory and the Pattern of Fascist Propaganda" (1951), developed Fromm's thesis further by emphasizing the sadomasochistic attraction of fascism.[10] Fascist leaders such as Hitler display ordinary weaknesses. But this does not detract from their appeal, since unreflective persons in mass society do not experience conflict between themselves and the ego ideal that they project onto their leader. Moreover, there is sadomasochistic pleasure in such identification. For while one must diminish one's own self-worth in submission to the leader, one can enhance it by dominating those below. Here the distinction—between in-groups and out-groups—enables the formless mass of ego-weak subjects to achieve a kind of negative integration, or self-effacing conformity. They project their own sense of inferiority onto the very persons they secretly envy and, therefore, resent—intellectuals, minorities, and other nonconformists.

Adorno maintained that the sadomasochistic tendencies at the root of fascism also manifest themselves in the consumption of cultural "commodities." By "cultural commodity" is meant any work of art, literature, or music whose intellectual content—that aspect which provokes critical reflection on the imperfections of everyday life in contrast to the utopian yearning for complete freedom and fulfillment—is foresaken in favor of its marketable surface effect, which provokes feelings of immediate gratification. Adorno noted, for example, that the consumption of art, in capitalist society, is geared toward providing compensatory release from the repressive regimen of work. The "culture industry" was the term he used to capture *both* the debasement of "high culture" to mindless entertainment and consumer commodity *and* the corresponding manipulation of consumer preferences—from above—by advertising agencies seeking to integrate mass behavior around the uniform expectations of the market.

Yet the kind of pleasure afforded by the culture industry is less fulfilling than distracting. One is invited to experience, however *vicariously*, the excitement, adventure, and glamour denied one in everyday life. But going to the movies, buying fancy sports cars and fashionable clothing, and taking expensive vacations serves only to remind one of what one doesn't *have*. Hence, these pleasures are accompanied by the pain of envy and diminished self-worth. To compound the pain further, the merchandise comes with a price tag that must be paid for with longer hours at work.[11]

"High culture," Marcuse noted, also ideologically affirms existing reality by lending it the appearance of beauty. In contemplating, say, a seventeenth-century Dutch painting depicting the quaint life of a merchant's family, the modern-day urbanite can experience "fulfillment," too. This is, in spite of the ugly poverty, racism, and crime threatening to close in on the serene environs of the museum-shrine, wherein such contemplation occurs.[12] At the same time, however, Marcuse acknowledged that the high "bourgeois" culture of the nineteenth century also contained a transcendent "truth" content that is missing in popular forms of contemporary mass culture.

Focusing his attention instead on popular and high modern art forms of the twentieth century, Adorno noted that forms of modern art don't provide explicit visions of transcendent freedom and harmony—of the sort found in artistic representations of the nineteenth century. Jazz, he argued, reinforces the spatiotemporal fragmentation and mindless distraction of assembly-line or office routine by eliminating the need for the listener to focus attention on the formal unity of the composition. In this instance, art no longer even pretends to transcend existing reality toward affirmation of a potentially better and freer life, but imitates reality directly.[13] However, not all art forms that violate the law of aesthetic harmony, affirm reality. As a progressive instance, he mentions the formalist work of art. Adorno, who was an accomplished pianist and composer as well as music critic and sociologist, favored the atonal compositions of Arnold Schönberg and the dissonant classicism of Gustav Mahler. In such formalist works of art, unity and reconciliation are juxtaposed to fragmentation. In listening to them, one is forced to engage in active reflection rather than passive distraction. For it is by reflecting on such dissonance, that one is led to critical ruminations about the inhumanity and alienation of everyday life.

In retrospect, Adorno, like other members of the Frankfurt School, became increasingly disillusioned with Marxism's promise of the inevitable collapse of capitalism. Their studies of the working class and the modern state led them to the opposite conclusion. Above all, their reading of Freud convinced them that the ideological forces, sustaining passive deference to authority, were more deeply entrenched in the dynamics of psychological development than Marx had ever suspected. These forces included the stupifying effects of mass culture, a sphere of life traditionally ignored by Marxist economists.

I have argued that one way to view the Frankfurt School's reception of Marxism is in light of the theory/practice problem which Marx inherited from the Enlightenment. In rejecting the scientistic interpretation of Marx, typical of orthodox and "revisionist" schools, they found themselves returning to the philosophical heritage of German idealism. The need to integrate philosophy and science was made clear by the problem of ideology. By fashioning an interdisciplinary research program uniting philosophy, law, economics, history, and psychology they thought that a realistic assessment of the truth-value of cultural ideas could be made, one that would render them functional for guiding critique.

Of course, it still remains unclear how such a program of enlightenment can succeed. How can one distinguish between "true" and "false" needs and interests? How can one bridge moral philosophy and empirical science, what ought to be the case and what is the case, in a way that might enable us to speak meaningfully about "true" interests at all? Clearly, we need a better understanding of the way in which Freudian psychoanalysis helps to "enlighten" us about these matters—a task that was explicitly undertaken later only by Marcuse and Habermas. However, it might be argued, against the use of psychoanalysis as a method of critical enlightenment, that the validity of interests is best determined democratically, in everyday practice, rather than "monologically," through the clinical application of theory. If so, the Frankfurt School's attempt to remedy the anti-individualistic and antidemocratic tendencies in orthodox Marxism will have to address the problem of community and its peculiar form of communicative practice. These issues, which ultimately impact upon the possibility of resolving the theory/practice problem, will be treated in greater detail in the chapters to come.

Before discussing these issues further, however, we must first look at another problem that cuts to the core of critical theory. Throughout much of the thirties the Frankfurt School assumed that a philosophically enlightened social science was possible. By the end of the Second World War their optimism had noticeably waned. Most distressing was their growing conviction that the rationalist heritage of the Enlightenment could not be realized, and that the tensions between philosophy and science, morality and facticity, ideality and reality, freedom and natural necessity, and individual and society could not be resolved. Moreover, they began to think that the cause for this failure extended beyond capitalism itself—to the very heart of rationality.

The most important strand of social scientific thought—greatly influencing their growing pessimism—was the theory of social rationalization developed by Max Weber. Following Hegel, Weber showed how reason emerged in the unique religious worldview of the Occident and actualized itself in objective social institutions. Yet, following Kant, he argued that scientific, moral, and aesthetic rationality denoted incommensurable types of activity that could not be reconciled under a higher philosophical idea. Such a conception not only implied a separation of theory and practice but, as we shall see, it drew into question the very possibility of moral autonomy as such.

NOTES

1. Karl Marx, *The Poverty of Philosophy* (1847).

2. V.I. Lenin, *What Is To Be Done?* (New York: International Publishers, 1929). Originally written and published in 1902.

3. See Herbert Marcuse, "Philosophy and Critical Theory," *Negations* (Boston: Beacon Press, 1968), p. 143; and Max Horkheimer, "Traditional and Critical Theory," p. 250. Both of these essays are reprinted in *Critical Theory: The Essential Readings* (*CTER*).

4. The study, "Revolt of the Blue-Collar and White-Collar Workers," was published in 1930–31. See Helmut Dubiel, *Theory and Politics. Studies in the Development of Critical Theory*, trans. Benjamin Gregg (Cambridge, Mass.: 1985), for further discussion of the early and middle periods of the School.

5. Friedrich Pollock, "State Capitalism: Its Possibilities and Limitations," *The Essential Frankfurt School Reader*, ed. Andrew Arato and Eike Gebhardt (New York: Continuum, 1982), pp. 71–94.

6. Neumann argued (against Pollock) that the Third Reich represented a type of totalitarian monopoly capitalism in which the economy (the profit motive) still held sway over the political. See Franz Neumann, *Behemoth: The Structure and Practice of National Socialism, 1933–1944* (New York: Oxford University Press, 1944); and

Otto Kirchheimer, "Changes in the Structure of Political Compromise," *The Essential Frankfurt School Reader*, pp. 49–70.

7. Although Pollock's theory of state capitalism led Adorno, Horkheimer, and Marcuse to postulate the eventual convergence of fascism, communism, and New Deal capitalism in a monolithic, relatively conflict-free totalitarianism, his conviction that economic contradictions reappear as political contradictions later supported the "structural" or nontotalitarian view of the capitalist state defended by Claus Offe and Habermas.

8. See, for example, Max Horkheimer,"The Authoritarian State" (1941) reprinted in *The Essential Frankfurt School Reader*, pp. 95–117; Theodor Adorno, "Society" reprinted in *CTER*, and Herbert Marcuse, *One-Dimensional Man* (Boston: Beacon Press, 1964).

9. Erich Fromm, "The Method and Function of an Analytic Social Psychology," *The Essential Frankfurt School Reader*, pp. 477–97.

10. Theodor Adorno, "Freudian Theory and the Pattern of Fascist Propaganda," *CTER*.

11. See Theodor Adorno and Max Horkheimer, *Dialectic of Enlightenment* (New York: Herder and Herder, 1947). Selections from the first essay included in *Dialectic of Enlightenment*, "The Concept of Enlightenment," are reprinted in *CTER*.

12. Herbert Marcuse, "The Affirmative Character of Culture" (1937). Reprinted in *Negations*.

13. Theodor Adorno, "On the Fetish Character in Music and the Regression of Listening," *The Essential Frankfurt School Reader*, pp. 270–99. Also see Adorno's essay, "How to Look at Television" reprinted in *CTER*.

SELECTED BIBLIOGRAPHY

Freud, Sigmund. *An Outline of Psycho-Analysis*. Trans. James Strachey. New York, 1949.

——*Civilization and its Discontents*. Trans. James Strachey. New York, 1960.

——*Group Psychology and the Analysis of the Ego*. Trans. James Strachey. New York, 1960.

——*Totem and Taboo*. Trans. James Strachey. New York, 1962.

Lenin, V.I. *State and Revolution*. New York. International Publishers, 1974.

——*What is to be Done?* New York. International Publishers, 1929. Originally published in 1902.

Marx, Karl. Selections from the works mentioned in this chapter may all be found in *Karl Marx. Selected Writings*, ed. David McLellan (Oxford: Oxford University Press, 1977).

Works by critical theorists cited in this chapter: Works by Adorno, Fromm, Horkheimer, Kirchheimer, Marcuse, and Pollock are reprinted in their entirety in *The Essential Frankfurt School Reader*, eds. Andrew Arato and Eike Gebhardt (New York: Continuum, 1982).

Commentaries: The best historical treatment of the Frankfurt School in the thirties is Helmut Dubiel's *Theory and Politics. Studies in the Development of Critical Theory*, trans. Benjamin Gregg (Cambridge, Mass.: MIT Press, 1985). Also highly recommended: Martin Jay's *The Dialectical Imagination. A History of the Frankfurt School* (Boston, 1973).

THREE

WEBER AND THE DIALECTIC OF ENLIGHTENMENT

The problem of relating theory to practice haunts twentieth-century critical theory. Kant was perhaps the strongest believer in the power of reason to affect widespread popular enlightenment. Even Hegel and Marx, who more fully grasped the social, economic, and ideological forces limiting enlightenment, agreed with Kant's view that human history shows a pattern of irreversible, rational progress in the attainment of universal freedom.

By the thirties, the members of the Frankfurt School no longer believed that emancipation was imminent. The revolution which they, following Marx, thought to be necessary for bringing about a truly free and just society could be undermined or, worse yet, perverted into a totalitarian nightmare. Ideology, it seemed, could prove too powerful even for modern, secular societies. This pessimistic appraisal was reinforced by Freud's discovery of the unconscious and its instinctual dynamics. In this reading, reason seems ever subordinate to the operation of aggressive drives.

Despite their realistic appraisal of the ideological forces preventing revolutionary enlightenment, the members of the Frankfurt School nonetheless believed in the power of reason to enlighten and emancipate. Decisive, in this regard, was their attempt to develop an interdisciplinary research program combining philosophy and social science. Although they harbored no illusions about the capacity of theory to promote the popular dissemination of enlightenment among the working classes, they still believed that its conjunction of theory and practice could help aid progressive forces in combatting ideology and pinpointing areas of resistance.

However, their reception of Freud had already anticipated some of the problems that would later dampen their enthusiasm. The most disturbing feature of Freud's prognosis of humanity's fate was his belief that reason itself operates through mechanisms of repression and domination. As we shall see, this view struck a sympathetic chord with Adorno, Horkheimer, and Marcuse regardless of their insistence that rational enlightenment was nonetheless desirable. This became the predominant theme of the school from the forties on.

The *dialectic of enlightenment*—the expression introduced by Adorno and Horkheimer to describe this reversal—seemed to justify a pessimistic view of history. For while the progressive spread of scientific enlightenment certainly dispels the unfreedom born of dogmatic prejudice, it also contributes to the enslavement of imagination, the leveling of individuality, and the hierarchical regimentation of social life under the law of efficient administration.

Of course, none of this was totally unfamiliar to Hegel and Marx. But, unlike later critical theorists, they were inclined to blame the irrationality of scientific enlightenment on an *incomplete* and, therefore one-sided, realization of reason's emancipatory potential. The problem we must address in this chapter, then, is how first-generation critical theorists could have extended this limited critique of scientific rationality to the point of seriously jeopardizing the interdisciplinary program they had developed during the thirties. The answer to this question, I shall argue, is to be found in the Frankfurt School's reception of Max Weber's sociology of modern life.

No introduction to critical theory can ignore Max Weber's contributions, in setting forth the internal tensions within rationality that underlie the theory/practice problem. Nor can it neglect to mention his highly influential study of the Protestant Ethic, references to which appear throughout the work of critical theorists. In particular, there are three areas of his sociology that impinge directly on the theory/practice problem.

First, Weber developed a theory of social action that attempted to show the peculiar psychological nexus linking transcendent cultural ideals, subjective ideas, and concrete material interests. His analysis of the "elective affinity," linking Protestantism and capitalism, exemplified this connection in a way that proved decisive for the school's own attempt to come to grips with the positive and negative elements underlying bourgeois moral idealism. Second, the theory of social action provided Weber with a methodology for both understanding and causally explaining social phenomena. This method helped the school understand how philosophical interpretation of and reflection on cultural meanings could be wedded to scientific explanation of social phenomena. Above all, it enabled them to conceive ideological false consciousness along the model of a fixed and unfree form of reflex-patterned behavior. Finally, Weber's analysis of rationality tended to reaffirm the sorts of dichotomies between rational form and prerational content, scientific proceduralism and moral idealism, that had led Kant to problematize the relationship between theory and practice. Ironically, this analysis severely compromised the synthesis of idealism and materialism, implicit in Weber's own theory of social action, thereby indirectly contributing to the school's abandonment of its former faith in the possibility of constructing an interdisciplinary research program uniting philosophy and science. More seriously, it led to a pessimistic diagnosis of rational society that would later insinuate itself into the school's writings from the late forties on.

WEBER, REASON, AND THE GERMAN PHILOSOPHICAL TRADITION

Max Weber (1864–1920) is considered by many to be one of the great founders of modern sociology and political science. His monumental studies on world religion, law, and political economy are informed by a keen awareness of the positive and negative yield of a secular, scientific culture. As might be expected from one so influenced by the German philosophical tradition of Kant, Hegel, and Marx, he was also deeply interested in the prospects for a truly free, just, and rational society.[1]

Although Weber was highly critical of the metaphysical elements of Hegel's philosophy, there is a sense in which he, too, could be said to hold an idealistic view of rational progress. He and Hegel both maintained that ideas influence the course of history. Contrary to some of Marx's mere polemical statements, ideas are not, Weber insisted, mere ideological reflections of economic interest. Weber also shared Hegel's view that some *worldviews*, or systems of ideas that influence a given culture's global outlook on life, are more rational than others. In this respect, the Judeo-Christian worldview was esteemed by Weber as containing a higher potential for evolving into a rational ethics than, say, the antihumanistic worldview of Buddhism.

Despite his agreement with Hegel, Weber was sufficiently moved by Marx's critique of idealism to deny that the content of ideas was alone capable of affecting historical change. Ideas prove ineffective unless there exists an *elective affinity*, or correspondence, between them and prior socioeconomic interests. Furthermore, it is not the explicit meaning of ideas that often motivates, but the unintended—and largely unconscious—psychological effects that arise from their affinity with economic interests. In the final analysis, ideas and material interests are mutually interrelated. The pursuit of material interests is selectively governed and legitimated by ideas, but ideas achieve their effect in and through material interests.[2]

Weber's attempt to steer a course between economic determinism and cultural idealism was favorably received by members of the Frankfurt School. Like Weber, they held that any satisfactory account of human action had to take into consideration the subjective ideas—and objective cultural ideals—underlying a person's decisions to act one way rather than another. From an idealist perspective, a person's going to the supermarket would be explained in terms of that person's own beliefs about what it is he or she is doing—say, buying some fruit to make a liquor cocktail, making a cocktail for a party, and so on. Of course, people are often unaware of the *unintended* influence exercised by their beliefs over their behavior. As we shall see below, Weber and later critical theorists thought that such an elective affinity obtained in the case of early Protestantism and capitalism. Members of Protestant sects were compelled to engage in entrepreneurial activity for reasons which, though unknown to them, were nonetheless *implicit* (subconsciously) in their religious beliefs.

The need to *understand* and *interpret* the *subjective meaning* of social action as *intended* or otherwise *implied* by the actors in question was regarded by Weber and the school as the most significant methodological consequence of cultural idealism. Yet, as we have seen, they were also materialists who acknowledged the role of instinctual dynamics and economic factors in determining behavior. Commercial transactions produce unintended side effects that confront the transactors as lawlike, objective forces. In this instance, it is appropriate to regard behavior as less the outcome of deliberate intentions and conscious beliefs than the effect, more or less predictable and involuntary, of some impersonal causal pattern. This is precisely how Marx tended to view the alienated and objectified, crisis-ridden operation of the market. The methodological consequence of this way of viewing social action is obvious. As critical theorists, following Weber, realized, such reified behavior must be *causally explained* in terms of impersonal economic laws, not merely understood and interpreted.[3]

As we shall see, the methodological implications of Weber's combined idealist/materialist approach played an important role in the Frankfurt School's attempt to formulate a scientific method of *ideology critique*. On one hand, persons acting out of ideological false consciousness do not act freely and deliberately in the fullest sense. They deceive themselves regarding the true motives underlying their behavior. In so deceiving themselves, they allow a causal factor (a hidden, unconscious motive) to determine their behavior in ways that contradict their true interests. Since, as Freud argued, repressed motives manifest themselves in the form of compulsive and rigid behavior, it was logical for members of the school to regard ideologically motivated actions as instances of causal *laws*. This was made all the easier by the school's analysis of modern culture as a sphere of covert manipulation, unconsciously programming individuals with uniform and invariant habits of thought.

On the other hand, Weber's insistence on the need for subjective interpretation struck them as a necessary antidote to a one-sided orientation toward objective, causal explanation. A sociology restricted to causal explanation, they realized, can only *describe* social behavior as a necessary and predictable outcome of the existing system. It cannot also *criticize* such behavior as the effect of ideological *false* consciousness. It cannot, in other words, regard the lawlike behavior of social actors as historically conditioned and changeable through efforts of enlightenment. This would require an *understanding* of subjective ideas and objective cultural ideals motivating action, as well as their *evaluation* in terms of furthering an *objectively* existing rational (emancipatory) potential.

We will turn to the school's attempt to formulate a scientifically responsible critical theory, founded on insights drawn from psychoanalysis, in chapter six. Presently, it is important for us to examine the Kantian roots of their conception of reason, for it is the latter which eventually led to their pessimistic view of enlightenment. Like Kant, they accepted logical distinctions between form (concept or ideality) and content (sense experience or reality), universal and individual, and, most important, value and fact.

Kant had argued that questions of value, above all, questions of morality, were irreducible to questions of knowledge, which pertained to the description and causal explanation of facts. Quite simply, Kant held that what *ought* to be could not be decided by what *is*. Both Weber and the Frankfurt School accepted this logical distinction between "ought" and "is." The school, as we have seen, nevertheless felt compelled to unify moral philosophy and descriptive science as a prerequisite for resolving the theory/practice problem. Weber went further, than either Kant or the school, in equating reason with competencies that were almost exclusively related to the acquisition of causal knowledge rather than the prescription of critical ideals. Kant maintained that pure reason was a faculty of *ultimate ends*, or unconditional (categorical) moral commands. Weber, by contrast, insisted that it could only be a *formal procedure* for *calculating* the causally most-efficacious *means* for bringing about *prerational* ends.

Despite their retention of a critical conception of reason, Adorno, Horkheimer, and Marcuse were profoundly influenced by Weber's conviction that only "instrumental" reason finds a niche in modern social institutions. Strangely, this conviction is based upon Kant's own conception of reason. Kant had argued that reason is activity in accordance with universal *forms* of thought. So abstract and general are these forms, or *procedural rules*, that no particular content, or meaning, can be derived from them. The rules of deductive logic that govern valid inference are like this. I can validly infer "*A* is *C*" from the statements "*A* is *B*" and "*B* is *C*," regardless of the particular content substituted for *A, B*, and *C*. By parity of reasoning, Kant held that the category of causality and the categorical imperative were pure forms of thought which apply, respectively, to sense experience and free action.

Significantly, Kant realized that the categorical imperative does not *pre*scribe (or *pro*scribe) any *particular* action. At most, the categorical imperative prescribes a *general, repeatable procedure*. This procedure involves restricting our behavior to actions that all persons could perform without society self-destructing. Kant himself likened it to the Golden Rule: Do unto others as you would have them do unto you. For example, Kant argued that I ought not break any promise, for if everyone universally broke their promises whenever they wanted to, the trust, necessary for making promises in the first place, would be destroyed. In effect, I would have contradicted myself by willing the nonexistence of what I will. Moral rationality here functions solely as a *formal procedure* for testing the consistency of what are otherwise arbitrary ends. Like the principle of democracy, it does not prescribe any particular policy, but only a *valid rule* for arriving at policies generally.

If reason consists of *universally* valid *forms* of thought, then it cannot prescribe any *particular* manner of action, policy, or value. Weber, too, sometimes suggests that there is a distinct kind of *value rationality* that operates in a manner analogous to the categorical imperative. However, he interprets it in a way that paradoxically implies the irrationality of all values! For Weber, there are but three procedures for reasoning about values. First, I can test the internal consistency of values. A person who claimed to believe in democracy, but who wanted to suppress views that deviated from his own, would be contradicting himself. His value system would be logically incoherent. Second, I can infer specific courses of action from values. If I believe in democracy, then it follows that I ought to tolerate the expression of views which deviate from mine. Finally, I can choose values on the basis of their consequences. Indeed, the greater part of practical reason just consists in prudently calculating the most efficient means for realizing our ends, regardless of what they are.

Significantly, Adorno, Horkheimer, and Marcuse often follow Weber in reducing practical (but not critical) reason to instrumental, means/ends calculation. These are capacities which Weber groups together under the umbrella heading of *purposive rationality*. Here we should be careful to note the deviation of Weber and critical theorists from Kant's moral thought. Kant maintained that some values (in particular, rational, moral values) were *unconditional*, or prescribed *ends* that had to be pursued regardless of consequences. This notion of reason, as commanding ultimate (absolute) ends, is regarded by Weber and the others as a contradiction in terms. *Formal reason*, they insist, always makes the pursuit of any given end dependent upon the calculation of consequences. They further note that unconditional commitment to an end (or value), for its own sake, is actually a residue of *dogmatic religious conviction*—precisely the sort of thing that rational enlightenment dispels.[4] Once again, we must keep in mind that critical theory is premissed on the idea that moral philosophy and predictive social science ought to condition one another.

Still, there is a paradox in this reduction of practical reason to purposive rationality. Weber and members of the school realized that *if* the validity of any given value is dependent on consequences, *and* if the assessment of consequences is relative to arbitrarily given needs, then even the most universal, formal values—such as truth, moral goodness, and beauty—are irrational.[5] This is to say that there can be no *absolute* rational justification of reason itself. Consequently, acting rationally may *not* be the most efficient way to achieve long-term happiness, *if that is our end*. As we shall see, later critical theorists sought to avoid this paradox by specifying fundamental human needs and interests in light of which consequences could be rationally assessed.

THE IMPLICATIONS OF THE PARADOX OF REASON FOR MODERN SOCIETY

That rationality may not be productive of happiness, as defenders of enlightenment have maintained, is but one of the messages conveyed to us by the school. This pessimistic appraisal, which stems from their Weberian analysis of modern society, should not obscure the extent to which the school continued to believe in the possibility of a rational assessment of basic needs and interests. Yet, we cannot ignore their pessimism either. Despite its scientific and moral achievements, modern society is characterized by them as an iron cage in which persons routinely pursue their vocations without the assurance of any higher, absolute meaning. In this respect they, no less than Weber, bore the influence of another great German philosopher, Friedrich Nietzsche (1844–1900).

Nietzsche believed that the modern age had ushered in the "death of God." Taken to its extreme, rational enlightenment undermines all metaphysical absolutes. The result is *nihilism*, or the *negation* (devaluation) of values as such. Positively speaking, however, Nietzsche believed that, by destroying the illusion of value absolutism, enlightenment enhanced the activity of *valuation*, or the *free creation* of values.

According to Nietzsche, all values—even the "rational" values of objective truth and moral rightness—are *subjective illusions* whose sole worth resides in furthering life. Reason, too, is justified only to the extent that it enhances our *power* over the meaningless chaos of nature. Yet, Nietzsche also realized that rationality comes with a price. It requires a self-restraint and discipline that often works against the interest of life. This is especially true of those universalistic moral codes that descend from the Judeo-Christian tradition.

For Nietzsche, Kant's categorical imperative and the socialist ideal of universal equality *are* but *rationalizations* of baser motives. These motives are traceable to the envy and resentment felt by the masses with regard to the superior power of truly creative, "noble" spirits. Resentment gave rise to law and punishment (revenge as exchange and restoration of equality). Eventually, the desire to dominate, which is inherent in everyone, is repressed, or introjected (literally, turned back upon its originating source). Thus, the birth of moral conscious and rational self-control is coeval with the will to self-punishment.[6]

Nietzsche's unmasking of the deeper psychological motivations underlying rational moral conceptions had a profound influence on the kind of ideology critique developed by later critical theorists. This occurred, despite their reservations regarding his glorification of power for power's sake. Much of that influence, however, was transmitted indirectly in the writings of Freud and, of course, Weber. In perhaps his most famous work, *The Protestant Ethic and the Spirit of Capitalism* (1904–5), Weber argued that there exists an *elective affinity* between the moralistic doctrines of certain Protestant sects and the selfish, competitive pursuit of profit for its own sake, characteristic of modern capitalist society.

Medieval Catholicism represented a serious obstacle to institutionalized capitalism, since it condemned the pursuit of material wealth and mandated a rigid class structure—thereby restricting upward mobility. Yet, the Church was also a paternalistic force which sought to protect the poor and encouraged the selfless commission of "good works" (the taking of sacraments as well as the giving of charitable donations). Protestant theology, by contrast, was radically individualistic. Accepting St. Augustine's view of eternal predestination, which held that one's salvation or damnation was decided by divine foreknowledge at the beginning of time, Calvinists, Lutherans, and Methodists believed that no amount of good works or sacraments would guarantee one's "election."

However, since unwavering faith was considered necessary for salvation, it was only natural for members of these sects to look for some confirmation of their election in this world. Interpreting literally the Old Testament stories, in which God rewards the faithful with material goods, they came to regard the pursuit of wealth in a totally different light than their Catholic brethren. Of course, this was an *ascetic* pursuit. These Protestant capitalists rationalized their unbrotherly, selfish competition by segregating themselves from the less fortunate (who were stigmatized as lazy and God-forsaken), and devoting their enterprises to the greater glory of God.

The Protestant work ethic is just one of the manifestations of Western society's progressive assimilation of rational attitudes. For Weber, it was "progressive" in the sense that the extreme psychological isolationism imposed upon the early adherents of Protestant sects made them respond to the "calling" of their God through inwardness of faith rather than through displays of outward compliance with Church sanctions. The individualism born of this ethic of conscience was gradually transformed into a rational *ethic of responsibility*.

By assuming responsibility for their own moral values, individuals in modern society achieve the freedom and initiative necessary for pursuing a specialized vocation. Such initiative, Weber argued, fulfills a necessary requirement for modern capitalism, in which persons are legally permitted to do what they want, compatible with a like freedom for all. Yet, far from entailing license, freedom from social and religious constraints enjoins that we take responsibility for actions that might affect others adversely.

Despite its progressive aspects, the Protestant work ethic, the Frankfurt School realized, imposes excessive renunciation. As Weber had shown, work for God's sake demands narrow specialization and repression of individuality and imagination. In this respect, it is but a symptom of a larger phenomenon—the loss of meaning and freedom, which necessarily accompanies modern, rational society.

According to the school, modern society is the product of a long process of *rationalization*. "Rationalization" is Weber's term for the dissemination of rational modes of conduct throughout all spheres of culture and society. In the West, rationalization first made itself felt in the dissolution of the Judeo-Christian worldview, which culminated in the Age of Enlightenment. Prior to rationalization, questions of truth, moral justice, and aesthetic value were not sharply distinguished. Rather, they were treated as religious concerns resolvable by appeal to the unitary will of God. Nature, for example, was regarded as a hierarchically ordered chain of Being, symbolically exhibiting the intrinsic moral goodness and beauty of divine purposes. What masqueraded as universal reason, under these circumstances, was but a thinly veiled appeal to religious dogma as the unquestioned cipher of natural law (God's will as revealed in nature).[7]

Rationalization changes all of this by emancipating science, law, and art from religious dogma and grounding them in distinct formal-rational procedures. Questions of knowledge are now treated exclusively by scientists, in accordance with the "value-free" (purposive-rational) methods of deductive reasoning and experimentation. Questions of justice are dealt with by trained legal experts and ethicists in accordance with "value-rational" procedures designed to test the universal validity, consistency, and effectiveness of norms and laws. And questions of taste are taken up, by professional artists and art critics, in ways that further the development of creative techniques and the appreciation of expressive values.

The internal development of each of these *cultural value spheres* in turn issues in distinctly modern attitudes and institutions. Take truth (knowledge), for example. Prior to the rise of modern science in the sixteenth and seventeenth centuries, nature was regarded as a harmonious unity of *purposes* reflecting divine agency. Science, however, "disenchants" nature. That is to say, it reduces nature to *spiritless* matter in motion. Having been reduced to abstract mathematical laws, nature ceases to express the value and dignity of a higher subjectivity. Objectified and deprived of intrinsic value, meaning, and purpose, nature becomes susceptible to scientific predictability and technological domination.

A similar transformation occurs in the cultural value spheres of justice (morality/law) and beauty (art/eroticism). Having been secularized, or freed from the authority of religious dogma, law and morality take on worldly, utilitarian functions. Legal and moral conceptions are now justified *rationally*, in terms of their efficiency in producing desired consequences. Since the efficiency of profitable production lays stress on individual freedom and the "free" competition of ideas, rational society permits the legal toleration of differing moral views as expressions of *private conscience*. This separation, of public law and private morality, also plays an important role in the maintenance of democratic institutions. For it is only by allowing the free expression of dissenting views that a generally popular consensus regarding the public good emerges. In turn, democracy functions as an efficient means for holding officeholders accountable and procuring loyalty to the state.

Finally, the rationalization of culture permits the specialization of art around expressive values. The most obvious instance of this is avant-garde art since the late nineteenth century. Freed from religious constraints, art need not function as an ideological medium for enforcing a particular moral code or representing reality truthfully. Modern works of art are appreciated for their expression of the artist's personal vision, even if this sometimes runs counter to conventional moral attitudes and ways of perceiving.

The process of cultural rationalization described above finds parallel expression in the societal differentiation of economy, state, and family. With the institutionalization of private property and contractual law, a market economy comes into being whose primary organizational unit, the business firm, disposes over purposive-rational methods of accounting, management, and production in the calculated pursuit of profit. Gone are the days in which the family functioned as a self-sufficient economic unit and the Church regulated wages, prices, and profits according to preestablished patterns of justice. The organizational core of the modern state, the bureaucratic administration, uses the same techniques of rational accounting and management to secure its monopoly over the use of force in maintaining law and order.

Here again, the legitimacy of the state is detached from familial lineage (monarchy) and vested in formal democratic procedures of procuring consent and ensuring accountability. Moreover, both government and business administration are regulated internally by formal procedures for delegating authority, processing information, and organizing the flow of communication within an overall economy of efficiency. Finally, the nuclear family functions as the primary mechanism by which value-rational attitudes are instilled in the individual.[8]

Our sketch of rationalization, so far, has focused on its liberating effects. Scientists, artists, jurists, administrators, and entrepreneurs are free to ply their trades unencumbered by religious constraints. Yet, the school's Weberian perspective reveals a darker side to modern life: the inevitable erosion of freedom and meaning. I have already alluded to the nihilistic implications of Weber's reduction of reason to formal rationality. Not only are rational undertakings such as science and jurisprudence ultimately without rational foundation—and are thus, metaphysically speaking, "meaningless—but the various orders of life, which gravitate around these cultural value spheres, actually come into conflict with each other. The "new polytheism" of conflicting values is reflected in the religiously inclined moralist's disdain for modern science and modern art. Likewise, the businessman and bureaucrat attuned toward efficiency for efficiency's sake will look askance at the moral fanatic's unbending imperatives and the equally useless claims made on behalf of pleasure and art.

Ultimately, it is the moralist who is least able to find accommodation in modern society.[9] With the decline of religion, individuals cease to think of themselves as moral agents who orient their conduct toward absolute values. What remains, Weber tells us, is a life oriented toward survival, a life of work and consumption ruthlessly organized around the purposive-rational imperatives of efficiency and success. The loss of freedom for those engaged in specialized, methodical work, is epitomized by the professional bureaucrat.

The bureaucrat, Weber tells us, "is only a single cog in an ever-moving mechanism which prescribes to him an essentially fixed route of march."[10] Yet, lurking behind this "specialist without spirit," is the proverbial "sensualist without heart"—the romantic aesthete who abjures work for the pleasures of beauty.

Herein lies the mutual affinity between ceaseless toil and insatiable consumption that is so pervasive in capitalist society. This dismal conclusion, which was first reached by Weber, is repeated endlessly by the Frankfurt School in its paradoxical formulation that, in advanced capitalist society, evergreater gratification is purchased at the expense of ever-greater denial. In the final analysis, the "iron cage" of modern society consists in the only "rational" calling remaining in a spiritless society—the sacrifice of moral autonomy to the twin Gods of capitalism: the blind necessities of work and consumption.[11]

CRITICAL THEORY AND THE DIALECTIC OF ENLIGHTENMENT

Later critical theorists became increasingly receptive to Weber's gloomy diagnosis of modern society as fascism strengthened its stranglehold over Europe. In the thirties, the Frankfurt School's diagnosis was still largely informed by the enlightenment view that progress in science and technology paved the way for greater economic and political emancipation. More importantly, it was guided by an interdisciplinary vision of a practical theory in which philosophy and science are equal contributors. Although this view was never entirely absent from their subsequent writings, it nonetheless receded behind a very different theory: that scientific reason had become the dominant force underlying modern totalitarianism. Corresponding to this shift was a greater reliance on philosophical reflection and/or pure speculative theory.

The role played by reason in maintaining domination was thus the chief paradox to which critical theorists addressed themselves from the forties on. How could rational enlightenment cease to be a force for emancipation and become an instrument of total domination? The answer they gave is already anticipated in Weber's ambivalent analysis of rationalization. On one hand, Weber maintained that reason could be conceived only formally, as a procedure of deductive inference and efficient calculation. As such, reason is "value neutral"—a useful tool for bringing about any conceivable end whatsoever. On the other hand, Weber himself equated rational society with a particular sociopolitical formation—capitalism. Here, reason ceases to denote an abstract procedure and takes on the full-bodied meaning of a particular concrete set of values. As a "concrete universal"—Hegel's expression for a rational potential that has been objectively institutionalized—reason denotes a *substantive end*, efficient *technological domination* of all natural and social processes.

Critical theorists were radical enough, in their political orientation, to reject Weber's easy identification of reason and capitalism.[12] And for good reason. Had not Weber's own diagnosis confirmed Marx's opinion about the irrationality of capitalist society? If reason continues to have any *critical* meaning at all, it must refer to *substantive values*, concrete social and political ends, which transcend the limitations of capitalism. Yet—and this is perhaps the greatest paradox—critical theorists also came to accept Weber's belief that, as a *social* force, enlightenment had degenerated to formal rationality. And they further believed that, once having degenerated to formal rationality, reason then became synonymous with *substantive* political values of domination.

Most important of all, the school radicalized Weber's diagnosis by extending his analysis beyond its narrow focus on the instrumentality of reason for capitalist society. Formal reason, they noted, is not merely an efficient means for realizing profitability. With the ascendance of advanced, industrial capitalism, it exists as the dominant end governing all other ends—profitability included. Technological domination for the sake of domination becomes *totalitarian* and, in fact, achieves its quintessential articulation in the totalitarian regimes of fascism and bureaucratic socialism.

As we noted earlier, many members of the school were convinced that advanced "state" capitalism was but a forerunner of fascism. This conclusion, I have just argued, is compelled by the school's own Weberian analysis of rationality. No doubt, the greatest and most original development of this line of argumentation is contained in the Adorno/Horkheimer masterpiece, *The Dialectic of Enlightenment* (1947), which they (with the help of Leo Löwenthal) composed in California between 1942–44.

This, the key document of the school's "middle period," takes up a strand of argument that had been developed by one of the school's early mentors, Georg Lukács (1885–1971). As I mentioned earlier (in chapter two), Lukács' *History and Class Consciousness* (1923) was an important contribution to the Hegel renaissance in Western Marxism. Yet, Lukács was also a student of Weber and had accepted the latter's equation of *formal* rationality and capitalism, while reserving the title of critical reason for dialectical thought. For Lukács, formal rationality refers to a global "form of objectivity," in this instance, the *commodity* form of capitalism.

Marx had observed that the defining feature of any commodity is its *exchange* value, or reducibility to an abstract, *numerical equivalence* (e.g., the amount of time required to produce it). As embodiments of "abstract labor time," commodities are comparable to one another; they are equivalent, or *identical*, to the extent that they can be fairly exchanged. According to Lukács, this reducibility to abstract identity is also the essence of formal rationality. Consistency and, above all, calculation of costs and benefits, requires the reduction of all qualities to quantities which are comparable according to a single, objective measurement, and predictable according to constant numerical regularities (laws). As Adorno and Horkheimer put it:

> . . . Enlightenment recognizes as being and occurrence only what can be apprehended in unity: its ideal is the system in which everything follows. . . . Formal logic was the major school of unified science. It provided the Enlightenment thinkers with the schema of the calculability of the world. . . . Number became the canon of the Enlightenment. The same equations dominate bourgeois justice and commodity exchange. . . . Bourgeois society is ruled by equivalence. It makes the dissimilar comparable by reducing it to abstract quantities. To the Enlightenment, that which does not reduce to numbers, and ultimately to the one, becomes illusion. . . . The destruction of gods and qualities alike is insisted upon.[13]

For Lukács, formal rationality is not only a procedure for efficiently calculating profitable exchanges. It is also identical to an objective social form (the commodity) which permeates and structures society *in its totality*. Lukács thus accepted Marx's analysis of commodity fetishism, which shows that capitalist society is essentially an *abstract*, mechanical system, regulated by the impersonal, lawlike fluctuation of numerical exchange values.

Horkheimer and Adorno take Lukács's analysis one step further. Lukács still believed that a capitalist society, structured along the lines of formal rationality, would find its critical limit in the practice of the proletariat, the last refuge of a substantive, dialectical form of rationality. Because of its advantageous position in industry, the proletariat can perceive the contradictions lurking beneath the "objectified" appearances of a social life, held together solely by the ever-constant and seemingly immutable laws of the market. For Adorno and Horkheimer, on the contrary, the domination of formal rationality in all areas of life is *total*. Indeed, so complete is the bureaucratic regimentation and technological fragmentation of the labor process, that workers are the least likely to escape the illusion of fatefulness that permeates every aspect of capitalism. Firstly, to cite the authors of *Dialectic*:

> Knowledge, which is power, knows no obstacles. . . . Technology is the essence of knowledge. It does not work by concepts and images . . . but refers to method, the exploitation of others' work, and capital. What men want to learn from nature is how

to use it in order to dominate it and other men. That is its only aim (4). . . . The division of labor to which domination tends serves the dominated whole for the end of self-preservation.

Through the division of labor imposed on them, the power of all members of society . . . amounts over and over again to the realization of the whole, whose rationality is reproduced this way. What is done to all by the few, always occurs as the subjection of individuals by the many: social repression always exhibits the masks of repression by a collective. It is this unity of the collectivity and domination, and not direct social universality, solidarity, which is expressed in thought forms (21–22).

Secondly, Adorno and Horkheimer locate the origins of the dialectic of enlightenment in the dawn of civilization itself. In this reading, capitalism (and the commodity form) are only recent articulations of an *anthropocentric* tendency dating back to the birth of civilization. Reason shows itself to be the quintessential *power* of self-preservation—the domination of inner and outer nature requisite for the constitution of the self as self-identical *subject* standing over and against a self-identical *object*. Paradoxically, this means that the "freedom" of the individual is obtained at the cost of tremendous repression, and culminates in a repetition compulsion. At this stage, the "return of repressed nature" takes the form of a totalitarian eclipse of individuality in the dark night of fascism. Again, to cite *Dialectic*:

Myth intended report, naming, narration of the Beginning; but also presentation, confirmation, explanation. . . . Myth turns into enlightenment, and nature into mere objectivity. Men pay for the increase of their power with alienation from that over which they exercise their power. Enlightenment behaves toward things as a dictator toward man. He knows them insofar as he can manipulate them (8–9). . . . Just as myths realize enlightenment, so enlightenment with every step becomes more deeply engulfed in mythology. . . . It wishes to extricate itself from the process of fate and retribution, while exercising retribution on that process.

But as the magical illusion fades away, the more relentlessly in the name of law repetition imprisons man in the cycle—that cycle whose objectification in the form of natural law he imagines will ensure his action as a free subject. The principle of immanence, the explanation of every event as repetition, that the enlightenment upholds against mythic imagination, is the principle of myth itself (12). . . . Not only are qualities dissolved in thought, but men are brought into actual conformity. . . . The unity of the manipulative collective consists in the negation of each individual. . . . The horde which so assuredly appears in the organization of the Hitler Youth is not a return to barbarism but the triumph of oppressive equality (13).

The *Dialectic of Enlightenment* proceeds to argue its case by defending the following theses:

(a) Enlightenment leads to the replacement of "objective" (teleological) reason with formal rationality.

(b) Formal rationality is identical to instrumental or "subjective" reason. Its sole end or value is self-preservation at all costs.

(c) Self-preservation manifests itself in mythic narrative, which already attempts to reduce the chaos of nature to regular forces which are capable of being controlled.

(d) The reduction of natural chaos is a necessary condition for the birth and preservation of (self-)consciousness. The identity of the ego depends upon the repression of unconscious instinctual drives (the *id*).

(e) Nature repressed returns in the form of compulsive aggression. Reason reverts to myth in the fatalism of mechanical social relations. The emancipation of the individual from the domination of natural forces culminates in the domination of the individual by the totalitarian state.

Adorno and Horkheimer deny that reason is capable of discerning absolute moral ends. Such an *objective*, or teleological, notion of reason rests on the mistaken view that values possess a metaphysical (objective) existence. This is expressed, for example, in God's will—independent of the relativistic vicissitudes of human (subjective) valuation. Following Weber, they argue that only a form of reason, which is restricted to the deduction and confirmation of causal laws in controlled, value-free observation, approximates scientific knowledge. However, since this notion of rationality provides only for the prediction and *instrumental* control of nature (and *not* its complete and perfect representation), its validity resides exclusively in furthering a *subjective* value—*self-preservation*. Hence, it is but a *technological* means by which the *subject* dominates what is otherwise a chaotic and meaningless world.[14]

Reason, then, is but a subjective illusion—in Nietzsche's sense—for mastering nature. Once its instrumental value is recognized, it is not hard to see it already at work in the earliest myths. This seems paradoxical, since we are accustomed to thinking of enlightenment and myth as *opposed* categories. Myths are stories which depict nature anthropomorphically, as consisting of spirits and demons which escape human control. Yet science, too, is but a projection of the subject. And myth, with its systematic reduction of nature's complexities to identifiable agencies and repeatable cycles, already anticipates science. Indeed, conceptual classification (representation) is just one way in which humans attempt to distance themselves from, and thereby control, the natural forces which impinge upon them. Concepts are here understood as tools for subsuming particular things under general patterns of thought. Such subsumption is then conceived as a form of instrumental domination of the particular by the universal.

This idea, which was developed most fully in Adorno's late masterpiece, *Negative Dialectics*, was used to explain the paradox underlying enlightened, bourgeois conceptions of morality. The repression of particular passions and desires, which ostensibly enslave the human will, involves harnassing human "nature" to the universal laws of a higher, rational will. The self achieves its freedom and identity only by rationally mastering (and thereby repressing) its "inner nature."

This is a theme that Adorno and Horkheimer develop in discussing the sadomasochistic aspects of Kantian morality. For Kant, the moral subject is free because he obeys only himself. For Adorno and Horkheimer, however, the freedom of the subject is but another name for the subjugation of the subject by itself—or rather, by that part of itself (the superego) representing the internalized authority of society's collective will. The Kantian moral subject is thus characterized as an *impersonal* self—the *abstract* bearer of *universal* rights and obligations. Here, *rational* identity is manifested as the formal (logical) self-consistency of being true to one's own conscience. Therefore, it stands opposed to the particular needs, feelings, and traits which make up *personal* identity. The price paid for rational self-control is thus repression of natural spontaneity and real individuality in the name of a higher, moral law—reason as the instrument of social conformity.[15]

Ultimately, the rational subject celebrated by liberalism is neither individual nor free. Within the parameters of formal rationality, the only value capable of motivating action is self-preservation. This becomes the sole universal with which all can identify and agree upon. Thus, enlightened bourgeois society is fragmented into isolated, egoistic bearers of property rights who, ironically, lack any *substantive* properties that might imbue their personalities with a sense of moral purpose. What identities they do possess are shaped by the collective forces that surround them—publicity being the most important.

This latter aspect is developed in detail in the section entitled "The Culture Industry: Enlightenment as Mass Deception." According to Adorno and Horkheimer, the identity of the individual in liberal society is a *mass* identity, imposed from without by the consumer-oriented entertainment of the "culture industry":

In the culture industry the individual is an illusion not merely because of the standardization of the means of production. He is tolerated only so long as his complete identification with the generality is unquestioned. . . . On the faces of private individuals and movie heroes put together according to the patterns on magazine covers vanishes a pretense in which no one now believes; the popularity of the hero models comes partly from a secret satisfaction that the effort to achieve individuation has at last been replaced by the effort to imitate (155–56).

The death of the bourgeois individual is explained by the authors as an offshoot of cultural degeneration. Prior to the nineteenth century artists worked for wealthy patrons. Although they were often commissioned to produce works that glorified the wealth, education, and achievements of their patrons, they also produced works that reflected the tension between universal, humanistic ideals and the hypocrisy of class society. This tension is also reflected in the Kantian opposition between the rational moral self and the egoistic personal self.

However, with the decline of aristocracy and the rise of capitalism, art lost its independence from the market. Deprived of its autonomy, art becomes a commodity whose appeal reaches only to the most common and ordinary desires. Its purpose is no longer to enoble the spirit and, thus, to mirror the contradiction between ideality and reality. It now serves to amuse and distract (130,157). With the rise of art forms dependent on processes of *mechanical reproduction*—film, lithography, photography, television, radio, etc.—the work of art loses its *individuality* as well, and can be functionalized for any purpose whatsoever. A medieval painting, whose religious significance was once bound up with its location in a cathedral, can now be reproduced photographically to sell clothing or music.

Mass-produced culture, however, also reinforces standardized forms of style and behavior. The appearance of diversity is deception: "Marked differentiations such as those of A and B films, or of stories in magazines in different price ranges, depend not so much on subject matter as on classifying, organizing, and labeling consumers" (123). Likewise deceptive is the appearance of consumer autonomy. The notion that popular culture reflects the democratic selection of conflicting consumer preferences is belied by the culture industry's manipulation of consumer needs. As the authors note:

The stunting of the mass-media consumer's powers of imagination and spontaneity does not have to be traced back to any psychological mechanisms; he must ascribe the loss of those attributes to the objective nature of the products themselves, especially to the most characteristic of them, the sound film. . . . Those who are so absorbed by the world of images, gestures, and words—that they are unable to supply what really makes it a world, do not have to dwell on particular points of its mechanics during a screening. All the other films and products of the entertainment industry have taught them what to expect; they react automatically (127).

The deception does not stop here, however. "Real life," the authors observe, "is becoming indistinguishable from the movies" (126). The theatrical staging of presidential campaigns and the election of actors masquerading as wise leaders is but a contemporary confirmation of this tendency. The "dream" reality in which we live is further reinforced by television, whose consequences, the authors predicted as early as 1944, "will be quite enormous and promise to intensify the impoverishment of aesthetic matter so drastically, that by tomorrow the thinly veiled identity of all industrial culture products can come triumphantly into the open" (124). Above all, television is the culmination of that "development of the culture industry," which "has led to the predominance of the effect, the obvious touch, and the technical detail over the work itself—which once expressed an idea, but was liquidated together with the idea" (125).[16]

Finally, deception is reflected in the false idea that culture debased to entertainment provides escape from the monotony and tedium of work:

What happens at work, in the factory, or in the office can only be escaped from by approximation to it in one's leisure time. All amusement suffers from this incurable malady. Pleasure hardens into boredom because, if it is to remain pleasure, it must not demand any effort and therefore moves rigorously in the worn grooves of association. No independent thinking must be expected from the audience: the products themselves prescribe every reaction. . . . Any logical connection calling for mental effort is painstakingly avoided. . . . As far as possible developments must follow from the immediately preceding situation and never from the idea of the whole (137–38).

The remarkable conformism induced by the culture industry is, of course, but one side of liberal society. The competitive antagonism of self-interested egos, as well as the specialization of tasks, requires the coordination of passive wills "from above." As Marcuse put it, "the technical democratization of functions is counteracted by their atomization, and the bureaucracy appears as the agency which guarantees their rational course and order."[17]

It is the need for centralized, rational coordination that leads mass society in its liberal phase to enter into more sinister, totalitarian configurations. Coupled with the excessive repression requisite for vocational life, it is not surprising that this tendency issues in that peculiar "revolt of nature" (as Horkheimer put it), characteristic of modern forms of barbarism.[18] In fascism there occurs a "satanic synthesis of reason and nature" in which aggressive drives commonly associated with paranoid and manic behavior are unleashed in lawless, but technologically sophisticated, forms of violence. One need only recall the meticulous detail in which Jews, gypsies, homosexuals, and other so-called "misfits" were "efficiently" exterminated in concentration camps.

More radical still, the authors go so far as to suggest that, far from being mere reactions against enlightenment, anti-Semitism and racism are its apotheosis. For the ideal of universal humanity, they claim, is itself governed by a totalitarian logic of *purity, unity* and *identity* that encourages conformity and punishes nonconformity.[19]

To sum up: Between 1939 and 1941, a noticeable shift occurred in critical theory's attitude toward reason. From believing unequivocally in the emancipatory potential of reason—a view that is entirely consonant with the German Enlightenment from Kant through Marx—the Frankfurt School came to suspect a more sinister, totalitarian side. The key to this interpretation resides in their reception of Weber's Kantian analysis of reason. According to Weber, so long as reason is conceived in purely procedural terms, it is incompatible with any unconditional moral idealism. Instead of showing how this might encourage a conditional idealism mediated by scientifically enlightened practice, Weber concluded that moral idealism and scientifically enlightened practice were simply incompatible. Thus, formal reason is identified by Weber and the others with scientific procedures of instrumental calculation. Consequently, Weber could not but insist that the Enlightenment—the rationalization of society—was incompatible with the survival of moral attitudes and institutions. The result is a modern society in which bureaucratic, machinelike efficiency and amoral materialism, oriented exclusively toward self-preservation and consumption, come to prevail. The tensions revealed by the Enlightenment between individual and society, freedom and necessity, science and morality resolve themselves in a dystopia in which freedom, individuality, morality, and community are all but extinguished.

As we shall see in the next chapter, it is this one-sided realization of the Enlightenment legacy that leads Marcuse to declare that science and technology have become ideological. For Marcuse, the formal rationality embodied in the scientific method was never neutral, or even entirely devoid of substantive content. In the eighteenth and nineteenth centuries, science was an "emancipatory" force working on behalf of a "universal" reason and, thus, opposed religious ideology. Today, thanks to the consolidation of economy, polity, culture, and technology in advanced capitalism and bureaucratic socialism, science works on behalf of a different set of substantive values. These values belie its universal, emancipatory pretensions and expose it, not religion, as the most prevalent and sinister ideology of the modern age. Indeed, Weber's and Lukács's identification of formal reason, with the particular historical institutions underlying capitalism, already implied that procedures of calculation were not neutral, but were essentially related to a system oriented toward domination for domination's sake.

If reason has become a partial weapon in the service of domination, how can Marcuse and the others continue to appeal to it? The answer, I shall argue, resides in their insistence that an emancipatory type of reason continues to live on in the aesthetic imagination which, they believe, has been repressed by social rationalization. The values esteemed by the Enlightenment—freedom, individuality, equality, community, etc.—may still be legitimate. Perhaps, rightly understood, the Enlightenment contains the idea of higher philosophical reason, which dialectically incorporates the achievements of both science and morality. However, as Hegel noted, this is a reason that cannot be reduced to formal procedures of calculation but, rather, consists of concrete images of happiness. Thus, it would imply an idea of reconciliation in which persons no longer confront one another or nature as an object to be dominated and possessed. The other is allowed its freedom and otherness— its difference if you will—without, thereby, ceasing to communicate with us. Thus, autonomy and communicative solidarity (receptivity and openness) are projected in a manner which avoids reduction to totalitarian identity or abstract opposition.

All of this, of course, raises new questions. Can a dialectical reconciliation of opposed tendencies be achieved at the level of real, concrete practice? Or must it remain simply at the level of philosophical and artistic (imaginary and utopian) speculation? What precisely would an emancipated society look like in which not only individual and society, but also freedom and nature—both internal and external—were reconciled? Wouldn't this require eliminating science and technology or at least changing them so fundamentally that they could no longer function in a predictive manner?

Or again, maybe the conclusions reached by Weber and first-generation critical theorists are simply too premature. Although modern society does suffer from some of the ills diagnosed by them, there is plenty of evidence indicating that the moral—and that means individualistic and democratic— aspects of the Enlightenment heritage are alive and flourishing. As of this writing, the peoples of Eastern Europe are rallying for reforms that will provide greater individual and democratic freedom within a socialist context. Here in the West people have extended the democratic principle, beyond participation in multiparty elections, to include local grassroots organization of peace, environmental, and antinuke demonstrations. Assuming that Weber was right about the formal nature of rationality, wouldn't these events suggest that it, too, might find institutional embodiment in morally significant ways? I have in mind, for example, those formal rules governing democratic procedural justice—freedom of speech, equal participation in public-opinion formation and so on, which appear to contain an ideal significance. Such rules suggest the possibility of reconciling theory and practice, individual and society, not only at the level of everyday political life, but also at the level of social theory itself. Perhaps critical theory should attempt to reconstruct these "regulative ideas" scientifically as well as philosophically, instead of retreating to the dialectical terrain of a purely aesthetic and philosophical rationality. These, then, are just some of the issues that will be joined in the remainder of our examination of critical theory.

NOTES

1. Weber was a member of the committee that submitted the first draft of the constitution of Germany's first republican government (the Weimar Republic of 1919–1933). He was a liberal who supported democracy for pragmatic reasons and remained highly distrustful of bureaucratic socialism. While at times an ardent nationalist and imperialist, he nonetheless assimilated much of Marx's critique of capitalism and, therefore, empathized with the plight of the working class. For a general analysis of the political realm in modern society, see Weber's "Politics as Vocation," in *From Max Weber: Essays in Sociology* (*FMW*), trans. and ed. H.H. Gerth and C. Wright Mills (New York: Oxford University Press, 1946), pp. 77–128.

2. According to Weber, worldviews determine "the tracks along which action has been pushed by the dynamic of interest" (*From Max Weber*, p. 280).

3. See *Max Weber on the Methodology of the Social Sciences*, ed. and trans. E. Shils and H.A. Finch (Glencoe, Il.: Free Press, 1949).

4. M. Weber, *Economy and Society*, ed. G. Roth and C. Wittich (Berkeley: University of California Press, 1970), vol. 1, pp. 24–25, 36–37, 869.

5. M. Weber, "Science as Vocation," in *From Max Weber*, p. 143 ff.

6. These arguments are developed in two of Nietzsche's most famous books, *Beyond Good and Evil* (1886) and *The Genealogy of Morals* (1887).

7. M. Weber, "Religious Rejections of the World and Their Directions," in *From Max Weber*, 323–59.

8. *Economy and Society*, pp. 289–99, 809–15, 866–71.

9. See "Politics as Vocation," "Science as Vocation," and "Religious Rejections of the World and Their Directions," in *From Max Weber*.

10. *Economy and Society*, p. 988, cited from *From Max Weber*, p. 228.

11. *The Protestant Ethic and the Spirit of Capitalism* (New York: Scribner, 1958), pp. 181–82.

12. See H. Marcuse, "Industrialization and Capitalism in the Work of Max Weber," in *Negations: Essays in Critical Theory* (Boston: Beacon Press, 1968), pp. 201–226;

and J. Habermas, *The Theory of Communicative Action. Volume One. Reason and the Rationalization of Society*, trans. T. McCarthy (Boston: Beacon Press, 1984), pp. 201–226.

13. M. Horkheimer and T.W. Adorno, *Dialectic of Enlightenment* (New York: Continuum, 1974), pp. 7–8. This passage is excerpted from "The Concept of Enlightenment" reprinted in *Critical Theory: The Essential Readings (CTER)*.

14. See M. Horkheimer, "Conflicting Panaceas," in *The Eclipse of Reason*, 61–62, 80–82; "Means and Ends," reprinted in *CTER*; and *Dialectic of Enlightenment*, trans. John Cumming (New York: Seabury, 1972), pp. 21–23. The latter passage is excerpted from "The Concept of Enlightenment" reprinted in *CTER*.

15. *Ibid.*, p. 81 ff.

16. See Theodor Adorno,"How to Look at Television," reprinted in *CTER*.

17. H. Marcuse, "Some Social Implications of Technology," in *The Frankfurt School Reader*, p. 154.

18. M. Horkheimer, "The Revolt of Nature," in *The Eclipse of Reason*, pp. 92–127.

19. *Dialectic of Enlightenment*, pp. 170–72.

SELECTED BIBLIOGRAPHY

Adorno, T.W. & Horkheimer, M., *Dialectic of Enlightenment*. Trans. John Cumming. New York: Seabury, 1972.

Habermas, J. *The Theory of Communicative Action. Volume One. Reason and the Rationalization of Society*. Trans. by T. McCarthy. Boston: Beacon, 1984.

Horkheimer, M. *Eclipse of Reason*. New York: Seabury, 1974.

Marcuse, H. "Industrialization and Capitalism in the Work of Max Weber." In *Negations: Essays in Critical Theory*. Boston: Beacon, 1968.

———"Some Social Implications of Technology." In *The Frankfurt School Reader*.

Nietzsche, F. *The Genealogy of Morals*. Trans. by F. Golffing. Garden City, N.Y.: Doubleday, 1956.

———*The Will to Power*. Trans. by W. Kaufmann and R.J. Hollingwood. New York: Random House, 1967.

Weber, M. *Economy and Society* (2 vols.). Edited by G. Roth and C. Wittich. Berkeley: University of California Press, 1970.

———*From Max Weber*. Edited by H.H. Gerth and C.W. Mills. Oxford: Oxford University press, 1969.

————*The Protestant Ethic and the Spirit of Capitalism.* New York: Scribner, 1958.

Commentaries: Those interested in reading further about Weber should consult Reinhard Bendix, *Max Weber, an Intellectual Portrait* (London, 1966), and A. Giddens, *Capitalism and Modern Social Theory: An Analysis of the Writings of Marx, Durkheim and Max Weber* (Cambridge: Cambridge University Press, 1971). In addition to the commentaries on the Frankfurt School mentioned in chapter two, I refer the reader to Zoltán Tar's *The Frankfurt School: The Critical Theories of Max Horkheimer and Theodor W. Adorno* (New York: Schocken Books, 1977) and P. Connerton's *The Tragedy of Enlightenment: An Essay on the Frankfurt School* (Cambridge: Cambridge University Press, 1980).

FOUR

MARCUSE AND THE NEW POLITICS OF LIBERATION

In the preceding chapter, I argued that the Frankfurt School's reliance on Weber's theory of rationalization led them to embrace a starkly pessimistic vision of modern society. This is not to deny the powerful impact that exile and wartime events had upon their diagnosis. Yet, the experience of fascism and modern genocide cannot explain the remarkable fascination that the dialectic of enlightenment held for them even after the war, when the threat of totalitarianism appeared to be waning.

What explains this fascination? Adorno and Horkheimer had cast their gloomy diagnosis in the form of a philosophical anthropology. In this reading, totalitarianism and genocide appear to be the inevitable outcome of a process of rationalization extending back to the dawn of human consciousness. The thesis itself is formulated in such a way that the facts seem all but indisputable. Rationalization involves the replacement of *objective* reason, with its unconditional prescription of particular *substantive ends*, with *subjective*, or instrumental, reason. In the absence of absolute values, the only end worth pursuing is self-preservation. Adaptability, or technological domination for the sake of domination, becomes synonymous with reason. In the final analysis, technological rationality not only conceives reality as a unified, mathematical system. It actively constitutes it as such.

The totalitarian implications of rationality need not be overt. The elimination of social conflict and all other differences, as well as the suppression of dissent, is built into the very system of rationalized production. The efficient division of labor into atomized tasks requires global coordination "from above." This administrative logic, in turn, empowers technological elites who possess the special skills and superior knowledge requisite for making decisions.

Juxtaposed to the hierarchy of domination, however, is the democracy of consumption. The *standardization* of production, dictated by technically efficient methods of mass production, requires a mass market composed of persons possessing uniform (standard) needs. The insidiousness of this "soft" form of totalitarianism is reflected in both the homogeneous identity of mass consumers and the manipulative manner by which it is inculcated. The resulting assimilation, of high culture to entertainment and advertising, not only deprives persons of opportunities for developing critical, analytical tools, but also enforces patterns of passivity and submissiveness that make domination acceptable and pleasurable.

No other critical theorist, in recent memory, followed through the consequences of this new form of domination to the extent that Herbert Marcuse did. His most popular work, *One-Dimensional Man* (1964), contains one of the strongest indictments of the narcotic effects of advanced capitalism ever written.[1] Yet, interspersed throughout its disheartening depiction of one-dimensional humanity are glimmerings of hope. Marcuse never quite succumbed to the degree of pessimism contained in the writings of his colleagues. Throughout the late sixties and early seventies, he continued to have faith in a revolutionary vanguard. It was one, however, composed of middle-class college students rather than workers. Moreover, unlike Adorno and Horkheimer, Marcuse freely speculated about the utopian contours of the emancipated society that he saw emerging in the countercultural life-styles of the New Left.

Marcuse, of course, could not have maintained such a hopeful stance without, at least partially, relinquishing the thesis of totalitarian reason developed by Adorno and Horkheimer. Indeed, neither he nor they ever abandoned their commitment to emancipatory reason entirely. The critical, dialectical reason—that technological society suppresses—continues to live on, they believed, in the aesthetic unconscious (imagination).

Yet, serious questions remain. What implication does the retreat into aesthetic imagination have for resolving the theory/practice problem? If resolving the problem depends on actualizing the emancipatory heritage of the Enlightenment in objective social and political institutions, would it not appear that reason actualized really is totalitarian in the way described by Adorno and Horkheimer? However, there are other interpretations of *Dialectic of Enlightenment* which suggest alternative responses. The authors of this work do not simply condemn the accomplishments of the bourgeois era. In some sense, technology and individualism are emancipatory. Yet, they are also fundamentally ambiguous, in that emancipation is purchased with increased domination. An even more radical interpretation suggests that the objective accomplishments of the Enlightenment contradict the emancipatory ideals which continue to live on in art and philosophy. In that case, actualization of the Enlightenment might involve radically transforming, if not abandoning altogether, the formal-rational achievements of science and technology. But what would a nonobjectifying, nondomineering form of science and technology be like?

At the very worst, the Enlightenment appears as an inherently dialectical phenomenon whose aspirations can never be fully realized. Either scientific or moral rationality may be realized—but not both. From a methodological perspective, it is clear that the school's decision, to opt for the latter alternative, led them to drastically rethink their original interdisciplinary synthesis of philosophy and science. Yet, despite the problematic nature of this synthesis in light of the dialectic of enlightenment, even the most radical members of the school, Adorno and Horkheimer, continued to rely on scientific insights in their social criticism, albeit, in a manner increasingly divorced from their philosophical speculations.

These philosophical speculations found expression in two very different tendencies. The first, developed by Adorno in *Negative Dialectics* (1966), problematizes any attempt to actualize reason in a way that will resolve its tensions. The second, developed by Marcuse in *Eros and Civilization* (1955) and *One-Dimensional Man* (1964), not only attempts to ground reason but also suggests positive ways in which reason—both scientific and moral—might be actualized. Despite their differences, both tendencies converge in the agreement that aesthetic rationality, or dialectical imagination, is the principal place in which emancipatory reason is to be located. Such reason is conceived as a form of communication in which oppositions between subject and object, individual and society, freedom and nature, universal and particular are at least maintained in their integrity, if not resolved.

In the following chapters, I propose to examine in detail the arguments made in two of Marcuse's most influential works, beginning with an analysis of *One-Dimensional Man*. Before preceding to that discussion, however, I will briefly touch upon Adorno's work during the fifties and early sixties. This work illustrates well the possibilities and limits inherent in the school's dialectical position with respect to the theory/practice problem. In particular, it provides a stark contrast between a critical theory that fully integrates the insights of social scientific research and a critical theory that doesn't.

FROM THE AUTHORITARIAN
PERSONALITY TO NEGATIVE DIALECTICS

The most important project undertaken by the Frankfurt School during and immediately after the Second World War was its study of fascism, entitled

The Authoritarian Personality (1950). Directed by Max Horkheimer, who was working under the auspices of the American Jewish Committee, the study combined the psychoanalytic model that had been deployed ten years earlier in the school's *Studies on Authority and Family* (1936), with empirical methods of data-gathering, questionnaires, depth interviews, and projective tests. Perhaps no other research, undertaken by members of the school, better exemplified the interdisciplinary synthesis of philosophy and science, which had inspired the school during the thirties. It is noteworthy, too, that Adorno, the school's major contributor to the project, was chiefly responsible for interpreting the statistical data which had been gathered by coworkers affiliated with the Berkeley Public Opinion Survey Group.

Once again, anti-Semitism provided a convenient point of departure for analyzing the prototypical antidemocratic ideology. The initial investigation confirmed that anti-Semitism, as measured by psychological propensities to view Jews as aggressive, offensive, threatening, seclusive, intrusive, and deserving of segregation, is "a general frame of mind." This was followed by an investigation which established that anti-Semitism was part of a larger ethnocentric prejudice which discriminates against members of all out-groups, including Jews, Blacks, radicals, and members of lower socioeconomic groups. The next series of politico-economic investigations established a positive correlation between conservatism and ethnocentrism, with fascism representing the extreme limit of antiliberal intolerance.

The final study combined the above results in a new measure to test antidemocratic, authoritarian tendencies. The so-called F scale (F = fascism) consisted of nine psychological variables. The most important of these were:

conventionalism (rigid adherence to middle class values)

authoritarian submission (uncritical attitude toward idealized moral authorities)

authoritarian aggression (suspicion and condemnation of people who violate conventional values)

anti-intraception (opposition to the subjective and imaginative)

superstition and stereotypy (mystical belief in fatalism and the tendency to think in rigid categories)

power and toughness (preoccupation with dominance-submission)

projectivity (projection outwards of unconscious impulses and paranoid beliefs)

The study concluded that the roots of authoritarianism lie in early childhood development. Children raised by parents who enforce rigid discipline and submission to authority are likely to feel helpless and inferior, while projecting their repressed hostility onto out-groups. Surprisingly, the authors suggest that the solution to the problem lies in reeducation and individual psychoanalysis. Such faith in the power of a theory, combining philosophical and scientific enlightenment, clearly deviated from the pessimistic conclusion set forth in the school's theory of rationalization. At the same time, Adorno's reticence, in addressing the historical and economic factors underlying authoritarianism, showed how detached his psychoanalytic critique of culture had become from its original base in Marxist ideology critique.

The tendency toward speculative, ahistorical theorizing, which first manifested itself in *Dialectic of Enlightenment*, became more pronounced in the school's later writings. We have already noticed how the historical specificity of such phenomena as fascism was gradually effaced in the school's research. By the late forties, fascism and bureaucratic socialism—not to mention advanced capitalism—were seen as variations of one and the same process of technological rationalization. Regarded from this highly abstract perspective, *all* modern social formations could be regarded as totalitarian—*economic, political, and ideological differences notwithstanding*.

Ironically, this tendency toward abstract metaphysical speculation culminated in the very sort of abstract idealism criticized by Marx as "ideological." In 1949, following their return to Frankfurt, Adorno and Horkheimer continued to encourage empirical research among their associates (the Frankfurt Institute for Social Research was reopened in 1951). However, their own work displayed just the opposite tendency. This is especially so in the case of Adorno's last masterpieces, *Negative Dialectics* (1966) and *Aesthetic Theory*, which was left unfinished at the time of his death in 1969.

Negative Dialectics is written in a loose, fragmentary way—and deliberately so. Adorno explicitly sought to dispel the impression that the "Theory of Society," proffered therein, could aspire to a totalizing, systematic presentation. What one finds instead is a use of conflicting methods: *dialectical* philosophy and *formal-scientific* analysis. According to Adorno, rationalized society must be conceptualized as a closed totality, or reified system, but only negatively so. That is, it constitutes a *false* totality containing inherent contradictions. Ironically, even dialectical thought, which presupposes the category of identity as much as nonidentity, is impugned as a reflection of the totalitarian identity underlying the commodity relationship. Indeed, the subsumption of sensuous particularity, under conceptual categories of any kind, is viewed as a type of subjective domination.

With *Negative Dialectics*, critical theory seems to have painted itself into a corner. Dialectical reason was supposed to have provided a universally valid basis for criticizing a society rationalized in a one-sidedly technological manner. However, the very category of totality, which it deploys, reveals a penchant toward identity and harmony that is just as false and totalitarian as the reified rationality it criticizes. Contrary to Hegel, dialectical reason cannot be put to practical purposes and realized without destroying its essential truth—that freedom demands nonidentity, or the "autonomy" of the other. In the words of Adorno, "philosophy, which once seemed obsolete, lives on because the moment to realize it was missed."[2]

The retreat of critical theory from political practice signals a profound break from Marxism. As Lukács put it in 1963: "A considerable part of the leading intelligentsia, including Adorno, have taken up residence in the 'Grand Hotel Abyss' which I described in connection with my critique of Schopenhauer as 'a beautiful hotel, equiped with every comfort, on the edge of an abyss. . . .' "[3] The "beautiful hotel" in Lukács's critique is a reference to Adorno's seeking refuge in aesthetic contemplation, as the last bastion of a critical reason protected from the harsh realities of reified life.

According to Adorno, authentic works of art—especially modern works—embody a formal unity of opposed differences. The most important of these dialectical tensions, or "force-fields," is that between subject and object. In everyday cognition, subject and object are related as opposed terms. "Nature" appears as an independent power, resistant to the satisfaction of subjective needs. This "contradiction" is resolved in favor of the subject, who imposes a unitary conceptual schema on nature, for purposes of controlling its chaos. Thus, abstract opposition leads to abstract conceptual unity. The subject "swallows up" nature, which is henceforth objectified as a mere conceptual and practical construct of the subject.

The progressive domination of an objectified nature by a sovereign humanity was regarded by Hegel and Marx as the key to emancipation. For Adorno and other critical theorists, however, it is implicitly totalitarian. The domination of nature, they argued, extends to humanity itself, in the form of psychological repression and social engineering. So long as subject and object are seen as opposed terms, enlightenment can but serve only to increase domination.

According to Adorno, art and aesthetic contemplation seem to avoid this dialectic. In the work of art, nature, in the form of unconscious impulse, and subjective consciousness—the source of rational unity—are related in a nonreductive manner. The work of art is neither pure feeling and emotion (nature), nor pure form (thought). Rather it is a "constellation," or juxtaposition, of the two. Art requires philosophy—conceptual analysis and synthesis—for the articulation of its truth, while philosophy requires artistic truth for its emancipatory content. Thus, the "reconciliation" of natural content and rational form, in this instance, does not signify an identity (harmony) without difference (conflict). The maker and viewer of the art relate neither to their own inner nature, nor to the outer nature of the artistic media, as use objects. Conceptual thought, infected with the concrete materiality of textual imagery incorporating the aesthetic object, does not permit it.

The convergence of the aesthetic and the philosophical in the essay form—Adorno's preferred medium of critical writing—is reflected in rhetorical tropes (metaphors, similes, allusions and so forth) that establish figurative rather than logical connections between concepts and the concrete properties of the work of art. Meaning is conveyed in the form of unstable thought-images that provoke continuous reflection.

Finally, the emotional impulses of the artist/spectator engage the rhythms and textures of the artistic media in a kind of passive/active *imitation*. Despite this harmony, thought (form) and feeling (content) remain conjoined in critical tension. In one of the last essays he wrote, "Subject and Object" (1969), Adorno speculated that such a relationship would involve a dialogical reciprocity, or communicative interchange, between autonomous agents that might serve as a cipher for true social solidarity:

> If speculation on the state of reconciliation were permitted, neither the undistinguished unity of subject and object nor their antithetical hostility would be conceivable in it; rather, the communication of what was distinguished. Not until then would the concept of communication, as an objective concept, come into its own. The present one is so infamous because the best there is, the potential of an agreement between people and things, is betrayed to an interchange between subjects according to the requirements of subjective reason. In its proper place, even epistemologically, the relationship of subject and object would lie in the realization of peace among men as well as between men and their Other. Peace is the state of distinctness without domination, with the distinct participating in each other.[4]

As we shall see, the notion of *communication* will assume importance in both the writings of Marcuse and Habermas. In authentic communication, two or more interlocutors "participate" in a common field of language constituted by their own mutual openness and receptivity toward one another. The "other" opposite one is neither an object nor a totally sovereign, self-contained subject. He or she is a partner—passive and active—in an *intersubjective* game of dialogue. Each partner, in turn, questions and is questioned by, the other in a *critical* process aiming at a noncoercive agreement. And it is this agreement that produces the distinct identities of the participants. These identities are born of a *mutual* effort of *critical reflection*, not of a *monological* act of domination.

MARCUSE AND ONE-DIMENSIONAL MAN

We noted above that Adorno never entirely abandoned the notion of critical reason, even in his most pessimistic moments. Although dialectical reason succumbs to totalitarian tendencies, it does so only if it is conceived *positively*, as it was by Hegel and Marx. Conceived positively, it is an activity whereby a subject imposes order, unity, and identity on nature, which is seen as resisting the subject's will. The sovereignty of the subject, that is, its freedom and self-sufficiency with respect to nature, is procured by dominating nature. The subject projects its ideas onto nature, transmits its powers into nature, and literally transforms itself and nature into an object of rational self-control. Nature infused with the unifying ideas and ordering powers of the subject thereby ceases to confront the subject as a hostile "other." A total identity between self and nature is established. The self can now find itself in nature, and can appropriate nature as its own creation. Yet "naturalized" subject and "subjectivized" nature do not confront one another as free individualities, but as objectifications of an impersonal, deterministic force—reason as universal lawgiver.

If reason's dialectical activity is conceived positively, the result is a total identity between subject and object (nature). The self takes on the objective qualities of a fixed and stable nature. Nature, in turn, appears as a mere projection of the subject. By contrast, if reason's dialectical activity is conceived negatively, the result is a kind of dialogical communication in which both sides, subject and nature, self and other, retain their independence or difference from one another. Such a dialogical relationship, Adorno believed, obtained in art and in the aesthetic contemplation of nature. In aesthetic contemplation, the viewer does not seek to use or dominate nature. Nature is not viewed as something alien that needs to be objectified and controlled. Rather, the needs and feelings of the subject spontaneously resonate with the (natural) rhythms of the aesthetic form and vice versa. This mimetic or imitative relationship points in the direction of a utopian reconciliation of humanity and nature. At the same time, however, it reminds us of the irreducible differences separating reason and feeling, universal concept and particular existent, human striving and natural passivity. Nature ought to be granted its own dignity as an independent realm of particularity. Humanity ought to become more receptive. And society ought to approximate a democratic community, in which respect for the individual *as other*, is combined with *solidarity with the other*. So construed, the negative dialectic embodied in aesthetic rationality functions as one of the main points of *resistance* against totalitarian society.

Because of his insistence on the seemingly utopian and negative nature of aesthetic enlightenment, however, Adorno never envisaged what the concrete contours of an emancipated society would be like. Nor did he believe that critical reason could ever become a practical force in social and political life without degenerating into instrumental domination. As Lukács disdainfully noted, Adorno had buried the theory/practice problem by relegating critical reason to the depoliticized sphere of art and aesthetic contemplation.

Marcuse, by contrast, was more daring in his attempt to address the new vanguard of student revolutionaries which emerged in the sixties. And he was by no means reticent when it came to propounding the utopia, which he believed to be implicit in the current state of affairs. Nevertheless, he was hardly consistent on this point, continually vacillating between hopefulness and despair while seeking refuge in the "aesthetic dimension."

No work of Marcuse better exemplifies this tension than *One-Dimensional Man*. This book takes up the analysis set forth by Adorno and Horkheimer in *Dialectic of Enlightenment*. "The analysis," Marcuse tells us, "is focused on advanced industrial society, in which the technical apparatus of production and distribution (with an increasing sector of automation) functions . . . as a system which determines *a priori* the product of the apparatus as well as the operations of servicing and extending it."[5] The result is a one-dimensional society in which all forms of oppositional resistance to the status quo are eliminated. What *ought* to be is no longer clearly distinguished from what *is*. Imagination of new possibilities is increasingly truncated in favor of adaptive response. The inner subjectivity of the individual is absorbed into, and obliterated by, the impersonal mechanism of the system. As Marcuse notes:

In this society, the productive apparatus tends to become totalitarian to the extent that it determines not only the socially needed occupations, skills, and attitudes, but also individual needs and aspirations. It thus obliterates the opposition between private and public existence, between individual and social needs. Technology serves to institute new, more effective, and more pleasant forms of social control and cohesion. The totalitarian tendency of these controls seems to assert itself in still another sense— by spreading to the less developed and even to the preindustrial areas of the world, and by creating similarities in the development of capitalism and communism.

In the face of the totalitarian features of this society, the traditional notion of the "neutrality" of technology can no longer be maintained. Technology as such cannot be isolated from the use to which it is put; the technological society is a system of domination which operates already in the concept and construction of techniques . . . it shapes the entire universe of discourse and action, intellectual and material culture. In the medium of technology, culture, politics, and the economy merge into an omnipresent system which swallows up or repulses all alternatives (xv–xvi).

According to Marcuse, industrial society is more ideological than its predecessor, "inasmuch as today the ideology is in the process of production itself" (11). The advanced industrial society which began to emerge at the turn of the century is distinguished by the fact that, for the first time ever, the natural and social sciences enter directly into the production process—as its primary determinants. This transformation culminated in today's military-industrial complex and its characteristic concentration of wealth and power:

Concentration of the national economy on the needs of the big corporations, with the government as a stimulating, supporting, and sometimes even controlling force; hitching of this economy to a world-wide system of military alliances, monetary arrangements, technical assistance and development schemes; gradual assimilation of blue-collar and white-collar population, of leadership types in business and labor, of leisure activities and aspirations in different social classes; fostering of a pre-established harmony between scholarship and national purpose; invasion of the private household by the togetherness of public opinion; opening of the bedroom to the media of mass communication (19).

Two major factors are identified by Marcuse which perpetuate this "soft" form of totalitarianism. First, the creation of an atmosphere of anti-Communist paranoia serves to justify the suppression of political dissent from the Left as well as encourage a close collaboration between government and big business (51). Second, the rising standard of living experienced by all sectors of society threatens to obscure the growing disparities in income between rich and poor. Automation tied to techniques of data processing results in a more educated class of "nonproductive" workers occupying "white-collar" jobs. These workers passively acquiesce in supporting the hierarchical arrangements of the management system, since this system is no longer obviously connected to the physical exploitation of heavy labor by capitalists (22–34).

Stated bluntly, the main source of opposition in liberal capitalist society—the industrial proletariat—has been thoroughly assimilated to the technological apparatus. This has become possible, Marcuse claims, because domination itself has assumed pleasurable forms. "The machine process in the technological universe," he observes, "breaks the innermost privacy of freedom and joins sexuality and labor in one unconscious, rhythmic automatism" (27). Likewise, the wasteful pleasure of consuming ever-vaster quantities of commodities—sold to the public on the basis of their sexual allure—is combined with the domination of longer work hours. This process has been abetted by what Marcuse calls *repressive desublimation.*

Sublimation was the term used by Freud to designate the rechanneling of sexual energy away from its primary object toward a "substitute," which provides a more socially useful type of pleasure. The substitute satisfactions Freud had in mind included professional (especially creative) work and largely intellectual endeavors. Marcuse, following Freud, agrees that the products of high culture and art, which exhibit imagination and beauty, are sublimations. Although they delay, and to that extent suppress, *immediate* gratification, such products figuratively articulate a life of harmony and fulfillment which is incompatible with the oppressive, utilitarian features of technological society. In the words of Marcuse, "what they recall and preserve in memory pertains to the future: images of gratification that would dissolve the society which suppresses it" (60).

Marcuse, as we shall see, deviates from Freud in regarding sublimation as less a form of repression than a source of liberation. For him, sublimation can serve to extend the principle of pleasure, beyond the narrow compass of genital sexuality, to include the full development of the subject's powers, faculties, and needs. It can also generate intense feelings of social solidarity and yearnings for aesthetic peace and harmony with nature. So construed, sublimation would demand the creation of a society without domination, oriented toward aesthetically pleasing forms of work and receptivity.

By the same token, *de*sublimation can issue in forms of "freedom" which are, in fact, repressive. The integration of sex into work and consumption serves to deny sexual fulfillment—even while promising it. Sex becomes an all-encompassing obsession which constrains us to behave and look certain ways. This is, no doubt, a great boon to the mind-manipulators employed by the cosmetics, tobacco, and automobile industries. But the empty fulfillment of loveless, genital copulation provides a false substitute for true erotic fulfillment. It makes it easier to tolerate the unpleasurable, *an*aesthetic features of our everyday work environment. Moreover, it allows us to neglect our genuine needs for intellectual, aesthetic development—in favor of gratifying unhealthy needs for wasteful consumption. Blinded by the allure of immediate gratification, the "happy consciousness" of today's consumer tolerates the suffering of others, even while mindlessly colluding in his own domination as well as their's (71–81).

IDEOLOGY, SURPLUS REPRESSION, AND ONE-DIMENSIONAL LANGUAGE

Perhaps the most original aspect of Marcuse's book is its treatment of ideology. Ideological false consciousness is a state of mind characterized by a systematically induced failure to identify one's true needs and/or interests. " 'False' needs," Marcuse says, "are those which are superimposed upon the individual by particular social interests in his repression: the needs which perpetuate toil, aggressiveness, misery, and injustice" (4–5). Examples are "the overwhelming need for the production and consumption of waste; the need for stupifying work where it is no longer a real necessity; the need for modes of relaxation which soothe and prolong this stupification; the need for maintaining such deceptive liberties as free competition at administered prices." This involves "a free press which censors itself (and a) free choice between brands and gadgets" (7). The distinction between true and false needs is not arbitrary:

The judgment of needs and their satisfaction, under given conditions, involves standards of *priority*—standards which refer to the optimal development of the individual, all individuals, under the optimal utilization of the material and intellectual resources available to man. These sources are calculable. "Truth" and "falsehood" of needs designate objective conditions to the extent to which the universal satisfaction of vital needs and, beyond it, the progressive alleviation of toil and poverty, are universally valid standards. But as historical standards, they do not only vary according to area and stage of development, they also can be defined only in (greater or lesser) *contradiction* to the prevailing ones. (6)

"In the last analysis," Marcuse concludes, "the question of what are true and false needs must be answered by the individuals themselves, but only in the last analysis; that is, if and when they are free to give their own answer." The problem, of course, is that the kind of freedom, required for making rational choices about needs, is unavailable in a society that demands so much repression.

Repression is the price that all societies must pay for surviving under conditions of *scarcity*. However, as technology develops and scarcity decreases, the need to toil under oppressive conditions should decline. Marx himself believed that, with the advent of complete automation (the application of science and technology), the amount of time people would have to devote to work could be reduced to a minimum. Workers could stand outside the production process as supervisors and regulators. They would thus be able to develop themselves intellectually, aesthetically, and socially without the need to produce more commodities. Moreover, as Marcuse notes, the technological division of labor envisaged by Marx actually opens up new possibilities for democratizing the labor force and breaking down the division between manual and intellectual labor. However, neither job rotation, worker democracy, nor freedom from labor due to decreased scarcity have come about.

According to Marcuse, the existing level of *surplus* repression, which extends well beyond what is necessary given the technological resources currently available to humanity, is sustained by repressive needs. These needs are functional for the existence of capitalism, which survives by encouraging ever-greater consumption and exploitation. In turn, they are reinforced by the system and its prevailing ideology of freedom. As Marcuse observes:

Under the rule of a repressive whole, liberty can be made into a powerful instrument of domination. The range of choice open to the individual is not the decisive factor in determining the degree of human freedom. . . . Free election of masters does not abolish the masters or the slaves. Free choice among a wide variety of goods and services does not signify freedom if these goods and services sustain social control over a life of toil and fear. (8)

One of the most pernicious mechanisms for reinforcing the ideology of freedom is the distortion of the very language in which persons reason about their needs. According to Marcuse, everyday language is increasingly drained of its critical content through assimilation to mass media. Mass media technology combines everyday language with images. Some of these are subliminal in ways that induce emotional, automatic responses rather than rational reflection. The telescoping and abridgment of syntax used in government propaganda and commercial advertising "cuts off the development of meaning by creating fixed images which impose themselves with an overwhelming and petrified concreteness" (91). Examples of such telescoping include the kind of "doublespeak" analysed by George Orwell (recall Ronald Reagan's dubbing the ICBM missile the "peacekeeper"), the use of emotional "buzz" words and "impact lines" (notice the way politicians drape themselves in the flag, appeal to "family values," and evoke images of "the evil empire," in avoiding talk about substantive issues), and the repetitive, hypnotic incantation of formulaic expression (the constant association of democracy and capitalism, for instance).

According to Marcuse, the manipulative use to which language is put in the mass media is symptomatic of a more general tendency evident in modern science itself. This concerns the reduction of linguistic meaning to concrete *operations*. In the metaphysical tradition of philosophy extending from Plato through Hegel, concepts denoted *universal* qualities shared by a plurality of particular individuals. As universal, they were believed to transcend, or point beyond, the individual which possessed them. In this reading, to say that *a* flower is *beautiful*, is not to identify any *particular* flower with beauty as such. Of course, what we mean by "beautiful" varies, depending upon the context of its use. A painting is not beautiful in the way that a person's personality is. Yet, beauty as such—the universal common to all beautiful things—designates a transcendent quality, however vague, which is irreducible to any particular context.

Marcuse further notes that, in the philosophical ascription of *essential* (necessary or definitive) properties to individuals, judgments are made that combine description and evaluation. When Aristotle says that human beings are essentially rational beings, he is ascribing the universal "rational" both *factually* and *prescriptively* to human beings. Human beings are born with a *universal* potential (rationality) which, being peculiar to themselves, *factually* distinguishes them from all other animals. Yet, insofar as rationality designates a *potential* which may be furthered or frustrated, it also prescribes an *ideal goal* to be achieved. Thus, the essential predication of universals to particulars in the tradition of metaphysical philosophy always implied *critical* standards. Indeed, it was thought that nature itself "prescribed" the necessary potentials and limits—according to which all beings could be judged more or less perfect. Thus, concrete reality could be criticized for not being fully adequate to its own essence.

Modern philosophy eliminates the dialectical tension between existence and essence, reality and ideality, particularity and universality, description and prescription which inhabits metaphysics. It does so by reducing meaning to just the factual and particular. This is especially true, Marcuse believes, of the ordinary language tradition commonly associated with G.E. Moore, the late Ludwig Wittgenstein, Gilbert Ryle, and J.L. Austin. These philosophers seek to explain away philosophical paradoxes and dilemmas by ridding us of essentialist misconceptions about language. Philosophy, they argue, serves this "therapeutic" function by getting us to accept the predominantly nonrepresentational, *pragmatic* function of language. Following this approach, the meaning of any term or expression would be bound up with its *particular context of use*. To return to our earlier example, there would be as many different meanings of "beauty" and "beautiful" as there are uses of these terms, without these meanings sharing anything in common. Beauty would cease to refer to a transcendent universal possessing ideal, prescriptive content.

Marcuse illustrates the problem of this approach, with reference to Gilbert Ryle's *The Concept of Mind*. According to Ryle, to say that someone possessed a brilliant mind would not mean that one possessed a special kind of universal mental "substance" distinct from the body. Such a metaphysical way of viewing the mind, Ryle argues, is based upon a category mistake originating in the grammatical parallel such statements have with genuine ascriptions of substantive properties. Simply stated, people don't "possess" brilliant minds in the same way that they possess long noses. Rather, they possess them *figuratively*, in the form of *behavioral dispositions*. For Ryle, to say that person P has a brilliant mind is really to describe P's *behavior* (e.g., P's tendency to solve math problems with greater facility than other persons).

Marcuse regards Ryle's reduction of the human mind to brute behavior as symptomatic of a false conception of ordinary language. It is false, as Hegel would say, because it *abstracts* from the *totality* of background conditions— social, cultural, and political—which lend ordinary language its ideological *and* critical import. Meaning, in everyday speech, is not reducible to context-bound operations or behavioral dispositions. When I say that P has a brilliant mind, I also *indirectly imply* what society at large takes to be a sign of brilliance (mathematical as opposed to critical aptitude). I imply the whole hierarchically structured economic and social structure, which makes possible P's elite education while, at the same time, perpetuating ignorance among members of the underclass.

Finally, I imply the existence of a *consciousness*, which is capable of behaving in the expected manner of one trained to be a mathematician, but which might also rise above the limits of this socially ingrained role and do something wholly unexpected. Marcuse sums up one aspect of the dual ideological/critical polarity of everyday speech accordingly:

In speaking their own language, people also speak the language of their masters, benefactors, and advertisers. Thus they do not only express *themselves*, their own knowledge, feelings, and aspirations, but also something other than themselves. . . . "What people mean when they say . . ." is related to what they *don't* say. Or, what they mean cannot be taken at face value—not because they lie, but because the universe of thought and practice in which they live is a universe of manipulated contradictions. (193–94)

The aim of critical theory, Marcuse insists, is "to make the established language itself speak what it conceals or excludes, for what is to be revealed and denounced is operative *within* the universe of ordinary discourse and action" (195).

Marcuse insists that everyday language implicitly indicts its own ideological operation insofar as it retains a metaphysical, or speculative residue of the sort articulated in traditional philosophy. The word "democracy," for example, still possesses a prescriptive meaning that cannot be reduced to descriptions of actual existing democracies—attempts by positivistically minded political scientists notwithstanding. Voting at the polls for candidates representing two or more parties may suffice to distinguish democratic from dictatorial regimes. However, it leaves out the ideal expectation implicit in the democratic notion of *free, rational* consent. That is, we assume that the voters are educated, well-informed, have actively participated in the selection of candidates and issues, and are acting independently of ideological indoctrination and manipulation (114–20).

Thus, ideology critique proceeds by turning the ideal (metaphysical) signification of ordinary speech against its real (context-bound) function, or pragmatic use. The historically contingent reality is found to be deficient on its own terms. Yet the criteria of social critique are not ahistorical. Reality is not criticized simply because it fails to live up to utopian expectations. Rather, it is criticized because it fails to approximate these ideals to the extent possible, given available resources. Thus, historically *immanent* critique and historically *transcendent* project coalesce in the following criteria of rationality:

(1) The transcendent project must be in accordance with the real possibilities open at the attained level of material and intellectual culture.

(2) The transcendent project, in order to falsify the established totality, must demonstrate its own *higher* rationality in the three-fold sense that:

(a) it offers the prospect of preserving and improving the productive achievements of civilization;

(b) it defines the established totality in its very structure, basic tendencies, and relations;

(c) its realization offers a greater chance for the pacification of existence, within the framework of institutions, which offer a greater chance for the free development of human needs and faculties (220).

PROSPECTS FOR EMANCIPATION: THE QUESTION OF TECHNOLOGY

What, then are the prospects for a nondomineering "pacification of existence"? By "pacification of existence," Marcuse means a mastery of nature which would liberate nature from its own violence and cruelty:

Cultivation of the soil is qualitatively different from destruction of the soil, extraction of natural resources from wasteful exploitation, clearing of forests from wholesale deforestation. Poverty, disease, and cancerous growth are natural as well as human ills—their reduction and removal is liberation of life. Civilization has achieved this "other," liberating transformation in its gardens and parks and reservations. But outside these small, protected areas, it has treated Nature as it has treated man—as an instrument of destructive productivity (240).

The pacification of existence, described above, would require cutting back on both population and economic growth, since these latter tendencies, both inherent in the capitalist system of production, create ever-greater pollution, waste, and environmental destruction. Yet, the real key to the pacification of nature, not to mention the resolution of the dialectic of enlightenment generally, would require, Marcuse contends, a qualitative transformation of technology itself.

With the "mechanization of all socially necessary but individually repressive labor," technology could be used to liberate human potentialities by providing free time for the satisfaction of vital needs (230–31). In doing so, it would cease being identified with the political end of domination, and would conform much more closely to its original, metaphysical end. For the Greeks, *techne* was virtually synonymous with art. And art, as Plato and Aristotle taught, was ultimately oriented toward life itself. The supreme art—the art of living well—encompassed all other arts and had as its ultimate end: individual and societal happiness. Thus transformed, technology, Marcuse speculates, would remain tied to substantive political values, but they would be essentially aesthetic in nature, oriented toward the imaginative projection and realization of new possibilities, sensibilities, faculties, etc.

To be sure, Marcuse himself sometimes suggests that only political ends would be transformed while technology, conceived as a neutral instrument for efficiently realizing ends, would remain the same: "One may still insist that the machinery of the technological universe is 'as such' indifferent towards political ends—it can revolutionize or retard a society . . . an electronic computer can serve equally in capitalist or socialist administrations; a cyclotron can be an equally efficient tool for a war party or a peace party . . ." (154). However, elsewhere he says that the very structure of science and technology itself would be transformed: "Its hypotheses, without losing their rational character, would develop in an essentially different experimental context (that of a pacified world); consequently, science would arrive at essentially different concepts of nature and establish different facts" (166–67).

What would this structural transformation of science amount to? Marcuse, following the German philosopher Edmund Husserl, argues that science represents a historical "project" dating back to classical antiquity, but only fully inaugurated since the seventeenth century. Literally speaking, science "projects" an interpretative scheme, or manner of conceptualization, in which all natural and social processes are seen as "objective raw material" for technical control.[6] From antiquity through the Middle Ages, nature had been conceived as consisting of *independent substances* whose behavior was thought to arise from an internal movement of self-realization—the purposive striving to "actualize" a universal essence.

Galileo and Descartes shattered this metaphysical view of nature by proposing that substances be conceived as abstract units of spatial extension and motion. The motion of these units was conceived to be externally generated by mechanical causes, whose uniformity and regularity could be analyzed *mathematically*. However, the *measurability* of nature, Husserl observed, has a prescientific, *practical* presupposition. It is because of a *prior* need to *anticipate the future* for purposes of instrumental adaptation and survival that mathematical exactitude is required. The calculation of future effects, stemming from human interference in nature, depends upon the discovery and confirmation of *replicable patterns*, or *identities*. In turn, replicability, which is basic to experimental science, presupposes the *reduction* of *qualitatively* distinct types of events to *quantitatively* similar ones (163–69).[7]

Although mathematical (or pure) science, is not explicitly undertaken with technical application in mind, its practical presupposition remains just as rooted in a technological interest as applied science. It is not surprising that philosophers of science have sought to demonstrate this fact by attempting to reduce all objective properties to recursive operations. To say, for example, that diamonds are hard is tantamount to saying that *if* one were to *do* certain things to or with diamonds, certain effects would follow. Marcuse maintains that this instrumental objectification of nature as manipulable matter is but a contingent historical project that might be changed. Presumably, an emancipated science would not conceptualize nature this way. But what would this mean?

Writing four years after the publication of *One-Dimensional Man*, Habermas had this to say about what he took to be the mystifying aspects of Marcuse's alternative vision of natural science:

Instead of treating nature as the object of possible control, we can encounter her as an opposing partner in a possible interaction. We can seek out a fraternal rather than an exploited nature. At the level of an as yet incomplete intersubjectivity we can impute subjectivity to animals and plants, even to minerals, and try to communicate with nature instead of merely possessing her under conditions of severed communication.[8]

The idea that a nondomineering relationship to nature and society would require the transcendence of the subject-object relationship as such was one that Adorno also proposed. However, the implication that such a *communicative* relationship would replace the instrumental attitude, that has hitherto prevailed in the scientific project, strikes Habermas as highly problematic. It is not the transcendence of instrumental reason, and its attendant subject-object relationship, that bothers Habermas. As we shall see, he, too, will accord a privileged place to communication as the locus of emancipatory reason. Yet, unlike Adorno and Marcuse, he will conceive this relationship as pertaining exclusively to rational agents, not between humanity *and* nature. Indeed, his acceptance of a dualistic conception of rationality consisting of both instrumental and communicative reason will enable him to *ground* these distinct orientations more firmly in *invariant* human competencies.

To recapitulate, the period extending from the mid-forties through the sixties witnessed two divergent tendencies in critical theory. One tendency, reflected in the thought of Adorno, problematized the notion of enlightenment as well as the concept of dialectical reconciliation. The other tendency, reflected in the thought of Marcuse, sought to appropriate the tradition of philosophy and enlightenment in a more positive manner, suggesting ways in which science and technology might be transformed in accordance with philosophical moral imperatives. In general, Marcuse remained optimistic about the possibility of wedding philosophical enlightenment to social and historical science, thereby making critical theory a real practical force in restructuring society. To be sure, Marcuse will also follow Adorno in locating critical (dialectical) reason in the aesthetic imagination. However, he will deviate from him in envisaging an aestheticized technological rationality aiming at liberation. Just how aestheticized production is to be conceived will be addressed in the next chapter, where the utopian dynamics of Marcuse's appropriation of Freud become more apparent.

In any case, the notion of an aestheticized technology is closely linked to another deviation in Marcuse's thought. Marcuse believed that the system necessarily generates a base of resistance comprising, "the outcasts and outsiders, the exploited and persecuted of other races and other colors, the unemployed and the unemployable," as well as a growing mass of well-off students who begin to question the work and consumption ethic (256). Whether this resistance—what Marcuse calls the "Great Refusal"—will be crushed by the overwhelming forces of the system remains debatable, even for Marcuse. As he himself noted, Fascist barbarism is not to be excluded as a possible outcome of the impending confrontation. Also not to be excluded, however, is a stalemate between contradictory forces tending toward the sort of chronic legitimation crises as diagnosed by Habermas.

Aside from these empirical questions, there remains the question of critical theory itself. Marcuse's approach, as we have seen, is vulnerable to objections posed by Adorno and Habermas. Adorno's analysis of the negative dialectic implicit in the philosophical tradition renders Marcuse's faith in philosophical essentialism highly problematic. If philosophy, as Adorno himself observed, cannot avoid making essentialist claims—even the virulent antiessentialism of ordinary language philosophers seems caught in the paradox that their own assertions about linguistic meaning claim to be universally if not necessarily true—it hardly follows that such claims are valid. Their transcendence of contextual particularity also endows them with an illusory, if not false and ideological cast, that needs to be criticized by the very social sciences and descriptive linguistic approaches that Marcuse seems to reject. In all fairness to Marcuse, one could cite passages where he acknowledges this difficulty. Yet, at the very least, Marcuse's reappropriation of myth and philosophy often appears "naive" when compared to the more sophisticated—if, indeed, convoluted—treatment of philosophy and art found in *Negative Dialectics* and *Aesthetic Theory*. It is not until Habermas that critical theory will again address the tension between philosophical transcendence and scientific historicity, universality and particularity, necessity and contingency, at such a high level of sophistication.

NOTES

1. It should be noted that Marcuse's main object of criticism is *advanced industrial society*, which includes bureaucratic socialism.

2. T.W. Adorno, *Negative Dialectics*, trans. E.B. Ashton (New York, 1973), p. 3.

3. G. Lukács, *Die Theorie des Romans* (Neuwied, 1963), p. 17. Cited from Zoltán Tar, *The Frankfurt School* (*loc. cit.*), p. 174. Arthur Schopenhauer (1788–1866) was a German idealist, influenced by Kant. His pessimistic view of a world represented and constituted by a transcendental Will, and his belief that aesthetic contemplation provided release from the suffering of life generally, had a powerful impact on the school (especially Horkheimer) as it had had previously for the young Nietzsche.

4. T.W. Adorno, "Subject and Object," in *The Essential Frankfurt School Reader*, pp. 499–500.

5. H. Marcuse, *One-Dimensional Man* (Boston: Beacon Press, 1964), p. xv.

6. Marcuse's formulation of this "project" is especially beholden to the existential philosophies of Jean-Paul Sartre and Martin Heidegger. For Marcuse's discussion of an alternative technology, see chapter 9 of *One-Dimensional Man*, "The Catastrophe of Liberation," reprinted in *Critical Theory: The Essential Readings (CTER)*.

7. Marcuse's analysis is largely indebted to Husserl's study of the origin of geometry in antiquity. See Edmund Husserl, *The Crisis of the European Sciences and Transcendental Phenomenology*.

8. J. Habermas, "Technology and Science as Ideology," in *Toward A Rational Society*, trans. J. Shapiro (Boston: Beacon, 1970), p. 88. This essay is reprinted in *CTER*.

SELECTED BIBLIOGRAPHY

Adorno, T.W. *Aesthetic Theory*, trans. Christian Lenhardt. London. Routledge & Kegan Paul, 1984.

———*Negative Dialectics*. New York. Seabury Press, 1973.

———"Subject and Object." In *The Essential Frankfurt School Reader*.

———et al. *The Authoritarian Personality*. New York. Harper and Row, 1950.

Habermas, J. "Technology and Science as Ideology" *Toward a Rational Society*. Trans. J. Shapiro. Boston. Beacon, 1970.

Marcuse, *An Essay On Liberation*. Boston. Beacon, 1969.

———*Counterrevolution and Revolt*. Boston. Beacon, 1972.

———*One-Dimensional Man: Studies in the Ideology of Advanced Industrial Society*. Boston. Beacon, 1964.

Commentaries: The best commentaries currently available on Marcuse are Morton Schoolman's *The Imaginary Witness. The Critical Theory of Herbert Marcuse* (New York: New York University Press, 1980); and Douglas Kellner's *Herbert Marcuse and the Crisis of Marxism* (Berkeley: University of California Press, 1989). For a short, critical synopsis of Marcuse's work see Alasdair MacIntyre's *Herbert Marcuse: An Exposition and a Polemic* (New York: Viking, 1970). Besides Tar's *The Frankfurt School*, and Jay's *Adorno*, the best studies of Adorno's later work are Susan Buck-Morss's *The Origin of Negative Dialectics: Theodor W. Adorno, Walter Benjamin, and the Frankfurt Institute* (New York, 1977); and Gillian Rose's *The Melancholy Science: An Introduction to the Thought of Theodor W. Adorno* (New York, 1978).

FIVE

MARCUSE AND FREUD: THE INSTINCTUAL BASIS OF CRITIQUE

I noted earlier that the theory/practice problem is fueled by a need to actualize the moral ideals of philosophy. In order for the actualization of philosophy to occur, however, universal goals must somehow resonate with concrete historical interests. The philosophers of the Enlightenment were optimistic about the capacity of each and every individual to find the truth by appealing to innate reason and/or common sense. For Marx, the heritage of enlightenment no longer represented a transcendent force, but was seen as intimately bound up with the rise of capitalism. Its ideas were, therefore, suspect of ideological taint. Yet, Marx never ceased to advocate the Enlightenment's ideas of universal freedom and democratic self-determination. If the initial reception of these ideas was ideologically useful for advancing the class interests of the bourgeoisie, their true realization would better serve the interests of the proletariat.

The problem that Marx and Lukács faced was showing why the proletariat's particular interests were identical to *the* universal interests of humanity. With the decline of the working-class movement, and the absence of total class polarization, critical theorists could no longer make this simple identification. Who would be the new carriers of enlightened social practice? And why would their particular interests resonate with the emancipatory goals of philosophy? More importantly, by means of what criteria could one establish that their interests—indeed, anyone's interests—are the true interests of humanity? These are just some of the questions that Marcuse attempted to answer in his Freudian analysis of instinctual needs.

One-Dimensional Man concludes with an ambivalent diagnosis of modern society. Whether advanced industrial society will issue in totalitarian barbarism or liberation largely depends upon the resistance of persons whose needs, for whatever reason, have not been satisfied by the system. These would include persons who have not shared in the material wealth generated by the system. It would include, for instance, poor people living in urban ghettos and in underdeveloped parts of the world, or people who have developed needs that cannot be satisfied by the possession of material goods. This last group, Marcuse believed, would consist chiefly of radicalized students, from relatively affluent families, who no longer accepted the work ethic, and who had become aware of the unhealthy costs of maintaining the system. The sixties witnessed many of these students experimenting with alternative "communal" life-styles. Their simplicity and democratic egalitarianism opposed the stressful competition, repressive specialization, and authoritarian class domination built into capitalism. It also opposed the additional waste, pollution, and destruction generated by a wartime consumer economy.

For Marcuse, the needs that they sought to gratify were inherently rational in a way that was diametrically opposed to the technological rationality governing the existing system of needs.[1] That is, their rationality was not a function of some false, artificially induced compulsion to dominate nature. It was rather motivated by a *biologically based* desire to achieve a completely happy life. In Marcuse's judgment, the ultimate criterion for distinguishing true from false needs must appeal to a rationale that is largely instinctual (i.e., natural or innate). For only needs, which have this kind of universality and necessity, fully merit the title of rationality. Moreover, Marcuse was convinced that unless there existed a permanent, *biologically rooted* set of dispositions, there would be no way to account for the possibility of social resistance. Simply stated, a human nature, whose basic needs were totally maleable by the system, would be incapable of opposing it.

Marcuse's attempt to explain the biological foundation of critical reason is contained in *Eros and Civilization* (1955), a work that owes a great deal to some of the more speculative aspects of Freud's later writings.[2] From a theoretical standpoint, it represents one of the most ambitious attempts, by any *first-generation* critical theorist, to establish the rational grounds of critical theory. Nevertheless, as we shall see, its vision of the relationship between nature and reason is highly problematic.

THE INSTINCTUAL DYNAMICS OF REPRESSIVE CIVILIZATION

Eros and Civilization begins by taking up the dialectic of progress elaborated in Freud's *Civilization and its Discontents*. According to Freud, progress in science and morality is purchased at the cost of great instinctual repression. By "repression" Freud means the blocking and rechanneling (sublimating) of biological impulses. Sexual impulses, for example, are kept hidden from explicit consciousness by an unconscious censoring agency (the *superego*). Forced into the unconscious, these impulses are denied the kind of free, spontaneous expression they would otherwise assume. The severity of this repression is such that it causes pent-up aggression to explode in acts of unparalleled destruction. As society becomes more "civilized," generating ever more impersonal forms of *rational* domination, it becomes more barbaric. Genocide and the wartime devastation of civilian populations are the most glaring, but by no means the most typical, examples of such destruction. More typically, aggression serves the profitable exploitation of colonial peoples and the wanton ravaging of natural "resources."

Freud's gloomy diagnosis stands or falls with his theory of the instincts. By downplaying the importance of biological "destiny" in explaining human conduct, neo-Freudian "revisionists"—including Marcuse's former colleague, Erich Fromm—could eliminate the tension between nature and culture, which fueled the diagnosis.[3] If, as they maintained, the "instinctual" basis underlying human motivation is entirely shaped by social conditioning, then, of course, it no longer represents a permanent force of resistance that must be repressed. A nonrepressive civilization is then conceivable. In that case, the dilemma of nonrepressive (primitive) barbarism or repressive (civilized) barbarism is easily avoided.

The problem with this attempt to conceive a nonrepressive civilization, Marcuse claims, is that it eliminates the one factor that critically resists a repressive status quo—nature in its immediate, *presocialized* form. Once the nature/culture tension has been eliminated, psychoanalytic theory loses its critical thrust and becomes a therapeutic tool aimed solely at adapting "social deviants" to societal constraints. So construed, psychoanalysis functions as a vehicle for reinforcing domination and repression—rather than dissolving it.

Despite his desire to preserve the independence of biological impulses with respect to social conditioning, Marcuse concedes that social factors do play a role in shaping human instincts. Not to do so would be to accept the kind of nature/history dualism that is so inimical to resolving the theory/practice problem. Historical rationality would be opposed to biological "rationality," so that the latter could never become a political force, be it destructive or constructive. In fact, Marcuse believes that Freud's chief error lies in neglecting the way in which historical circumstances *transform* instinctual energies into destructive forces. The opposition between nature and culture, and therewith, the dilemma of having to choose either unrepressed barbarism or repressive civilization, is itself dictated by repressive society. Under truly civilized (i.e., nonrepressive) conditions, instinctual energies would assume the form of sensitizing agencies which could promote the full development of persons into loving, social beings. This reading of Freud distinguishes the subtle way in which nature and culture interact. Though not conceived as totally alterable by social conditioning, biological nature must nonetheless be seen as partially affected by it.

To see how this is possible one must turn to Freud's theory of human development, both at the level of individual maturation (ontogenesis) and at the level of social evolution (phylogenesis). According to Freud, the development of a conscious self, or individual ego, involves a process of *differentiation*. At birth, the mental life of the infant is characterized by what Freud called "primary narcissism." The infant's psyche is chiefly comprised of preconscious instinctual drives seeking immediate gratification. At this stage, the mental life of the infant is governed by the *Pleasure Principle*. Not only is its entire body experienced as a sexually charged field of pleasure; so is its outer environment. Body and world are thus experienced as mere extensions of its own psyche. Encompassing internal (bodily) and external sources of pleasure within its "oceanic," womblike interior, the infantile psyche is not yet a *subject* (an "I") standing *over* an *object* (nature as "other").

The birth of infantile personality conceived as self-conscious *identity* occurs when the ego splits off from the unconscious repository of bodily drives (*id*) which comprise the "oceanic" self. The objectification of one's own inner nature as "other" (the distinction between one's mind and one's body) parallels the objectification of outer nature as "other." The latter, of course, corresponds to the distinction between one's inner subjectivity and the outer world. What compels this split is the infant's experience of pain, which it projects outside of itself, and the need to come to terms with the external source of that pain: reality. The infant learns that it cannot satisfy all its desires by itself, but must get another (the mother) to aid in this endeavor. There is an experience of nonself-sufficiency, as well as the need to "work" for the assured, long-term satisfaction of desire. Thus, the infant learns to delay immediate gratification by manipulating maternal responses through crying. This, in turn, is the beginning of a process of *self-objectification*, which eventually issues in the split between ego and id, subject and object. However, the cost of relating to oneself, as an object whose biological urges need to be rationally controlled, is high. For much of this control is achieved by repressing one's bodily desires, treating them as if they were mere "objects"— something "other" than the free, responsible *subjectivity* of a calculating ego.[4]

The resistance and the necessity with which nature confronts humanity elicits an adaptive response. This is what Freud calls the *Reality Principle*. The latter requires delayed and indirect forms of gratification. Thus, to the extent that all culture is a response to a basic survival need, civilization and repression are indeed coeval. Nature and culture remain opposed. However, as Marcuse points out, the level of repression mandated of society at any given historical moment is relative to the level of *scarcity*. Scarcity, in turn, is relative to a society's given state of *neediness*.

To a society that is accustomed to the wasteful consumption of automobiles with built-in "planned obsolescence," the absence of new models and cheap, plentiful gas would constitute a scarcity. To a simpler society, it would not. Furthermore, scarcity, Marcuse observes, has never been distributed equally among all members of society. Those who toil for a living have generally worked for the greater comfort of the leisure class, while also carrying a greater burden of the repressive discipline and self-denial necessary for basic survival. Thus, Marcuse distinguishes between *necessary* and *surplus* repression. The former is necessary for the satisfaction of both basic survival needs (food, clothing, shelter) and higher, cultural needs which realize the life-enhancing biological potential inherent in human nature. Surplus repression, by contrast, is unnecessary and even obstructs the realization of life-enhancing biological potential (37ff and 87ff).

The transition from the Pleasure Principle to the Reality Principle effects a profound change in the system of instincts. Desire for immediate sexual gratification is *sublimated* into desire for meaningful work and spiritual growth. However, under the constraints imposed by modern society, the Reality Principle undergoes a further transformation. It assumes the perverse guise of what Marcuse calls the "performance principle," or social adaptation in accordance with the imperatives of competition, social stratification, and economic growth (44). Because the performance principle mandates social inequality and the creation of surplus wealth beyond that required for basic survival, it inevitably imposes *surplus repression*. The sublimated desire for meaningful work and spiritual growth is perverted into a sadomasochistic desire for increased consumption under conditions of alienated labor and domination over others.

Marcuse situates the historical transformation of humanity's instinctual nature against the backdrop of Freud's account of ontogenetic and phylogenetic development. I noted above that the transition from the Pleasure Principle to the Reality Principle in the individual might be understood in terms of a conflict between two sorts of basic needs (or instincts)—the need for immediate sexual gratification and the need for survival. However, toward the end of his life Freud distinguished two primary instincts—a *life* instinct (*eros*) and a *death* instinct (*thanatos*). He believed these were related to self-preservation in a fundamentally ambiguous way. At first glance, the two instincts appear to be diametrically opposed to one another. The life instinct seeks to preserve life by compelling the creation of "ever greater unities," or complex fields of vital tension. Such unification, exemplified in acts of sexual coupling and social organization, ultimately tends toward the elimination of resistance and antagonistic opposition. By contrast, under the rule of the death instinct the elimination of painful opposition is achieved by dissolving organic tensions into inorganic matter (22ff).

Despite their differences, Marcuse believes that life and death instincts tend toward the same goal: release from pain and suffering. This goal is *regressive*. It indicates an irresistible desire to return to (or repeat) an earlier stage of life—the peaceful state of harmony and oceanic unity characteristic of life in the womb (what Freud calls the *Nirvana Principle*). It is also *progressive*, in that yearning for a lost state of peace and harmony need not issue in the extinction of autonomous selfhood. It can also look ahead to a democratic society composed of individuals who are free, equal, and mutually fulfilled in communal harmony.

Given the regressive/progressive ambiguity implicit in this "repetition compulsion," Marcuse speculates that these instincts might work in collaboration with one another to further *either* life *or* death. The death instinct, for example, might work to enhance life to the extent that aggressive energy is channeled into liberated technology. Although technology in totalitarian society is an instrument of domination and destruction, in emancipated society it might function differently—by eliminating natural obstacles to life itself. The difference between liberated and unliberated technology is the difference between, say, modern medicine and ecology, on one hand, and modern marketing, management, and military-industrial expansion, on the other. Conversely, the life instinct might be perverted in such a way as to further annihilation. As we saw earlier, the survival achievements of a totalitarian system may well succeed in eliminating painful opposition under peaceful conditions of relative abundance, law and order, but only at the expense of repressing (annihilating) individuality and freedom (85ff).

While compelling ever-greater economic *growth*, the Performance Principle imposes the kind of surplus repression that inevitably results in the destructive release of aggressive energy. Here, Marcuse remarks, what should be means for the enhancement of life—the instruments of technological domination—become the all-consuming ends to which life itself is sacrificed. Under the weight of the performance principle, erotic energy is increasingly confined to the productive imperative of sexual procreation. What was once a life-force, energizing and sensitizing the entire body of the infant, is now pressed into service maintaining the monogamous, nuclear family. The "polymorphous perversions" of oral, anal, and corporeal sexuality, which Freud attributed to the infantile stage of development, are gradually repressed in favor of a highly restrictive genital sexuality.[5] This process ultimately culminates in the Oedipal complex. At this stage, the last vestiges of polymorphous sexuality—in particular, those inhabiting incestuous love for the mother—are extirpated by paternal domination (37ff, 48ff).

The repressive centralization of sexual energy, that accompanies individual maturation, is reflected in the centralized organization of a society structured in accordance with the performance principle. Conversely, Marcuse notes that the perversions "seem to give a *promesse de bonheur*" (promise of happiness), which recalls the time when pleasure and integral fulfillment— the goal of life and death instincts—was predominant (49–51). Consequently, it is the *memory* of this archaic moment, expressed in *aesthetic imagination*, that continually threatens to revolt against the existing order. In the words of Marcuse:

Imagination envisions the reconciliation of the individual with the whole, of desire with realization, of happiness with reason. While this harmony has been removed into utopia by the established reality principle, phantasy insists that it must and can become real, that behind the illusion lies *knowledge* . . . behind the aesthetic form lies the repressed harmony of sensuousness and reason—the eternal protest against the organization of life by the logic of domination, the critique of the performance principle. (143–44)

Freud speculated that the development of repressed individuality is itself a repetition of a long and painful evolution which the species, in general, underwent. The contours of this archaic heritage are laid out in Freud's account of the "primal horde." As I noted earlier, Freud's hypothesis of a primal horde must be understood as a largely *symbolic* attempt to account for the tremendous guilt and pent-up aggression inhabiting the civilized psyche. The overthrow of the patriarch by his sons represented the first revolt of the Pleasure Principle against the Reality Principle. The matriarchies, which immediately followed, celebrated this liberation by condoning incest between mother and son. This temporary return to the nirvanic pleasure of polymorphous sexuality threatened to disrupt the rational order, imposed by the primal father as a precondition for survival. Accordingly, the need to delay gratification found expression in a restoration of patriarchal domination, now *internalized* in the form of monotheistic religions such as Judaism and Christianity.[6] Thus, along with the incest taboo, was born a whole system of laws whose coercive power resided less in overt penal sanctions (no pun intended) than in the internal sanctions of a *guilty conscience*.

The restoration of the patriarchal principle, at the dawn of civilization, is relived by the individual who successfully resolves the Oedipal conflict. By renouncing his incestuous desires for the mother, he learns to introject the painful sanctions of the father (fear of castration).[5] Yet the birth of the *superego* is purchased at a high cost. For not only does the individual feel guilty for hating his father, but, as Marcuse points out, he must also feel guilty for *betraying* his instinctual revolt against patriarchal domination generally. In order to defend against these feelings, the individual and society must ensure that the victory of the father will be complete. Thus, every revolt is followed by a restoration that is *more repressive* than the previous domination. The incest between father and daughter, which still existed in the primal horde, is entirely eliminated in the legal contract uniting the brother clan. Similarly, in modern society, the total restoration of patriarchal authority is reflected in a totally administered society. In the words of Marcuse:

The father, restrained in the family and in his biological authority, is resurrected, far more powerful, in the administration which preserves the life of society, and in the laws which preserve the administration . . . (T)here is no freedom from administration and its laws because they appear as the ultimate guarantors of liberty. The revolt against them would be the supreme crime again—this time not against the despot-animal who forbids gratification but against the wise order which secures the goods and services for the progressive satisfaction of human needs. (91–92)

THE INSTINCTUAL RATIONALITY UNDERLYING EMANCIPATED SOCIETY

The "dialectic of civilization" issues in impersonal, rational forms of domination are more repressive than the brutality of earlier regimes. Indeed, they must be so in order to counteract the surplus aggression waiting to explode in acts of wanton violence. Freud believed that this aggression would eventually lead to the triumph of the death instinct. For, according to him, civilization requires the repression of the very life force—sexuality—which might offset this instinct. And in repressing this force, it contributes to ever-greater guilt and aggression.

Is there any way out of this dilemma? Marcuse points out that the above diagnosis rests on three questionable premises: First, it forgets that repression is relative to scarcity, and that surplus repression is a function of artificially induced scarcity. Given current levels of technological development, there is no reason to think that, with a more equitable distribution of wealth and a more modest standard of living, the need to work (and, therewith, the current level of surplus repression) might be reduced. Second, work need not be unpleasurable and alienated. Art and other forms of creative endeavor testify to the fact that productive activity can be inherently satisfying. Finally, aggressive instincts, like their sexual counterparts, can be sublimated in work. Technology and industry are constructive examples of how destructive energies can be safely discharged (129ff).

Of course, the possibility of avoiding Freud's dialectic depends upon transcending the Performance Principle in the direction of a truly emancipated society. According to Marcuse, such a society would liberate the polymorphous potential inherent in sexuality, but in a sublimated form. Persons would not regress in their sexual behavior, although there would be much greater tolerance of sexual diversity. Rather, they would become more sensitive, loving, creative, and spontaneous. Their receptivity toward themselves and others would also be reflected in their caring attitude toward nature, as well as in the pleasurable aesthetics of their domestic and work environments. Most importantly, the "return" to a stage of communal reconciliation with others would not mark a dissolution of selfhood in a nirvanic, totalitarian oneness. Instead, a nonrepressive individuality would emerge that would preserve the accomplishments of technological and formal rationality within the framework of an "aestheticized" instinctual rationality. This is the true exemplar of Hegel's reconciliatory rationality. Such a *sensuous reason*, Marcuse further observes, "contains its own moral laws" (228).

The possibility for such an erotic liberation is implicit not only in the metaphysical imagery of Western religion and philosophy, but also in the productive apparatus itself. The relative affluence, achieved through automation, has already paved the way for a transformation of instinctual needs in the direction mentioned above. However, as Marcuse himself acknowledges:

The material as well as mental resources of civilization are still so limited that there must be a vastly lower standard of living if social productivity were redirected toward the universal gratification of individual needs: many would have to give up manipulated comforts if all were to live a human life. . . . The reconciliation between pleasure and reality principle does not depend on the existence of abundance for all. The only pertinent question is whether a state of civilization can be reasonably envisaged in which human needs are fulfilled in such a manner and to such an extent that surplus repression can be eliminated (151).

"Such a hypothetical state," Marcuse continues, "could be reasonably assumed at two points, which lie at the opposite poles of the vicissitudes of the instincts: One would be located at the primitive beginnings of history, the other at its most mature stage." The need to "reverse" the process of civilization, to return to a simpler life with a lower standard of living, points in the direction of primitive society. There is little repression in primitive society because the satisfaction of basic survival needs does not yet require the efficient, rational production of an economic surplus. In such conditions work, technology, and art intermesh; absent a rational division of labor, persons remain integrated, unalienated "wholes." Here, at the extreme point where technology itself ceases to be an objectifying force and has taken on the communicative and expressive function of dance and magical invocation, nature itself appears as a spiritual force whose "face" is just as reassuring as it is threatening. However "beautiful" and "idyllic" such conditions may be, they are nonetheless, from the point of view of human rationality, less than satisfactory. For such reconciliation with nature is also accompanied by slavish dependence on nature with all its attendant evils. Consequently, it is the other need, pointing ahead to complete automation, reduction of labor time to a minimum and exchangeability of functions, that Marcuse especially emphasizes.

As we saw in the last chapter, Marcuse insists that this would also require a transformation of technology and science. Yet, it remained unclear there as to whether this would amount to a change in technological rationality as such or just a change in its application. Should we intensify the technological division of labor, to the utmost extent of efficiency, in order to guarantee more leisure time for developing ourselves aesthetically, socially, and intellectually? Or should we break down the division of labor so as to democratize, and thereby aestheticize, productivity—even if this means reducing automation? Perhaps the greater happiness of workers, who participate fully in managerial decisions and enjoy the benefits of job rotation, will encourage a division of labor that will be more technologically rational in the long run—yielding a higher and more efficient productivity—despite possible reductions in automation.

Marcuse seemed to countenance all of these options. His philosophy is torn—between developing an objectifying technology to its fullest extent or radically transforming it—so as to make it somehow less objectifying and more aesthetic. However, as our preceding discussion makes clear, this tension in his philosophy may well turn on whether we should continue or reverse the process of civilization itself. When Marcuse stresses the necessity of alienated labor, maintaining that progressive automation frees the individual from having to work in general, he seems to have in mind a civilization of relatively high complexity and affluence. But in that case, it is clear that the needs generated by such a society will be many and various. This would require, it would seem, more repression than that required in primitive society. If so, it would appear that even emancipated society would harbor, at least, some surplus repression.

No doubt, Marcuse would argue just the contrary: that primitive societies are, in some sense, more repressive than their advanced counterparts. The susceptibility of persons living in such societies, to *early* and often *painful* deaths, inherently lends their reality a repressive cast which is not lessened by the aesthetic, communal conditions of their existence. Appeal to religious conceptions of eternal life, reincarnation, and the suspension of time itself may help to dispel fear of the future. But it does so only in an ideological sense, by leaving untouched the reality whose painfulness produces such mythic dreaming.[8]

Also, Marcuse would point out that the many and various needs generated by an advanced society, while certainly artificial and (biologically speaking) unnecessary, nonetheless enable the full realization of erotic potential in a way that is precluded by primitive society. The historical generation of new needs may lead to the further enhancement of life (as Marx thought), and their satisfaction may likewise be effected through nonrepressive forms of productive activity. In the final analysis, Marcuse seems torn between the allure of a simpler, less-developed (but also less wasteful and less destructive) society, and a more technologically advanced one. As a result, he gives ample testimony to his own inability to satisfactorily deal with the nature/culture split in a way that might resolve the theory/practice problem.

One problem still remains. It is unclear how the criteria of instinctual rationality alone can serve to identify artificial needs which are not false. These criteria ultimately refer to *subjective* feelings pertaining to potentials of pleasure and happiness, not *objectively* measurable or definable states. Thus, the truth or falsity of needs cannot be theoretically proven. This issue can be decided only—as Marcuse himself points out in *One-Dimensional Man*—by the individuals themselves, *under conditions of rational communication*. Consequently, it would appear that criteria for distinguishing true from false should depend less on human biology (nature), as this is *theoretically* conceived, than on *social* conditions of *rational choice*. As we shall see in the next chapter, it is precisely for this very reason that Habermas will eschew Marcuse's biological grounding of critical theory, in favor of a more rigorous foundation in rational communication. The question we must next address, then, is whether language—as a historical and cultural achievement— points toward ideals of justice and happiness that transcend the limitations and distortions of actual speech.

NOTES

1. Marcuse's earliest defense of an ethics based on rational pleasure was highly critical of Kant's ethic of duty. See "On Hedonism" (1938) reprinted in *Critical Theory: The Essential Readings (CTER).*

2. The main contours of Marcuse's discussion of Freud and his relevance for critical theory are contained in the first chapter of *Five Lectures*, "Freedom and Freud's Theory of Instincts," reprinted in *CTER.*

3. See the Epilogue to *Eros and Civilization: A Philosophical Inquiry into Freud* (Boston: Beacon Press, 1966). According to Marcuse, neo-Freudians play upon the discrepancy between theory and therapy in psychoanalysis. Theoretically speaking, Freud traced individual neurosis back to the pathological repressiveness of civilized society. As a therapist, however, he saw his task as "curing" the individual so that the latter might function normally within repressive society (245). Although all revisionists downplay the importance of biology in determining human behavior in favor of culture and environment, they differ among themselves regarding the extent to which this is so. According to Marcuse, the most conservative "revisionists," such as Harry Stack Sullivan, have all but rejected the *universal* core of human instincts in favor of a cultural *relativism*. Having eliminated the critical tension between biology and culture, they end up advocating conformism to the status quo as the proper end of personal self-realization (255–56). Others, such as Erich Fromm, are more critical of the status quo. (Indeed, Marcuse acknowledges his debt to his former colleague, even while castigating his recent work.) However, they are accused of falling into an ideological *moralizing* when they imply that such progressive values as "inner strength," "integrity," and "productive love," can be achieved by individuals *within* a repressive society (262–65).

4. *Ibid.*, 12ff. See Freud, "Formulations Regarding the Two Principles in Mental Functioning," in *Collective Papers* (London: Hogarth Press, 1950), vol. 4; and *Civilization and Its Discontents* (New York: Norton, 1961), pp. 13–16.

5. As Marcuse notes (38), Freud maintained that the suppression of "proximity senses" of smell and taste in favor of sight corresponds not only to the development of an upright posture but also to the generalized taboo against *immediate* (polymorphous and undifferentiated), pleasure. Once survival dictated the change to an upright posture, the natural scents and tastes of the body—especially those associated with the genitals and organs of excretion—become objects of aversion requiring "desexualization." In Marcuse's opinion, however, the extent of repression required by this evolutionary development falls drastically short of that required of today's "human machine."

6. Marcuse remarks that anti-Semitism may have its source in an unconscious "revolt of nature" against the patriarchal domination associated with Jewish (and later

Christian) monotheism: "(Freud) believed that anti-Semitism had deep roots in the unconscious: jealousy over the Jewish claim of being the 'first-born, favorite child of God the Father'; dread of circumcision, associated with the threat of castration; and, perhaps most important, 'grudge against the new religion' (Christianity) which was forced on many modern peoples 'only in relatively recent times.' This grudge was 'projected' onto the source from which Christianity came, namely, Judaism" (69). See S. Freud, *Moses and Monotheism* (New York: Alfred A. Knopf, 1949—originally published in 1939), pp. 144f.

7. Marcuse is especially critical of Fromm's reinterpretation of the Oedipal complex, which tries (in the words of Fromm) "to translate it from the sphere of sex into that of interpersonal relations." In this reading, the incestuous desire of the child is under-stood as less a progressive desire for integral (sexual) fulfillment than a regressive desire for womblike security. Consequently, for Fromm the repression of this desire is a positive step toward freedom and not, as it is for Marcuse, a negative acceptance of socially imposed unhappiness. See *Eros and Civilization* (p. 269f) and Erich Fromm, *Psychoanalysis and Religion* (New Haven: Yale University Press, 1950), pp. 79f.

8. Marcuse speculates that death itself might become a "token of freedom," if it were understood as the liberating terminus of a *complete* life (i.e., a life of fulfillment, without pain, and subject to voluntary choice). The completeness of a life relived in peaceful memory would then constitute a kind of eternity within time—a contemplative repose in which time and death (reality) would cease to confront human beings as oppressive forces of fateful necessity (231–37).

SELECTED BIBLIOGRAPHY

Freud, Sigmund. *Civilization and Its Discontents*. Trans. and ed. James Strachey. New York: Norton, 1961.

Marcuse, Herbert. *Eros and Civilization. A Philosophical Inquiry into Freud*. Boston: Beacon, 1955. Second edition with a "Political Preface 1966," Boston: Beacon, 1966.

———*Five Lectures*. Trans. J. Shapiro and S. Weber. Boston: Beacon, 1970.

Commentaries: Readers are referred to the commentaries mentioned at the end of chapter four. Marcuse's critique of Freudian revisionism was published in *Dissent*, vol. 2, no. 3 (Summer 1955) and in vol. 2, no. 1 (Winter 1956). Fromm's response was published in *Dissent*, vol. 3, no. 1 (Winter 1956).

SIX

HORKHEIMER AND HABERMAS ON CRITICAL METHODOLOGY AND ITS RATIONALE: A SECOND LOOK AT FREUD

Jürgen Habermas (b. 1929) is unquestionably the most influential exponent of critical theory living today. Most *second-generation* critical theorists of major repute have taken their lead from him, even while disagreeing with him on substantive issues.[1] In turn, Habermas is greatly indebted to the legacy of his predecessors. His own attempt to resolve the theory/practice problem eventually led him to pursue an interdisciplinary research program not unlike that proposed by Horkheimer in the thirties. Indeed, his more recent formulation of critical theory as "rational reconstruction," explicitly unites the empirical data of social science, developmental psychology, and philosophical essentialism in ways that suggest a plausible interpolation of facts and values. He has also been greatly influenced by Marcuse's analysis of advanced capitalist society. For, despite his rejection of Marcuse's biologism, Habermas shares his hope that the Enlightenment legacy might be realized in a way that will free it from the dialectical tendencies hitherto recounted and generalized by Adorno and Horkheimer. Indeed, both he and Marcuse tend to blame the oppressive features of rational society on factors external to rationality. Neither feels that technological rationality as such *need be* destructive and dehumanizing. These latter features are attributed, rather, to the peculiar historical form in which reason was institutionalized in Western society, features cognate with the Performance Principle. At the same time, they follow Adorno and Horkheimer in appealing to a nontechnological, nonobjectifying type of critical rationality, specifying ideal conditions of freedom and communal reconciliation. Finally, both Habermas and Marcuse look to Freud for inspiration in grounding critical theory, albeit in different ways. Whereas Marcuse was chiefly interested in the speculative aspects of Freud's theory of the instincts and his theory of social evolution, Habermas is fascinated with the therapeutic and diagnostic advantages of psychoanalysis as a *methodological* model for ideology critique.

Despite their agreement, Habermas is sharply critical of Marcuse's attempt to ground critical reason in a theory of the instincts. Such a grounding, Habermas believes, relies too heavily on nonverifiable speculation regarding human nature. Although ostensibly designed to uncover the necessary and universal features underlying human motivation, such speculation invariably invokes the parochial religious imagery of Western civilization for confirmation. However, there is no reason to assume that the Oedipus and Orpheus myths of Greek antiquity are valid for non-Western cultures. In any case, the truth-content of these and other Occidental traditions—as Marcuse himself acknowledges—is itself ideologically suspect. Consequently, Marcuse's speculation regarding human nature falls victim to the very *cultural relativism* it criticizes in neo-Freudian revisionism, for whom such traditions are but the product of nongeneralizable, historically unique, circumstances.

Habermas is also critical of the inherent subjectivism and vagueness of instinctual conceptions of social rationality. Because it is prior to any *discursive* (publicly formalizable) conception of rationality, instinctual reason is incapable of generating any precise standards of critique. It is less critical reflection than immediate impulse. A better ground for critical rationality, Habermas believes, is everday speech. This view is rejected outright by Adorno and Horkheimer and seriously questioned by Marcuse. Not surprisingly, Habermas's attempt to provide a more empirically convincing justification of critical theory's value standards will lead him to embrace the very disciplines—science and analytic philosophy of language—that Marcuse and the others found to be so suspect.

Finally, Habermas questions Marcuse's relegation of science and technology to a *historically contingent* "project," whose objectifying, instrumental structure is susceptible to alteration. Marcuse, he claims, overestimates the degree to which this structure is alterable. The relationship between science, human nature, and history is complex. Rationality—be it technological or critical—designates progressive processes of knowledge acquisition, whose roots are somehow *both* natural (necessary, universal, and invariant) and historical (contingent, culture-specific, and variable). If historical circumstances play a predominate role in determining the structure of rationality, it will be most apparent in the case of critical, not technological, rationality. Habermas locates critical rationality in *communicative competencies*, institutionalized in *democratic structures*, which *evolve* in response to growing political oppression. These competencies, he believes, circumscribe necessary and universal structures of rational choice. Thus, they are the ultimate criteria for distinguishing true from false needs.

Habermas's career can be divided into two major phases: the first phase culminated in *Knowledge and Human Interests* (1968); the second, in *The*

Theory of Communicative Action (1981). Both works are characterized by their systematic nature. Both are also primarily concerned with resolving two theory/practice problems. The first concerns the *grounding* of critical theory in normative expectations and values that necessarily and universally govern human conduct. The second concerns the *articulation* of a scientific model of explanation which best captures the methodology of ideology critique. The former deals with the problem of *relativism*. How can critical theory justify its critique of society unless the standards of justice and social well-being, to which it appeals, can be shown to be nonarbitrary and, in some sense, universally binding for all? The latter is concerned with the problem of working out a *scientific method* that will endow social critique with a high degree of objectivity and precision.

In general, Habermas does not think that his predecessors succeeded in either of these tasks. In particular, he notes that their research during the postwar period was characterized by a certain hostility toward science and systematic thinking (recall Adorno's repudiation of systematic theorizing in *Negative Dialectics*). Furthermore, he observes that they never really succeeded in grounding critical theory in necessary and universal conditions. Marcuse's theory regarding the instinctual basis of moral reason may have come the closest in this regard, but it was vitiated by its residual biologism.

HORKHEIMER ON THE RATIONALE AND METHODS OF IDEOLOGY CRITIQUE

If there is anything basic in the work of his predecessors that Habermas appropriates, it is that model of systematic research associated with the Frankfurt School's activity during the thirties. The interdisciplinary nature and methodological structure of this program was summarized by Horkheimer in "Traditional and Critical Theory" (1937). In that key work, Horkheimer sought to distinguish the theoretical assumptions and methods of critical social science from "traditional" scientific theories. For Horkheimer, traditional theories possess a formal structure consonant with the analytical-deductive methodology elaborated by Descartes—who believed that all knowledge consisted of beliefs that are either known to be immediately and intuitively certain or logically derivable from some that are. One begins by analyzing one's experience into its simplest, necessary and universal presuppositions. One then proceeds to infer more complex statements from the combination of these primary elements (axioms), much in the same way that geometricians prove theorems.

For Horkheimer, modern scientific theories basically subscribe to this

Cartesian model. They aspire to a universal system of mathematical principles, from which particular causal laws can be derived and factual explanations proferred. Causal laws have the logical form of a *conditional* statement: "If circumstances *a, b, c*, and *d* are given, then event *q* must be expected; if *d* is lacking, event *r*; if *g* is added, event *s*, and so on."[2] The scientific *explanation* of *q* (or prediction, if *q* has not yet occurred) consists of *subsuming* a particular *fact* under a law. The event *q* to be explained (e.g., the explosion of a tank filled with gas), is the conclusion of an argument containing two premises. The first premise states a law (e.g., that whenever (if) gas in a pressurized tank possessing a volume X is heated beyond n degrees an explosion will occur). The second premise, which is subsumed under the first, states a fact, namely, that the gas in the tank under consideration, which happened to possess volume X, was (or is) heated beyond n degrees.

This model of scientific explanation also satisfies the other Cartesian requirement—that of *verifying* the law (and by implication the theory from which it is derived) with respect to observations possessing an *objective*, that is, universal and indubitable, certainty (193). Every successful explanation of a past event or prediction of a future event by means of the law can be observationally determined. In turn, successful explanations and predictions confirm the truth of the law and, therewith, the truth of the theory from which it is derived.

The main problem with traditional theory, Horkheimer notes, lies in its uncritical *objectivism*. It assumes that the validity and truth of its knowledge consists in *passively mirroring* a reality, whose form and content is given independently of the subject's activity. Above all, it falsely assumes that its perception of the facts is purified of all extraneous, subjective values and concepts. Appealing to the tradition of Kant, Hegel, and Marx, Horkheimer remarks that the "detached" perspective of the scientist is belied by the fact that:

The facts which our senses present to us are socially preformed in two ways: through the historical character of the object perceived and through the historical character of the perceiving organ. Both are not simply natural; they are shaped by human activity. . . . The perceived fact is therefore co-determined by human ideas and concepts, even before its conscious theoretical elaboration by the knowing individual. . . . The so-called purity of the objective event to be achieved by experimental procedure is, of course, obviously connected with technological conditions, and the connection of these in turn with the material process of production is evident. . . . Man's physiological apparatus for sensation itself largely anticipates the order followed in physical experiment.

As man reflectively records reality, he separates and rejoins pieces of it, and concentrates on some particulars while failing to notice others. This process is just as much a result of the modern mode of production, as the perception of a man in a tribe of primitive hunters and fishers is the result of the conditions of his existence (as well, of course, as the object of perception). (200–201)

Traditional theory becomes ideological, Horkheimer contends, by failing to acknowledge that its knowledge represents but one particular sociohistorical interpretation of reality which conditions, and is conditioned by, "the bourgeois world." The reduction of reality to a harmonious system of necessary and invariant laws, as well as the depiction of knowledge as a function of passive, neutral, and detached observation, reflect the *alienation* and *reification* of capitalist society. Not only does this type of theory tacitly "legitimate" the status quo, by clothing it in the mantle of natural necessity and universality, but it provides causal knowledge that can be used by the powers that be to predict and control social as well as natural processes (194, 203ff).

In contrast to traditional theory, whose chief aim and justification resides in providing technically useful knowledge for purposes of *domination*, critical theory reflects on ideas in order to reveal their ideological function in maintaining the system. For it is only by knowing the social causes and functions of our ideas that we are in a position to freely (i.e., rationally) accept or reject them. In unmasking ideology, critical theory dissolves the constraints imposed by false consciousness. It aims at *emancipation*. This applies to all domains of culture, including the scientific production of knowledge itself. By making transparent the hidden social context and underlying class contradictions of specific types of knowledge—including its own—critical theory dissolves the false notions of universality and necessity inherent in all forms of objectivism. It thereby enables the subject of knowledge and action to project new possibilities of knowing and acting that transcend those prescribed by tradition.

Methodologically speaking, critical theory incorporates some aspects of traditional theory: "the knowledge and prognosis of relatively isolated facts . . . the same logical form," etc. (216). These features will be useful in analyzing the behavior of bourgeois society, which approximates an *objective* system. In this reading, human action must be explained as both the (mechanical) cause and effect of an impersonal, self-maintaining organism (228–31). At the same time, the statistical data of descriptive sociology will be critically evaluated in terms of their deviation from ideal standards of social freedom, justice, and well-being which implicitly inform the *subjective* consciousness of historical agents. Such data will then be explained as the necessary product of historical contradictions, whose underlying conditions are alterable. Unlike traditional theory, critical theory assumes that members of society are potentially free subjects, whose enlightened political practice might overthrow the system. Therefore, rather than contemplate social reality from afar, critical theory seeks to change it—by proferring ideology critique (231ff).

Critical knowledge serves the function of emancipatory enlightenment. Because its own theoretical and methodological presuppositions are intimately bound up with the structural contradictions of modern society, its own "truth," *as a valid description of social life*, is *relative* to this peculiar, historical reality. Does the same apply to its standards of evaluation? Horkheimer suggests that the notion of a rational society, composed of free, integral subjects, is not a utopian fantasy that is detached from existing reality. If it seems like utopian fantasy, it is because "an image of the future which springs indeed from a deep understanding of the present determines men's thoughts and actions even in periods when the course of events seems to be leading far away from such a future" (220).

Here, *subjective understanding* of the actual *ideas* motivating human conduct is necessary. However, contrary to Weber, the critical theorist must not remain satisfied with "describing the psychological contents typical of certain groups" (214). Such contents always contain ideological distortions, which falsify their inherent rationality. Although critical standards of justice and freedom have "found expression in cultural creations," they "are not correctly grasped by individuals or the common mind" (212–13). What is required is a "certain concern" for the plight of the oppressed, as well as a "wider vision" of the social totality. Only the critical theorist possesses the concern and theoretical insight necessary for discerning the truth-content of those higher, cultural ideas, which ultimately motivate human action. For only the critical theorist possesses the wider vision necessary for exposing their ideological function and critical potential. As reflections of an imperfect society, they show themselves to be fundamentally ambiguous, true and false at the same time. To cite Horkheimer: "If we take seriously the ideas by which the bourgeoisie explains its own order—free exchange, free competition, harmony of interests, and so on—and if we follow them to their logical conclusion, they manifest their inner contradiction and therewith their real opposition to the bourgeois order" (215).

"Traditional and Critical Theory" provided the basic model for Habermas's first major work, *Knowledge and Human Interests*.[3] Habermas accepts its outline of the methods and aims of critical theory. Horkheimer's critique of objectivism, and his argument that the critique of knowledge must become social critique, is taken up by Habermas in a detailed discussion of the history of German philosophy from Kant through Marx—a history that we summarized in chapter one. In particular, there are two important ideas that Habermas appropriates from Horkheimer. These are the distinctions between three types of knowledge, in accordance with their underlying methods and aims, and the conception of critical theory as an interdisciplinary program combining understanding of meaning and causal explanation, philosophical reflection and scientific objectification. Thus, one can read *Knowledge and Human Interests* as an attempt to clarify in further detail the peculiar unity of theory and practice envisioned by Horkheimer.

However, Habermas goes well beyond Horkheimer in trying to show how these distinct types of knowledge are necessarily and universally—that is to say, transcendentally—implicated in the "natural history" of the human species. For one thing, Horkheimer does not claim that the experimental method represents an irreversible achievement that articulates a feature of the human condition that has remained constant from the beginning of human evolution. In Horkheimer's opinion, this method articulates a "rule of experience"—the anticipation of future events based upon observed causal regularities—that is largely an expression of a particular historical reality, bourgeois society. For Habermas, on the contrary, this "rule of experience" is deeply entrenched in a universal, "natural" disposition, the interest in achieving given ends through application of efficient means. This disposition is not only factually expedient for human survival, but it also designates a type of action—the trial and error feedback acquired in the course of intervening instrumentally in nature—that is transcendentally necessary for the causal ordering of a coherent and meaningful world of objects.

By tracing a peculiar form of knowledge back to necessary and universal presuppositions that "transcend" historical contingencies, Habermas shows himself to be much more Kantian than his predecessor. Secondly, Habermas feels that Horkheimer's method of ideology critique, which proceeds *immanently*, by showing how particular cultural ideas contradict themselves, is too *relativistic*. One cannot assume that the contents of tradition always contain a kernal of truth. Horkheimer himself sometimes suggests that the universal goals, in terms of which particular traditions are to be critically appropriated, must be derived from something that transcends such traditions, such as a general scheme of historical progress. Because of the ideological distortion affecting all tradition, Habermas will also appeal to a broader conception of historical progress. However, unlike Horkheimer, he will argue that the universal goals of historical progress, and therewith the ideal standards of critique, must be drawn from a more universal and permanent, "historically invariant" set of orientations—in this case, the necessary conditions for the possibility of spoken communication.

KNOWLEDGE AND HUMAN INTERESTS:
THE NATURAL BASIS UNDERLYING
ANALYTIC-EMPIRICAL SCIENCE AND TECHNOLOGY

Habermas's first major work, *Knowledge and Human Interests*, undertakes a justification of critical theory by showing that its standards are already implicit in knowledge. This argument is both transcendental and anthropological. It is transcendental, in that it attempts to show that knowledge presupposes certain necessary and universal conditions. The conditions underlying the possibility of objective knowledge, it will be argued, include those essential for the maintenance of free and undistorted communication. Ultimately, they imply a democratic society free of social inequality and domination. Seen from an anthropological point of view, however, we can say that such conditions are factually necessary for the self-preservation of the species at a certain stage in its evolution.

The distinction, between transcendental and anthropological perspectives, is important to maintain in trying to understand Habermas's argument. If one thinks that the ultimate justification of knowledge resides in its contribution to preserving the human species, then humans will obviously have a practical interest in achieving knowledge. In this case, knowledge and its moral presuppositions will be justified relative to a practical interest in self-preservation. However, Habermas wants to argue that the unity of theory and practice and, in particular, the unity between knowledge and morality, is drawn tighter than this anthropological connection suggests. Human beings have an interest in moral knowledge that transcends biological self-preservation. They have an interest in achieving an integral personal identity, or self-certainty, to use Hegel's terminology. One might continue to talk about this interest in self-identity as an interest in "self-preservation," but only in a very qualified sense. For individuals have been quite willing to sacrifice their biological existence for the sake of preserving their self-identity, their way of life.

This becomes clearer when Habermas, following Hegel, shows how the practical interest, in achieving an integral self-identity, ultimately engages an emancipatory interest in liberating oneself from prejudices and illusions that block one's understanding of oneself as an integral being. Thus, willingness to sacrifice one's biological existence for the sake of preserving one's self-identity makes sense only when what is being preserved (or achieved)—human freedom—is so integral to one's very being that it "transcends" life as such.

According to Habermas, transcendent freedom is the ultimate transcendental presupposition underlying knowledge and reason generally—a position that Kant and his successors, Johann Fichte and Hegel, also defended. Reason is essentially oriented toward emancipation (toward its own free use). Conversely, freedom is oriented toward transparent knowledge of self in its integrity, or reason. So construed, the moral conditions underlying the possibility of knowledge *and* self-identity coincide. Both knowledge and self-certainty presuppose undistorted communication. Therefore, although knowledge may be in the service of self-preservation, it is also in the service of freedom (as Plato taught). However, the interdependence between knowledge and freedom is explicit only when we turn to a particular kind of knowledge: reflection. The reader will recall that, for Hegel, reflection is the essential manifestation of reason as such. For Habermas, too, critical theory is the name we give to that reflection which emancipates us from prejudices and distortions obstructing self-understanding and communication generally.

Habermas will argue that the very reflection which links knowledge to emancipation reveals the interest-base of knowledge as such. It combines theory and practice in its very method. Critical theory must be preeminently scientific (descriptive and explanatory) and interpretative (prescriptive and interpretative). In its very functioning, it is a force of social and political enlightenment that brings about, or actualizes, the transcendental presupposition it shares with knowledge generally, in however an implicit or explicit form. Reason is revolutionary—to paraphrase Marcuse's gloss on Hegel's philosophy. This is a very strange notion of knowledge, indeed, and merits further scrutiny.

To argue that knowledge is grounded in practical (even political) interests runs contrary to *positivist* philosophy of science. By "positivism," Habermas has in mind the philosophical movement initiated by August Comte and later continued by the Vienna School under the name "logical positivism."[4] Positivism maintains that all forms of knowledge, including that proffered by social science, conforms, or ought to conform, to the kind of knowledge proferred by natural science (what Habermas calls *scientism*). This kind of knowledge involves the explanation of past events or the prediction of future events in terms of causal laws whose truth has been confirmed (or, at least, not falsified) by factual observation. Positivism assumes that the truth of a scientific fact consists in correspondence with a reality whose meaning preexists the selective perception and conceptual activity of the perceiver. Observation of this reality is thus assumed to be *purely objective*. That is, it is assumed to be freed from all practical values and interests that might lend it a *subjective, interpretative* cast. Its universal validity, or repeatability for all persons regardless of subjective differences, is to be guaranteed by the experimental reduction of all phenomena to measurable quantities.

Habermas clearly thinks that positivism is false as a *philosophical* theory about the essential structure of cognition generally. It defends an objectivistic conception of knowledge, which ignores the transcendental accomplishments of the knowing subject, in conceptually and behaviorally structuring experience. It neglects, as we shall see, the fundamentally interested nature of all knowledge. It is less clear, however, whether and to what extent Habermas thinks positivism gives a false account of scientific *methodology*. To the extent that positivism claims that the methods deployed in natural science are necessary for achieving knowledge in any field, it is false. Habermas claims that knowledge in the historical and cultural sciences as well as knowledge in critical social science necessarily presuppose the understanding and interpretation of meaning. Yet, in his opinion, the objectivity of such understanding and interpretation cannot be conceived along the lines of natural scientific methodology.

The matter is considerably less clear when Habermas talks about the natural sciences and the behavioral social sciences. Habermas believes that behavioral social sciences, such as experimental psychology, conform to the methodological canons of natural science. Sometimes he suggests that this poses no insuperable difficulty for them, so long as it is understood that behavioral social science provides a very one-sided form of social knowledge which should (but need not be) supplemented with interpretative, critical social science.[5] Elsewhere, however, Habermas suggests that behavioral social science is simply inadequate for explaining social action because, in the social domain, explanation necessarily presupposes understanding.[6]

The case of natural science is still more complicated. There can be little doubt that Habermas thinks that positivism gives an adequate account of two key methods of natural scientific *explanation*. These are: (a) the subsumption of the *explanandum* (the event to be explained or predicted) under the *explanans* (a general causal law formulated as a hypothetical conditional); and (b) the experimental confirmation of the *explanans* under conditions of controlled observation.[7] However, Habermas most certainly does not think that positivism gives an adequate account of the methods (or logic) of *discovery* characteristic of the natural sciences. The positivist notion, that general theoretical axioms and concepts can be reduced to observation statements or simple operations, is one he denies (despite his belief that observation statements can be reduced to operational statements). He also rejects the Humean idea that causal regularities are discovered by passive observation, rather than through operational activity guided by theoretical hypotheses.

Habermas concedes that a natural science, whose explanatory methods conform to the positivist account, can unmask the ideological content of certain beliefs.[8] These would include beliefs affirming as factually true statements that are disconfirmed by observation; statements that are nonfactual, or even meaningless, such as metaphysical or religious statements about God; and statements that are confirmed by observation, but which misidentify the cause of the fact asserted (e.g., attributing it to a condition that is natural and necessary, rather than historical and changeable).

Despite the critical value of positivistic science, Habermas points out that it is uncritical of its own philosophical presuppositions, especially those pertaining to its false, objectivistic theory of knowledge. Positivistic science claims to be *disinterested* and *value-neutral*. In reality, scientific knowledge is justified only because it fulfills *practical interests*. Anthropologically, knowledge furthers *values* deemed factually necessary for "survival." Transcendentally, knowledge furthers values requisite for realizing the emancipatory conditions underlying its very possibility. If the objectifying methodology of natural science is validated at all, Habermas claims, it is by efficiently advancing an anthropologically and transcendentally deep-rooted interest in technological control. This interest, however, is but one of the basic orientations securing self-preservation and freedom.[9] The others include an interest in communicative intersubjectivity and an interest in emancipation. These interests achieve satisfaction through fundamentally different types of knowledge, and therefore dictate different methodological strategies.

As we shall see, Habermas insists that a critical social science guided by an emancipatory interest is necessary for guaranteeing the objectivity, or intersubjective validity and usefulness, of knowledge generally. For only it can determine whether a claim, about which *needs* ought to be met and which *interests* ought to be pursued, is ideological or not. Positivistic science can expose the ideological basis of *descriptive* claims that pretend to be factually true, but are not. It cannot, however, accomplish the same task with respect to *prescriptions*. For what the latter putatively assert are not true facts, but "true" *value-judgements*.

The first part of *Knowledge and Human Interests* retraces the forgotten prehistory of positivism—the tradition of German philosophy from Kant through Hegel and Marx—to justify the claim that a critique of knowledge (in Kant's sense) must aspire to social (ideology) critique. Since I have already summarized the basic contours of this argument in chapter one, we shall concentrate instead on the second and third parts of Habermas's study. According to Habermas, the path of reflection leading from Kant to Hegel and Marx was not entirely suppressed in the annals of positivist philosophy of science. In the research of two Kant-inspired thinkers—Charles Peirce (1839–1914), the founder of American pragmatism, and Wilhelm Dilthey (1833–1911), the leading exponent of hermeneutic (interpretative) philosophy at the turn of the century—knowledge is shown to have a practical interest.

For these thinkers, reflection on the logic of causal explanation (in natural science) and textual interpretation (in historical and cultural science), reveals the life-preserving and freedom-enhancing activities and interests underlying two types of knowledge: *technically useful* and *morally binding* knowledge.

Peirce provides an important link between Marx and Hegel, on one hand, and modern science, on the other. The reader will recall that Marx and Hegel transformed Kant's notion of reason from synthetic activity occurring in the privacy of each individual's mind to social activity embodied in mental and physical labor. For Kant, the synthetic power of the mind produces causal unity in the world. Peirce shows how the production of a causally unified world, or rather, the production of a stable system of causal beliefs, is a function of labor (instrumental action). The discovery of causal regularities, he argues, occurs only in the course of instrumental interventions in nature. It is only by *actively* trying to bring about certain events, through effecting changes in our environment, that we isolate, by trial and error, real from apparent causes. Passive observation *alone* does not suffice to distinguish those observed regularities that represent noncausal connections (e.g., the rising of the sun being preceded regularly by the crowing of the rooster), from genuine causal connections. For Peirce, the kind of *experimental*, or trial and error, behavior necessary for the discovery of causal relations, forms the basic *logic* underlying scientific inquiry. Specifically, the logic of scientific inquiry consists of three types of instrumental activity:

discovery of causal laws via trial and error (abduction);
explanation, or inference of effects from antecedent conditions and causal laws (deduction); and
experimental confirmation of laws (induction).

These activities comprise a *methodologically* sophisticated set of *operations* that make possible the *cumulative* acquisition of causal knowledge—in ways that are convincing for all persons.

Especially significant for Habermas is the fact that causal knowledge acquires its *original meaning* and *validity* with respect to a *prescientific*, or methodologically unsophisticated, context of feedback-monitored, habitual behavior. The three operations mentioned above—abduction, deduction, and induction—correspond to more primitive behaviors which evolved in response to organic changes in the species. The need to adapt to changing conditions of scarcity, combined with the assumption of an upright posture, the development of opposable thumbs, and so forth, produced certain *reflex responses* to outer stimulii, which took the form of instrumental interventions. Changing one's environment in order to satisfy one's wants—in short, *working* for one's livelihood—could be successfully satisfied only by learning to anticipate the typical effects of one's behavior. Yet such predictions remained unreliable prior to the discovery of a procedure for isolating true causes from apparent causes. This lack was remedied by the discovery of the experimental method in the sixteenth century.

According to Habermas, scientific method transforms feedback-monitored behavior into a cumulative learning process by isolating causal chains under *controlled* conditions. Measuring procedures infuse instrumental actions with greater precision and intersubjective reliability. In Habermas's opinion, not only the *meaning* of descriptive statements and objective observations, but also their *power to convince others* (i.e., their power to generate intersubjective agreement and thereby secure their own "truth"), is grounded in the categorical framework of possible measuring operations (194–95). To paraphrase an example cited by Peirce, factual statements, such as "diamonds are hard," are reducible to conditional statements regarding the effects of instrumental interventions. "Diamonds are hard" = "If one performs operations x, y, and z on diamonds, effects possessing properties p, q, and r will occur." But properties themselves are also definable in terms of standardized measures. Heat, for example, is definable in terms of a volumetric increase of mercury.

The main upshot of Habermas's argument is that *nature* as it is conceived by science—as a system of mathematically definable causal laws—is itself the product of human measuring activity. *Objective* reality is just another name for that intersubjectively agreed-upon (because quantifiable) set of properties and relationships that reflects *one possible way of interpreting nature.* However, to say that it is an interpretation, or a *human* construct, is not to deny its *objective (intersubjective) validity* for all persons. For this interpretation reflects a "bias" that is rooted in an "anthropologically deep-seated" *technical interest* in securing and expanding control over *objectifiable* processes (91–139). Because this interest is fundamental to the preservation of the species, to the constitution of objective reality, and to the possibility of free action, one can say that it is necessary, universal, and hence valid for all human beings. By parity of reasoning, the same can be said of that peculiar manner of interpreting nature which most successfully satisfies it. Instrumental action represents nothing less than a transcendental condition for the possibility of experiencing any objective facts whatsoever. Without such a world, neither self-preservation nor free action would make any sense.

It is here where Habermas and Marcuse part company. As I noted at the end of chapter four, Marcuse ties the objectifying (instrumentalizing and quantifying) structure of science and technology to a particular sociohistorical formation, bourgeois society. Thus, he cannot envisage a radical transformation of society without also envisaging a radical transformation of this structure. Marcuse sometimes speaks as though the science and technology of an emancipated society would adopt a totally different attitude toward nature—communicative rather than objectifying.

Habermas does not deny the possibility of adopting such an *attitude* toward nature. Indeed, prior to Galileo and the emergence of modern, mathematical science, nature was conceived either as a spiritual force with whom one could communicate, or as a symbolic expression of divine purposes requiring a kind of textual interpretation. Nonetheless, he doubts that a communicative attitude toward nature could be compatible with the necessary presuppositions underlying *objective knowledge*. Above all, such a view ignores the fact that technology and science depend upon an objectifying methodology for their *validity*. For not only does this methodology secure the possibility of intersubjective agreement, but it articulates a *natural* form of adaptive behavior whose instrumental objectification of nature is indispensable for survival as well as free action.

So closely does Habermas tie objectifying technology and science to human nature that he notes that technological *development* is but a *self-objectification* (in the terminology of Marx and Hegel) of the subject's natural powers. In other words, technology and science can be understood as processes by which the human species unburdened itself of its own organic functions, namely, by "projecting them one after another onto the plane of technical instruments":

At first the functions of the motor apparatus (hands and legs) were augmented and replaced, followed by energy production (of the human body), the functions of the sensory apparatus (eyes, ears, and skin), and finally by the functions of the governing center (the brain). Technological development thus follows a logic that corresponds to the structure of purposive-rational action regulated by its own results, which is in fact the structure of *work*. Realizing this, it is impossible to envisage how, as long as the organization of human nature does not change and as long therefore as we have to achieve self-preservation through social labor and through the aid of means that substitute for work, we could renounce technology, more particularly *our* technology, in favor of a qualitatively different one.[10]

THE COMMUNICATIVE BASIS UNDERLYING MORAL KNOWLEDGE AND THE INTERPRETATIVE SCIENCES

The answer to the question, Why should we pursue natural science? has been answered. As a general enterprise, science possesses objective, intersubjective validity because, anthropologically speaking, it is the most efficient way of satisfying our necessary interest in technologically controlling nature for purposes of adaptive survival. Transcendentally speaking, its very structure exemplifies a type of activity which is necessary for experiencing that objective world without which we cannot act freely. However, further reflection on the nature of scientific knowledge suggests that another interest is at play. Peirce's account of the relationship, between scientific knowledge and instrumental action, still recalls the positivist idea that the truth of a law consists in its "correspondence" with observed facts. Yet, we also know from Kant that the "facts" are not given independently of the observer. Not only are they constituted by the measuring activity of the subject, they are *preinterpreted* by the conceptual categories of the scientific theory. "Facts" are descriptions that employ general concepts. The "truth" of the latter, Peirce would say, is a function of their pragmatic usefulness, not their correspondence with some uninterpreted "brute" sensation or reality. However, what counts as useful is a question of what needs and interests ought to be satisfied. Consequently, the "truth" of concepts, and therewith the truth of scientific facts, is also a question of value.

But in what does the validity of a value consist? Values imply prescriptions—purposes and ends that ought to be pursued. We know from our discussion of Weber that what *ought* to be is not validated by what is. Generally, we justify our prescriptions by appealing to the commonly shared beliefs of our society. *Intersubjective agreement*, then, seems to be a necessary condition for bestowing validity on our value judgments. Nevertheless, we know that the collective judgment of a society might be distorted by ideology. Consequently, only an ideal and absolutely unlimited, universal *consensus*, achieved through *rational communication*, will suffice to validate a value-judgment. That is to say, in stating that such and such a goal ought to be pursued, we tacitly imply that if all persons who ever lived possessed a complete, rational understanding of themselves and their world, they would agree with us in our judgment.

I shall have more to say about the conditions of rational communication below. What presently concerns us is the importance of rational communication in the justification of scientific theories. Peirce himself believed that the validity of scientific method resided in its unique capacity to generate universal agreement regarding "true" beliefs. However, in that case the real meaning of truth would reside less in pragmatic adaptation than in *rational consensus*. Habermas himself points out that the notion of an ideal universal agreement, which Peirce proposes as a substitute for the correspondence theory of truth, cannot be understood in abstraction from the *community of scientists* (135–39).

A belief or theory may *produce* successful predictions, as in the case of Newtonian mechanics, and yet not be true; that is, rationally justifiable in the long run. Indeed, Thomas Kuhn's study of scientific revolutions, which Habermas cites, indicates that the most basic propositions of a scientific theory are worked out in advance of evidential confirmation. This happens in *conversations* between scientists about what counts as a pressing problem, how such a problem ought to be conceptualized, and so forth. Such propositions are *irreducible* to empirical predictions. For it is only when they are taken in combination with one another that they yield testable hypotheses. Consequently, their "truth" would have to be captured in terms of an *ideal consensus*. Thus, "true" propositions are those which, according to Peirce, anyone would *agree to* in the long run, given sufficient time for rational reflection.

The fact that scientific truth presupposes the existence of a *communicative community* leads Habermas to consider the categorical framework in which intersubjective meaning, value and validity are constituted. It is obvious how predictive science is related to the context of instrumental action. It is also obvious that the anthropological usefulness and transcendental validity of science resides in its successful satisfaction of a technical interest. However, it is unclear what, if any, interest is satisfied by communication. Equally unclear is the relationship between communication and those "sciences of man" associated with history, literature, cultural anthropology, etc. Nevertheless, Habermas will argue that the kind of *textual interpretation* preferred by these sciences is essentially related to communication. The latter, in turn, will be shown to satisfy a *practical* interest in procuring intersubjective agreement, regarding shared norms and values. This is a necessary condition, not only for the creation and maintenance of personal and social *identity*, but also for the achievement of individual freedom.

Peirce provided the necessary link connecting the logic of causal explanation to Marx's notion of labor as an activity underlying self-realization and world constitution. Dilthey provides a similar link connecting communication and symbolic understanding to Hegel's master-slave dialectic. The reader will recall that this dialectic shows how one's identity is defined and confirmed through recognition by an other. For Dilthey, this dialectic is as essential to the methodological grounding of history, philology, and literary criticism—sciences concerned with understanding the spiritual life of humankind—as causal explanation is to the methodological grounding of the natural sciences.

The method of understanding grounding the human sciences is none other than the circular interpretation of textual wholes in terms of their parts, and the interpretation of these parts in terms of more inclusive wholes. This circular dialectic, as we shall see, also encompasses the interpreter. The interpreter is responsible for much of the meaning contained in the text. At the same time, the text is responsible for opening up new meaning for the interpreter. Stated somewhat paradoxically, text and interpreter mutually constitute one another as meaningful identities. This activity of *symbolic* reproduction, Habermas will argue, is capable of advancing moral knowledge. Yet, it can do so only to the extent that the dialectic between text and interpreter assumes the form of a simulated dialogue.

According to Dilthey, the understanding of the past, or the interpretation of an ancient text, is an elaboration of the sort of retrospective self-interpretation that an individual continually engages in, while reconstituting the continuity of his or her life history—the very substance of one's unique identity. To begin with, the generation and maintenance of a stable, personal identity involves assigning one's life experiences with a meaning related to the intersubjectively recognized norms and concepts of a broader linguistic community (context). This reiterates Hegel's point in the "master-servant" dialectic that our certainty, regarding our own identity as free subjects, depends upon recognition by others for confirmation. And this is mainly accomplished by communicating with others: saying "no" to their commands, learning to see ourselves in light of their descriptions of our behavior, participating in the same social and cultural institutions as they do, and so on.

It is at this point, Habermas notes, that everyday communication reveals an interpretative structure. The three classes of "life expressions" as distinguished by Dilthey—verbal utterances, actions, and nonverbal expressions (gestures, body language, and the like)—"interpret" each other in a circular manner. This is similar to the way in which sentences, paragraphs, and narratives interpret each other in the part/whole dialectic of textual interpretation. Linguistic understanding is (con)textual. The expression "I love you" can be understood seriously, facetiously, humorously, etc. depending on the occasion, the body language of the speaker, what he or she is trying to do, etc. Even a simple utterance such as, "close the door" may be understood in different ways (as a command, a request, a wish). Even aspects of reference (the door-object referred to) and address (the listener designated by the utterance) require further actions, gestures, etc. to be clearly understood (140–86). Therefore, to say that understanding is interpretative is just to say that it can never be completed. The hermeneutic circle is a never-ending process of contextual cross-referencing which yields indefinite possibilities for new understanding.

Dilthey's analysis of linguistic expression underscores the moment of textual interpretation in all communication and self-understanding. But, in what sense does the reverse hold true? How are history and cultural anthro-pology—interpretative sciences par excellence—related to communication and self-understanding? It is here that Habermas turns to the *philosophical hermeneutics* of Hans-Georg Gadamer. Gadamer's hermeneutics attempts to show the interpretative structure underlying all experience. Most importantly, it demonstrates that, even the most methodologically sophisticated forms of textual interpretation, are based upon a prescientific communicative com-petence.

Dilthey, Gadamer argues, mistakenly identifies textual interpretation with reproduction of the private intentions of the author. He commits, in other words, an objectivistic fallacy by presuming that the meaning disclosed by "correct" interpretation is identical to (corresponds with) the meaning originally intended by the author. This fallacy, Gadamer believes, renders both understanding and *intersubjective* (transcultural and transhistorical) "truth" incomprehensible.

According to Gadamer, understanding serves to *bridge* the cultural ho-rizons of interpreter and author by means of a *shared*, public language. A message is communicated whose meaningfulness, reasonablness, and truth ostensibly remains identical across time. Understanding of meaning is here conceived as a process of *reaching mutual understanding* between different cultural horizons. Gadamer sees the bridging of cultures as foundational for any *moral* relationship. As Kant taught, the essence of the moral point of view consists of identifying with perspectives other than one's own. Ulti-mately, the goal is to achieve a *universal*, cosmopolitan perspective in which the narrow boundaries of one's own native self-understanding are gradually *expanded*, or *opened up*, to include ever-broader points of view. Such a process of moral *enlightenment*, of discovering and generating *commonalities* of interest linking oneself with others, can only occur through *communicative understanding*.[11]

The agreement between communicating horizons is clarified by Gadamer in terms of the *dialogical* dynamics of textual understanding. The objectivity of textual interpretation, like the objectivity (intersubjective validity) of the moral point of view, is achieved by checking the distorting effects of one's prejudices. However, contrary to the objectifying methodology of analytic-empirical science, this is not accomplished by putting one's prejudices out of play. The attempt by Dilthey and others to cancel the influence of those values, preferences, and linguistic assumptions, that form the tacit background of their own understanding by immediately identifying with the mind of the author, is futile. These assumptions alone provide the familiar reference points, questions, etc. that are necessary for opening up a dimension of possible meaningfulness in the first place. Thus, textual meaning is not pre-given by the author's original intentions, but is partially constituted by the subjectivity of the interpreter.[12]

Does this then mean that textual interpretation is an act of arbitrarily projecting one's own prejudices onto the text; that is, reading into the text whatever one chooses to find there? If this were the case, there would be no difference between correct and incorrect interpretation. It would also be hard to conceive how understanding could serve the function of moral enlightenment (i.e., of discovering the moral truth embedded in cultural tradition), one's own as well as others.

It is only by conceiving textual interpretation along the model of simulated communication (dialogue) that objectivity and moral enlightenment can be accounted for. By resisting *easy* translation into the interpreter's horizon of understanding, a text drawn from the past or a different culture *questions* this horizon's range of validity. Conversely, by resisting *sustained* attempts at translation, the text may reveal those aspects of itself that are parochial and anachronistic. These are then *questioned* as to their validity in communicating a message, that can be understood as true and reasonable, by persons from other cultures. Thus, text and interpreter confront one another as participants in a Socratic dialogue. Each *critically reflects* its own horizon of understanding off the other, so to speak.

Moral knowledge and self-limitation, like objective interpretation and self-understanding, involve a process of *critical reflection* that can be provoked and sustained only dialogically, in communication with self and others. As we have just seen, the competencies requisite for ordinary *communication* are openness toward the other as an autonomous being worthy of respect, the simultaneous assumption of speaker (questioner) and listener (respondent) roles, dialogic reciprocity, and critical attitude toward self and other. These are precisely those that are required in assuming the moral attitude. Like Hegel's dialectic of reason, interpretation and communication are processes by which two opposing terms mutually define one another. Each term critically alters its opposite. Yet, it is only through such mutual "negation" that the "truth" inherent in both is "preserved" and raised to a higher universality (identity, or agreement).

EMANCIPATION AND CRITICAL SOCIAL SCIENCE

In Habermas's opinion, the interdependency between communication, interpretation, and moral knowledge has decisive consequences for critical social science. Interpretative sociology, he claims, can escape ethnocentrism only when the interpreter adopts a communicative—and inherently critical—attitude with respect to her own prejudices as well as those of the agent's whose actions she is trying to interpret. "We" must, in other words, critically assess what "they" count as good reasons for their action with reference to "our" own standards of rationality. Indeed, only then can we begin to discover the limits of our own *reason*, which, in contrast to the intimacy and community fostered by simpler cultures, emphasizes constant growth, increased division and hierarchical stratification of labor, and the reduction of nature to mechanical processes lacking any higher meaning.

Despite sharing Gadamer's views about the capacity of communication to expand our moral horizons and open up ever broader horizons of agreement and "truth," Habermas rejects his "ontological" understanding of interpretation generally. For Gadamer, all forms of knowledge and experience are basically interpretative and contextual. Although Habermas agrees that all knowledge ultimately rests on communicative understanding and, further, that all knowledge engages a prior set of interest-orientations, he insists that some of these orientations are transcendental, or noncontextual in nature. Moreover, he insists that the interpretative aspect of natural scientific knowledge should not obscure fundamental methodological differences between this type of knowledge and those preferred by the interpretative and critical sciences, properly speaking. Unlike objects in natural science, texts and text-analogues are linguistic constructions from the very beginning. Consequently, one can gain access to them initially only by interpreting them. One must, as it were, participate in their language in order to identify them as meaningful. However conceptually constituted objects in natural science may be, they can be directly observed from an objective distance. They can seem utterly meaningless and yet be measured, explained, etc.

As we shall see, the objectifying methodology of natural science plays a key role in Habermas's conception of critical theory. It is what enables the critical theorist to gain a critical distance from the linguistic and cultural prejudices that normally distort one's understanding in the course of participating in popular forms of social interaction. In particular, it enables the critical theorist to bracket the validity of conventionally agreed-upon interpretations and values and to check them against an objective social reality that is not itself reducible to these interpretations.

Before discussing Habermas's conception of critical theory further we must first understand how he proposes to ground pure interpretative science in a transcendental interest, since this is where he and Gadamer begin to part company. The connection between textual interpretation and communication enables Habermas to ground the historical-hermeneutic sciences in a *moral-*

practical interest in maintaining *unconstrained intersubjectivity*. As we noted in our discussion of Hegel, intersubjectivity without domination is necessary for the achievement of normatively binding solidarity (social integration), personal autonomy (individuation), and identity formation (cultural transmission).[13] Here the categorical framework of *ordinary language* constitutes the necessary conditions for maintaining a form of life dependent on meaning. Yet, implicit in the notion of a meaningful life, Habermas argues, is an ideal type of *rational communication*:

> What raises us out of nature is the only thing whose nature we can know—*language*. Through its structure, autonomy and responsibility are posited for us. Our first sentence expresses unequivocally the intention of a universal and unconstrained consensus. . . . (O)nly in an emancipated society whose members' autonomy and responsibility had been realized, would communication have developed into the non-authoritarian and universally practical dialogue from which both our model of reciprocally constituted ego-identity and our idea of true consensus are always implicitly derived. To this extent the truth of statements is based upon anticipating the realization of the good life (314).

The above passage announces a *second* interest implicated in communication. Besides being oriented toward the *renewal* of cultural tradition and the *preservation* of intersubjectively binding norms necessary for maintaining personal and social identity, *rational* speakers are oriented toward conditions of *unconstrained* reciprocity, or *emancipation*. The interest in emancipation appears to be dialectically related to the other two interests. Unlike the technical and practical interests, which are *organically* related to the preservation of biological and spiritual life, the emancipatory interest, Habermas notes, emerges only in the course of cultural evolution as a *reponse* to economic and political *domination*. In particular, it indicates the fact that the renewal of cultural tradition and preservation of normative solidarity in everyday communication is unreliable due to ideological distortion. Knowledge is rendered suspect, and one's identity is victimized by an unfree, false consciousness.

It is Habermas's contention that the *ideological distortion* of communication and self-understanding, by *power relations* that are as anonymous as they are diffuse, must be criticized by transcending the participatory context of everyday language—an achievement whose possibility Gadamer ultimately denies. Ordinary communicative competence may provide the basic reference points necessary for understanding the past. However, if ordinary language itself is permeated by ideological distortions, it no longer functions as a reliable medium of understanding. In this instance, the "gaps" in understanding are caused by something other than changes in languages brought about by the passage of time (216).

For Habermas, the closest analogy to ideological false consciousness is neurosis. Like neurosis, ideology manifests itself as a form of delusion. In particular, one is deluded regarding the meaning of one's behavior. One assumes that one's choices are the result of free, rational deliberation when they are, in fact, the result of subtle, largely unconscious, manipulation. Subsequently, one is also deluded as to the interests one pursues. One believes that the satisfaction of certain needs is necessary for the achievement of happiness. In fact, just the opposite is true.

Habermas is especially struck by the fact that both neurotic and ideologically compelled behavior exhibit a high degree of mechanical rigidity. As I mentioned above, this lack of freedom is to be explained by the fact that the real determinants of one's behavior operate below the threshold of rational, conscious deliberation. Following Freud, Habermas suggests that these unconscious determinations of behavior be understood as suppressed motives. Certain needs for freedom and fulfillment are deemed to be incompatible with the surplus repression demanded by society. They are subsequently suppressed through the agency of *linguistic censorship*.

Communication with self and others is thus *distorted* by the confusion and truncation of meanings (recall Marcuse's analysis of one-dimensional speech). One, for example, is no longer permitted to speak of freedom as a need for communal reconciliation and integral, bodily fulfillment, since this contradicts the kind of repressive freedom required by the Performance Principle. Nevertheless, these suppressed needs manifest themselves as unconscious motives that somehow manage to reappear in social behavior. They do not appear, of course, as explicit demands for social liberation. The system does not permit such a public and rational expression of what is forbidden. Instead, they appear as *pathological symptoms*, patterns of *cynical conformism* caused by vague feelings of alienation, meaninglessness, and lack of freedom (219–29).

Like neurosis, ideologically fixated behavior is a *symbolic* expression of *unconscious* motives which does not comprehend itself as such. These motives reflect suppressed needs and agency of suppression at once. The *real* meaning of such behavior cannot be rendered transparent in everyday communication. Indeed, language itself functions to distort it. Therefore, Habermas concludes that the ideological meaning of social behavior must be *interpreted* and *diagnosed* by relating it to the subterranean force fields of the economic and political "system." Ultimately, it must be interpreted from the vantage point of a *therapist*. For only a therapist is in a position to *understand* the emancipatory potential of a given society, in light of its socioeconomic development, while *explaining* the systemic causes motivating acceptance of substitute gratifications.[14]

Psychoanalysis exemplies the third, *critical* type of (social) science sought by Habermas. Marx, Habermas notes, misconceived his critique of political economy along the lines of a predictive, analytic-empirical science. Such a view reflected his belief that labor (instrumental action) was the primary vehicle of social evolution. Ultimately, this led to the economic determinism of orthodox Marxism and to the neglect of the political question: What is the true life interest motivating the establishment of a *democratic* socialism? We now see, however, that labor is only one of the media underlying social evolution. The other medium, linguistic communication, is the basis underlying moral evolution and identity formation culminating in fully democratic institutions.

However, because ideology works through the distortion of communication, its critical exposure cannot be obtained through analytic-empirical or historical-interpretative methods taken in exclusion from one another. Hence, Habermas accords a privileged status to psychoanalysis, which combines the explanatory methodology of natural science with the interpretative methodology of historical and cultural science. Like the latter, psychoanalysis aims at restoring the full context of a patient's life history. However, it does so by reincorporating repressed motives into the stream of consciousness. Once the neurotic understands that his or her behavior is a symbolic reenactment of a childhood scene, involving the painful suppression of some need by parental authority, the compulsion to repeat the behavior is dissolved.

According to Habermas, this kind of depth interpretation is distinguished from ordinary textual interpretation. In the case of psychoanalysis, the gap in understanding needing to be bridged has its source in an extralinguistic cause—an unconscious act of repression. Consequently, unlike textual interpretation, the understanding of neurotic and ideologically constrained behavior will involve tracing its source to some objective (consciously unintended) cause related to the systemic dynamics of either personality or economy. Thus, the methodological combination of subjective understanding and objective causal explanation is reflected in the very structure of critical theory itself (266).

The theoretical basis of psychoanalytic depth interpretation consists of general interpretations of psychodynamic development that specify lawlike phases. These phases involve the satisfaction of erotic needs with respect to certain erogenous zones (oral, anal, and genital, respectively) and with respect to certain persons (mother, father, and spouse/mate, respectively). Each phase leads to conflict and must be resolved in a certain manner in order to permit development to continue (259–73).

Like theories in natural science, general interpretations permit the deduction of invariant causal relationships between specific types of conflict and conflict resolution. Unlike theories in natural science, however, the lawlike succession of developmental stages retains a *teleological* dimension that can be understood only along the model of a narrative text. For the developing self is like an actor in a drama, struggling to achieve full moral identity, autonomy, and self-understanding.

The correct explanation of a causally necessitated mode of behavior, which is also the correct understanding of that behavior's concealed meaning, *dissolves the causal connection*. Moreover, because the "correctness" of the interpretation proferred by the analyst can be confirmed only by the patient himself, they cannot be empirically verified or falsified. It is confirmed only to the extent that the patient's change in behavior is an expression of the patient's own heightened self-understanding. The "predictions" which general interpretations make possible, regarding changes of behavior at the conclusion of therapy, transpire only if the patient completes the process of critical reflection provoked by the analyst in therapeutic dialogue.

On the surface, at least, Habermas's suggestion that critical social theory be conceived along the lines of psychotherapy seems promising. However, it seems less so in practice. Is the relationship between social theorist and society really analogous to the clinical relationship between doctor and patient? The latter relationship is built upon a mutually accepted asymmetry. The patient accepts his or her lack of rationality in turning to the doctor for enlightenment. The moral authority of the social critic, by contrast, would not extend beyond those groups who, by and large, already agree with her on the substantive ills of society. These groups might then appeal to her insight in explaining the ideological behavior of other members of society.

The privileging of the social critic's point of view is problematic for another reason. As Gadamer remarked, it tacitly encourages an elitist refusal to engage the "deluded" others in a critical debate on their terms. One renounces critical dialogue with others by prejudging their competence as rational speakers. Habermas claims that the validity of any set of agreed-upon terms, which hasn't been freely and consciously produced by fully rational agents, is questionable. But that would indicate that no language is above suspicion. Following through on this line of reasoning, the critical theorist would seem to be justified in refusing to engage in any mutual give-and-take with those who hold opinions different from his or her own. But, refusing to engage in such dialogue could amount only to a kind of moral obtuseness, to say the very least.[15]

Therefore, it is not surprising that whenever Habermas describes the process of ideology critique, it always involves a *monological* act whereby the lone critic identifies with the universal interests of society. To be sure, the critical theorist hypothetically imagines the various factions as participants in a perfectly rational discourse, in which their true interests are made known to them in light of economic scarcities. But this moral dialogue is *simulated* within the mind of the critic, who then compares the results with the actual interests being served by social, political, and legal institutions.[16]

In all fairness to Habermas, it must be conceded that whole societies have been deluded about their genuine interests and that sometimes the lone critic who stands outside the framework of day-to-day life may have a truer, more objective view of the way things really are. For persons of African-American or Native-American descent who feel that their needs for freedom and dignity do not find adequate expression in the dominant language of formal rights, for women and gays who feel that their needs for self-identity do not find adequate expression in traditional gender roles, and for workers who feel that their needs for justice do not find adequate expression in the contractual language of a wage agreement, refusal to enter into the established discourse may well represent a principled moral stance against oppression and injustice.

As an advocate for these marginalized and suppressed interests, the critical theorist's stance is not at all elitist, if what is meant by the latter is transcendent aloofness from and indifference to the voice of the people; for the people in question may speak in ways that point beyond the privileged language of the establishment. In that case, it would be best to see the critical theorist's refusal to engage in the dominant language as a gambit intended to expand and open up that language to the hitherto voice of the oppressed. As Habermas himself points out, critical enlightenment cannot aid us in deciding how we ought to act in particular situations. Its power is limited to dissolving illusions of the past that hinder present self-understanding. Yet, for all that, its validity is not cut off from practical confirmation. Therapists' insights must be validated by their patients and therapists, too, must undergo therapy. As we shall see, the essentially collaborative and dialogical effort of confirmation is the hallmark of Habermas's notion of critical theory as a reconstructive science.[17]

CONCLUDING REMARKS

In this chapter, I sought to address the theory/practice problem from the standpoint of the methodological and philosophical rationale underlying critical theory. Critical methodology presupposes a close collaboration between understanding and explanation, philosophical reflection and scientific methodology. Its philosophical rationale is based on mediating transcendent theoretical ideas and historical practice. Critical theorists disagree about the relative transcendence of theory versus practice, which is reflected in their respective notions of ideology critique. First-generation critical theorists were inclined to accept an immanent conception of ideology critique. They believed that the standards for criticizing ideological culture were somehow inherent in that culture. Like Hegel, they saw critical reflection as a means by which the ideal, utopian essence of tradition (especially, images of reconciliation and freedom embedded in art, religion, and philosophy), is turned against that tradition's ideological functioning in real life. Habermas, by contrast, eschews immanent ideology critique because cultural standards are not universally valid for all times and places. He also notes that culture may be so ideologically distorted as to preclude the interpretative discovery of moral insight. Consequently, in his first major work, *Knowledge and Human Interests*, he sought to ground standards of critique in necessary, universal conditions of knowledge.

Knowledge and Human Interests carries on the Kantian critique of positivist objectivism initiated by Horkheimer. It argues that there are three distinct types of scientific knowledge with their own peculiar methodologies: the analytic-empirical methodology of natural science; the interpretative methodology of cultural and historical science; and the explanatory (depth) understanding of critical social theory. These methodologies are not arbitrary, but constitute (or criticize) reality in ways that are universally valid. For they represent refined modes of specific types of everyday action—instrumental, communicative, and reflective—that are indispensable for the survival and self-determination of the species. Consequently, they are guided in advance by three sorts of basic orientations or interests: a technical interest in controlling natural processes, a practical interest in achieving intersubjective agreement among speakers, and an interest in emancipation from internal and external forms of domination.

Science is essentially a social enterprise. Therefore, all knowledge—even the analytic-empirical knowledge of natural science—is guided by a practical interest in achieving intersubjective agreement regarding the theoretical elaboration and confirmation of research. Furthermore, since rational communication among members of a scientific community presupposes the absence of external and internal ideological constraints, the pursuit of knowledge is also guided by an interest in emancipation. Consequently, the primary interest underwriting critical theory—freedom from domination—is shown to be a necessary condition for the possibility of objective knowledge. Truth can be conceived only as an ideal consensus among all rational (i.e., emancipated) persons, who confront one another as equal participants in an open dialogue. It is principally for this reason that critical theory is accorded a privileged place by Habermas. For only in critical reflection do knowledge for the sake of emancipation and emancipation for the sake of knowledge coincide.

Psychoanalysis is the preferred model for methodical reflection because it combines objective causal explanation with subjective understanding. It provides a deep understanding of the real, but hidden or unconscious motives underlying behavior. Guided by general patterns of psychic development and self-understanding, psychoanalytic interpretation proceeds by explaining motives, which function like causes. Once the "story" behind the repressed motive is understood by the patient, the motive's power to coerce, or to influence behavior unconsciously and mechanically, is dissolved.

We noted above the practical problems encountered by Habermas in trying to extend the clinical relationship between analyst and patient to the social arena. By assuming the role of moral authority, the critical theorist removes herself/himself from dialogue with those who are presumed in advance to be deluded. Instead of exposing her/his own prejudices to reciprocal critique in open dialogue, she/he prefers to explain their behavior objectively; that is, as if they were things rather than persons. However, we also noted that this type of explanation may be justified, given the mechanical refusal of ideologically duped persons to respond freely and openly to themselves and others. Moreover, the critical theorist does check her/his diagnoses against feedback from others. In the next chapter we shall see that Habermas's later formulation of critical theory deliberately avoids any hint of dogmatism. The critique of ideology yields to a critique of social reification. In the latter case, the critical theorist no longer attempts to hypothetically reconstruct the true interests of social agents, but rather seeks to explain the causes that prevent agents from doing so on their own.

Questions still remain about the methodological status of *Knowledge and Human Interests*. Is this work an example of critical theory? If so, it doesn't seem to possess the same structure as Freudian psychoanalysis. Habermas himself confirms this suspicion when he characterizes it as pure reflection, which moves immanently within the philosophical tradition it seeks to criticize. But lacking an objectifying, scientific explanation of social facts, how could it be fully critical? Might not this entire tradition be burdened with ideological presuppositions? In particular, might it not privilege the cognitive relationship, between knowing subject and known object, to the detriment of the communicative relationship between subjects? As we shall see, these questions lead Habermas to reformulate the relationship between theory and practice in a way that privileges communication over cognition. This reformulation, however, initially appears to jeopardize the intimate connection between philosophical reflection and emancipatory practice he once sought to defend. It remains to be seen whether this connection can be reestablished and, if so, how.

NOTES

1. Habermas's most well-known advocates include the German social theorists Albrecht Wellmer and Axel Honneth (and to a lesser extent, Karl-Otto Apel, who has exercised an equally powerful influence on Habermas); the Anglo-American political philosophers Thomas McCarthy, Richard Bernstein, Anthony Giddens, and Fred Dallmayr; and younger scholars such as Seyla Benhabib and Nancy Fraser.

2. M. Horkheimer, "Traditional and Critical Theory," in *Critical Theory: Selected Essays* (New York: Seabury, 1972), 194. The relevant sections of this essay are reprinted in *Critical Theory: The Essential Readings* (*CTER*).

3. For a concise statement of Habermas's indebtedness to Horkheimer, see his preliminary outline of *Knowledge and Human Interests*, "Knowledge and Human Interests: A General Perspective," reprinted in *Critical Theory: The Essential Readings* (*CTER*).

4. Habermas also has in mind the school of "critical rationalism" associated with Karl Popper, with whom he and Adorno debated in the early sixties. See T.W. Adorno et. al., *The Positivist Dispute in German Sociology*, trans. G. Adey and D. Frisby (London: Heinemann, 1976) for Habermas's and Adorno's contributions to the debate.

5. J. Habermas, "The Analytical Theory of Social Science and Dialectics," in *The Positivist Dispute in German Sociology*, trans. G. Adey and D. Frisby (London: Heinemann, 1976), pp. 131–62.

6. *Ibid.*

7. Habermas accepts Karl Popper's revisionism of the positivist theory of experimental verification. According to Popper, the empirical worth of a general law is proportional to the number of predictions derivable therefrom, that could in theory (if not in actual practice) be falsified. Since there are an indefinite number of conceivable and potentially observable states of affairs that might falsify, or disconfirm, a general law, no law or theoretical axiom can ever be confirmed, or proven infallible in light of future observations. Furthermore, Habermas would reject that version of the subsumption model of explanation, which construes general laws as ordinary hypothetical conditionals. Such a construal is intimately related to a positivist logic of discovery which holds that causal laws denote regular (but accidental) conjunctions of events based upon passive observation. For Habermas, on the contrary, causal laws have the form of counterfactual conditions possessing the form, "If X had not occurred,

then Y would not have occurred," where X is both necessary and sufficient for Y. Counterfactual conditional statements, he argues, are essentially grounded in operational modes of activity, which isolate true causal (necessitating) factors from those that are merely conjunctive (associative) and accidental. See below for his discussion of Peirce.

8. J. Habermas, "Technology and Science as Ideology," p. 99. This essay is reprinted in *CTER*.

9. Technologically useful knowledge frees us from the necessity of having to toil as well as from the fatalism of natural events, that appear to be beyond our control due to their unpredictability. This type of "emancipation" is qualitatively distinct from the kind of emancipation provided by reflective knowledge, which is explicitly guided by an interest in emancipation as such, independent of survival goals.

10. J. Habermas, "Technology and Science as Ideology," p. 87.

11. See H.-G. Gadamer, *Truth and Method* (New York: Crossroad, 1975), pp. 274–341.

12. *Ibid.*, 192–274; Habermas, p. 182.

13. Unlike Marx and Marcuse, Habermas does not appeal to the "master-slave" dialectic in Hegel's *Phenomenology of Spirit*, in support of the communicative structure of moral development. With its emphasis on labor as self-objectification and contemplative self-appropriation, the master-slave dialectic, he feels, best approximates the objectifying structure of technical domination and control. Unlike the *Phenomenology's* impersonal dialectic of World Spirit, the dialectic contained in the earlier *Philosophy of Spirit* of the Jena period (1802–1803), Habermas claims, locates the formation of individual moral identity in the interpersonal (love) relationship of the family. This relationship is distinguished from the subject-object relationship involved in labor, in that two autonomous subjects (husband and wife) recognize one another in a higher *intersubjectivity*, represented by the child. Hegel explicitly compares this intersubjective mediation with the activity of *speech*. See J. Habermas, "Remarks on Hegel's Philosophy of Mind," *Theory and Practice*, trans. and ed. J. Viertel (Boston: Beacon, 1973), pp. 142–69; and G.W.F. Hegel, *System of Ethical Life and First Philosophy of Spirit*, trans. H.S. Harris, and T.M. Knox (Albany: State University of New York Press, 1979), pp. 231–35 and 244–45.

14. For Habermas's critique of a purely hermeneutic social science see his 1970 review of Gadamer's *Truth and Method*, in F. Dallmayr and T. McCarthy (eds.) *Understanding Social Inquiry* (Notre Dame: University of Notre Dame Press, 1977).

15. This objection was voiced by Gadamer in "The Scope and Function of Hermeneutical Reflection," in *Philosophical Hermeneutics*, ed. D. Linge (Berkeley: University of California Press, 1976). For Habermas's response, see "The Hermeneutic Claim to Universality," in J. Bleicher, *Contemporary Hermeneutics* (London, 1980).

16. J. Habermas, *Legitimation Crisis*, trans. T. McCarthy (Boston: Beacon, 1975), pp. 113–17. This selection is reprinted in *CTER*.

17. For a detailed discussion of Habermas's treatment of the theory/practice problem see the preface to the second edition of *Theory and Practice*.

SELECTED BIBLIOGRAPHY

Habermas, Jürgen. *Knowledge and Human Interests*. Trans. J. Shapiro. Boston: Beacon, 1971.

———*Theory and Practice*. Trans. J. Viertel. Boston: Beacon, 1973.

———*Toward a Rational Society. Student Protest, Science and Politics*. Trans. J. Shapiro. Boston: Beacon, 1970.

Horkheimer, Max. *Critical Theory*. New York: Herder and Herder, 1972.

Commentaries: Among the best commentaries of *Knowledge and Human Interests* are Garbis Kortian, *Metacritique* (Cambridge: Cambridge University Press, 1980; and Richard Keat, *The Politics of Social Theory* (Chicago: University of Chicago Press, 1981). The best study of Habermas's work prior to 1978 is Thomas McCarthy's *The Critical Theory of Jürgen Habermas* (Cambridge, Mass.: MIT Press, 1978). For an excellent discussion of the Marcuse/Habermas debate on science, technology, and emancipation, see C.F. Alford, *Science and the Revenge of Nature: Marcuse and Habermas* (Gainesville: University of Florida Press, 1985).

SEVEN

COMMUNICATION AND SOCIAL CRISIS: HABERMAS AND RECENT CRITICAL THEORY

In the preceding chapter, we noted some of the ways in which Habermas returns to the original conception of critical theory, as outlined by Horkheimer in the late thirties. While the idea of critical theory as an interdisciplinary synthesis of philosophy and science was never totally absent from the work of the Frankfurt School during the postwar period, much of their research became increasingly divorced from empirical analysis. This was especially so in the case of Adorno's late masterpieces, which focused on the unresolvable dialectical tensions inherent in critical theory. Rather than construct a well-grounded, systematic approach of the sort favored by Habermas, Adorno problematized the relationship, between universal concept and historical reality, philosophy and science, in ways that seemed to undermine any hope of realizing the Enlightenment's goal of unifying theory and practice. If anything, Adorno's brooding reflection on the debasement of individuality, freedom, and community in rationalized "mass" society, led him to doubt the possibility of any enlightened political practice that might escape this fate. This explains his withdrawal, his retreat into philosophical reflection on the aesthetic, as a recollection of the lost promise of a mimetic reconciliation of self and other, freedom and nature.

In comparison to Adorno's pessimism, Habermas's reappropriation of Horkheimer's model of critical theory seems much more positive and constructive. In general, he has sought to show that the dialectic, as diagnosed by Adorno, fails to address important conceptual distinctions. To begin with, Habermas's approach to critical theory is marked by a high degree of analytic precision and systematic closure. Not only is he careful to draw distinctions between different kinds of knowledge and rationality, but he tries to show how they are grounded in universal interests. Second, his approach displays a greater appreciation of the role played by empirical science in critical theory.

Indeed, *Knowledge and Human Interests* develops the idea of a critical theory by reflecting on the necessary relationship between science, emancipation, and ideological critique.

Since the late sixties Habermas has emphasized other differences with his former colleagues over the prospects of unifying theory and practice. He repudiates the argument advanced by Adorno and Horkheimer, that enlightenment or rationality, is inherently dialectical. The alienation of modern society, he contends, is less a function of reason (social rationalization) than it is of factors external to it. These factors pertain to the peculiar dynamics of capitalist and bureaucratic socialist societies, which undermine moral-practical reason by encouraging the one-sided growth of technological reasoning. The proper aim of critical theory is to expose these factors so that the full potential of the Enlightenment, the moral-practical interest as well as the instrumental-technological, can be realized. By doing so, critical theory can foster the growth of grass-roots democratic associations that will politicize a passive and apathetic public, thereby furthering greater autonomy and self-determination.

The above difference reflects a new approach to grounding critical theory. Instead of grounding critical theory in universal human interests, which regulate the acquisition of scientific knowledge, Habermas's approach articulates moral-practical competencies rooted in everyday communication. We have seen that this idea is implicit in some of the statements made by Adorno and Marcuse. The latter sought to recover a speculative notion of reason that would incorporate an idea of communicative solidarity and autonomy. However, instead of seeking this relationship in everyday language, which they thought to be ideologically distorted, they sought it in the aesthetic contemplation of works of art.

Habermas does not deny the potential of art to enlighten in this way. Yet, he doubts whether aesthetic contemplation fully transcends the subject-object relationship at the heart of objectifying, instrumental reason. Although everyday language is susceptible to ideological distortion, its underlying *structure*, he believes, nonetheless anticipates an *ideal speech situation*—in which full reciprocity, solidarity, and autonomy are achieved.

The most distinctive feature of Habermas's recent work has been his attempt to develop a *communicative ethic*. This ethic performs several critical functions. First, it advocates an expansion of participatory democracy in ways that serve to question current needs and property relations. Second, it provides an ideal model of democratic procedural justice, which can be used to question the fairness of existing social institutions. By using this model to reconstruct hypothetically the genuine, but suppressed, interests of social agents, Habermas hopes to ground a relatively precise method of ideology critique. Finally, it articulates universal emancipatory needs, whose resistance to basic social trends in late capitalist society, helps to explain the existence of trenchant social crises.

A NEW APPROACH TO THE GROUNDING PROBLEM

Habermas's communication ethic is part of a much larger *theory of communicative action*. This latter program grew out of several difficulties which attended *Knowledge and Human Interests*. Chief among these was the status of that work itself. If an interdisciplinary method of ideology critique of the sort exemplified by psychotherapy defines the essential structure of critical theory, then in what sense is *Knowledge and Human Interests* an example of critical theory? There is little doubt that it is critical of positivism, whose suppression of more radical forms of reflection and whose functionality in maintaining uncritical forms of social and historical research, can be construed as ideological in a broad sense. Yet, the critique of positivism proceeds in a manner that appears to have little in common with psychotherapeutic ideology critique.

The critique of positivism proceeds at two levels. First, it proceeds as a form of reflection that is immanent within the positivist tradition itself. In Peirce and Dilthey, positivism reveals its own inherent incoherency. Second, this purely historical reflection forces a turn toward a deeper, transcendental level of reflection. Positivism is refuted by revealing the necessary and universal interest structures underlying distinct forms of knowledge. These forms of critique—the one representing a historical interpretation of a tradition, the other a philosophical interpretation of knowledge as such—simply lack the moment of causal explanation and symptomalogical diagnosis characteristic of psychoanalysis.

Habermas eventually realized that *Knowledge and Human Interests* represented a form of critical reflection that differed, in fundamental respects, from the type of emancipatory reflection characteristic of psychotherapeutic ideology critique. The theory of cognitive interests failed to distinguish adequately between two sorts of reflection, emancipatory and theoretical. Habermas now claims that pure theoretical reflection of the sort carried out in *Knowledge and Human Interests* is not immediately guided by any practical interest, be it instrumental, moral-practical, or emancipatory. Above all, the sort of philosophically enlightened theoretical reflection undertaken in that work aims at reconstructing *necessary* and *universal* conditions for knowing, speaking, and acting. Yet, knowing what *must* be the case, in order for persons to speak or act, does not help us to decide what we *ought* to say or do. For example, just because communication is necessary for the possibility of coordinating interaction, transmitting culture, and achieving a sense of self-identity, doesn't mean that we have to always communicate with one another, or that our communication must always take the form of open dialogue. Nor does it mean that we have to organize our society freely and democratically. Thus, the pursuit of pure theoretical knowledge is neither directly guided by an emancipatory interest, nor directly produces emancipatory results.

Theoretical reflection must therefore be distinguished from emancipatory types of reflection, such as psychotherapy, aimed at dissolving historical forms of inner domination. Thus, there is no *direct* connection between theoretical knowledge and practical emancipation. Yet there is an *indirect* one. For example, psychotherapy and ideology critique rely on theoretical knowledge to reconstruct the basic mechanisms and institutional forces underlying repression. Second, insofar as moral theorizing ultimately depends on public communication for confirmation, it is more directly linked to political emancipation than, say, theorizing in natural science.

Knowledge and Human Interests was deficient in another respect as well. It presupposed a kind of philosophical reflection which, in Habermas's opinion, was perhaps too speculative—or too detached from empirical evidence and historical understanding—to ground a transcendental theory of cognitive interests. At that time, Habermas thought that philosophical reflection was qualitatively distinct from empirical science and historical understanding. It was its transcendence from changing historical conditions that enabled it to ground these types of knowledge in invariant orientations claiming absolute necessity and universality. However, even then Habermas recognized that knowledge-constitutive interests straddle the line separating the purely rational (necessary and universal) from the empirical (historically contingent). This is especially the case with the interest in emancipation.

The reader will recall that the interest in emancipation is not as directly implicated in world constitution and survival as either the technical or the moral-practical interest. Interest in emancipation emerges with the growth of class society and its forms of social domination. In order to claim a transcendental status for this interest Habermas had to assume further that emancipation was not only a necessary presupposition underlying reason, or knowledge, but that it was an end in itself. He had to assume, in other words, that the final goal of history—conceived as the progressive attainment of moral and cognitive knowledge—was not mere self-preservation and happiness, but universal freedom.

This assumption proved highly problematic. As Thomas McCarthy pointed out, Habermas's attempt to view the natural history of the human species as aspiring toward a higher purpose conflicted with Habermas's own account of nature as a world of objects. According to Habermas, nature can only be known as a coherent and lawful order insofar as it is constituted by our interest in technical control. This interest, however, is rationally satisfied to the extent that nature itself is subsumed under objectifying categories of causality and material substance. If nature, and by implication the natural evolution of the human species, only appear as rational and coherent under mechanistic categories, then Habermas's attempt to view the natural history of the human species as aspiring toward a final goal—as if it were itself a purposive agency—would appear to be wholly speculative and rationally indefensible.

Habermas was aware of this difficulty in writing *Knowledge and Human Interests*. "Cognitive interests," he tells us, "mediate the natural genesis of mankind with the logic of its cultural development" (*KHI*:196). Yet, in claiming that cognitive interests "derive both from nature and from the cultural break with nature," Habermas seems to want it both ways. That is, he wants to claim that the emancipatory interest, which ultimately underlies knowledge and reason, can be understood as a result of natural selection—a purely causal mechanism which explains the relative permanence of mutations in terms of their functional contribution to survival. And he wants to claim that this very same interest can be understood as both a transcendental condition and a transcendent goal of cultural history, insofar as this is conceived as rationally motivated by ideas.

Given the conceptual difficulties inherent in his attempt to ground the emancipatory interest, it is hardly surprising that Habermas would undertake to redefine the relationship between nature and culture, science and moral philosophy, more carefully. Though rather schematic, his most recent conception of transcendental philosophy as *rational reconstruction* seems to be the most sophisticated attempt by any critical theorist to lay out the subtle linkage between philosophy and science. To put it crudely, *rational reconstruction* interprets the intuitive or implicit knowledge of competent (speaking, acting, and knowing) subjects with an eye toward explicating the "deep structures" or formal, procedural rules by which speech, action, and knowledge are generated in the first place. These conditions are *historically emergent*. What endows them with a transcendental status—or universal validity—is just their abstract formal structure.

Rational reconstruction is subject to empirical or dialogical verification. Habermas notes that "the procedures employed in constructive proposals, in gathering data, are in some ways like the nomological sciences."[1] Yet, a cursory reading of his writings, as McCarthy has shown, indicates that the formulation of reconstructive hypotheses relies at least as much on personal reflections, conceptual analyses, and interpretative appropriation of sociological and philosophical traditions. In any case, rational reconstruction differs depending on whether the competencies are natural (the result of natural selection) or cultural (the result of rational reflection). Empirical confirmation of lower stages of cognitive and moral development can achieve high levels of probability, since the competencies in question, such as the coordination of social perspectives by means of shared symbols and the ability to perceive objects as invariant through perspectival changes in their aspects, are organically, or naturally, based. The higher—nonnatural or reflexive— stages of development, however, cannot be confirmed through empirical observation, but are themselves the outcome of theoretical and practical conversations between competent test subjects and theoreticians. Here rational reconstruction attempts to make explicit, through questioning and systematically ordered examples, specific competencies which enable the ranking of different levels of moral and cognitive problem-solving. Regardless of whether rational reconstruction proceeds empirically or dialogically, it always remains fallible, or based on potentially falsifiable generalizations derived from potentially changeable responses. As such, rational reconstruction bridges the gap between theory and practice, philosophy and historical/empirical science, "ought" and "is," by playing off philosophical speculation, scientific data, and the informed judgment of everyday common sense in a kind of critical give-and-take.

Before concluding our discussion of the differences between the idea of critical theory elaborated in *Knowledge and Human Interests* and that contained in his most recent theory of communicative action, let us briefly recall the suspicion on which we concluded the preceding chapter. The earlier theory, I noted, represented a type of reflection that remained within the confines of an interpretative appropriation of a philosophical tradition whose principal task was to articulate the relationship between a knowing subject who is seeking cognitive mastery over some object, be it nature, language, or the subject's own identity. Consequently, in attempting to ground critical theory in the necessary and universal conditions of knowledge the earlier program also privileged this relationship.

Even the intersubjective dialogue between interpreter and text could be understood in this manner. The dialogue remains simulated, so that the interpreter as subject ultimately speaks on behalf of the text as object. The new program, by contrast, aims at substituting the intersubjective relationship of speaker and listener for the subject-object relationship of knowledge. This approach to grounding the emancipatory and communal ideals underwriting critical theory proves to be more successful, Habermas claims, since communication implicates both the autonomy and reciprocity of speakers oriented toward achieving unconstrained agreement.

IDEOLOGY, DEMOCRACY, AND LEGITIMATION: PRELIMINARY OBSERVATIONS TOWARD GROUNDING A COMMUNICATION ETHIC

I shall have more to say about the grounding of critical theory below. Before addressing that issue, however, I would like to turn to another side of the theory/practice problem, namely, the problem of resolving the tension between individual freedom and democratic self-determination that informs the political heritage of the Enlightenment. This problem is addressed by Habermas in his idea of a communication ethic, that he develops within the general framework of a critique of Western democracy. According to Habermas, democracy in advanced industrial society has functioned to procure mass loyalty at the cost of limiting the scope of rational self-determination to passive suffrage. This limitation is justified by appeal to the inherent egoism of human nature and the fundamental antagonism of particular interests.

Conflicting needs, interests, values, and conceptions of the good are assumed to be little more than expressions of personal preference and circumstantial caprice. Every opinion is held to be as valid as any other, so disagreement and conflict are normalized. This pluralism of particular interests encourages tolerance of different points of view. However, it also encourages competition among conflicting interests as the only mechanism for resolving serious disputes between them. The state protects private opinions as it protects private property. Yet, conflict between opinions, like conflict between property rights, is often resolved in favor of the most powerful.

Liberal democracy permits the most powerful to win at the polls because of the tacit assumption that elected legislators will enact laws that are in the interest of the majority, if not of everyone. But this is surely questionable. It is far from obvious that all opinions, even the most prevalent among them, are equally valid. Likewise, it cannot be assumed that all property rights are equally sanctified in view of the common welfare. What is truly in the common interest of all concerned would surely constitute the basis for an opinion that would claim a greater authority than others, one capable of adjudicating conflicts between competing property rights in a manner favoring justice rather than power. However, attempts to institutionalize democratic procedures aimed at discovering common interests goes against the pluralistic, conflict- and competition-oriented assumptions built into the present system. Such attempts are thought to be utterly futile, not to be undertaken for fear of inciting public intrusion into the private affairs of citizens.

Thus, the preservation of private property against public encroachment is the unquestioned *philosophical* presupposition underlying an important libertarian argument in favor of restricting democratic participation to passive suffrage. However, there is a *political* justification as well. Because "vulgar" forms of liberal political thought prejudge the irrationality of needs and interests, they tacitly assume that, for example, the needs of the coal industry to seek a profit at the expense of polluting the environment are just as "valid" (or no less "invalid") than the equally "arbitrary" needs of citizens for fresh air and acid-free rain forests.

Since the state has assumed responsibility for balancing the interests of private business and public welfare, it is not surprising that political debate regarding the rationality of particular interests is suppressed. The structural concealment of conflict is indispensable for procuring mass loyalty. The latter, in turn, is manufactured by a system which encourages apathy (especially among the poor and less educated) and discourages radical questioning. It deflects attention away from public debate about the validity of existing private-property rights to debate about candidates and their personalities. Participation is subsequently restricted to passive suffrage, in which elected officials and their appointees go about the task of drawing up *compromise* legislation which, more often than not, reflects the financial power of elite lobbies rather than the will of the people.

What Habermas calls *pseudo-compromises* ideologically prejudge the irreducible particularity, subjectivity, and validity of conflicting interests, all the while taking for granted the consensus supportive of the status quo. Since, to use the above example, the coal industry's interests and the environmentalist's interests are assumed to be equally valid, legislators representing the interests of these two groups work out compromise legislation providing for a few (mostly cosmetic) restrictions on the production and consumption of coal. By taking for granted the equal validity of conflicting interests, the system as it presently exists suppresses impartial debate over radical quality-of-life interests behind a strategic negotiation aimed at achieving a non-threatening *balance of power* favorable to the ruling elite.

Power, Habermas is fond of saying, does not constitute a sufficient basis for motivating voluntary compliance—unless, of course, all parties to the negotiation still disagree, *after* submitting their private interests to *impartial* public discussion aimed at reaching agreement on interests that are to each and everyone's advantage. Without having first participated in such discussion, why should I voluntarily consent to obey laws that reflect the powerful interests of an influential minority? Habermas admits that, in modern pluralistic societies, compromises, in which some private interests prevail over others, "possess a wholly undiminished worth." But, he adds, their worth is dependent on impartially determining which of the competing interests are compatible with the long-term interest of all concerned. Any compromise that hasn't been reached through fair, democratic procedures, designed to test the compatibility of particular interests with respect to the common interests of all, is a pseudo-compromise. Compromise legislation between the coal industry and the environmental lobby is of this sort. For, although there currently exists no consensus regarding the just distribution and control of wealth or the protection of natural resources, who's to say that one wouldn't arise, if all persons submitted their interests and needs—in short, their personal life-styles and notions of the good life—to impartial dialogical critique?

It is this line of reasoning that compels Habermas to conclude that the suppression of discussion regarding *generalizable* interests belies liberal democracy's own claim to *legitimacy*. Such a regime would be legitimate, or worthy of being recognized as morally binding authority, only if it institutionalized procedures for achieving fair results (i.e., just laws and policies that were in the *real* interest of *each* and *everyone* concerned). Such results, however, would have to be the outcome of a fair and impartial discussion among equally competent and privileged speakers aimed primarily at reaching rational consensus on substantive issues of common interest.[2]

As Rousseau noted, a truly equitable and rational democracy demands direct participation on the part of its citizens. So long as others are delegated to speak on our behalf, we fail to exercise a fundamental right to self-determination. From a moral perspective, representative democracy can begin to approximate this ideal only as long as it is guided by the informed consent of a rational and critical public. Habermas believes that democracy ought to establish procedures by which citizens can *reach agreement* on some *concrete* vision of *their* good. Unlike Rousseau, however, Habermas does not assume that general interests preexist public discussion. The uncritical postulation of a General Will can justify the suppression of particular differences—and thereby justify the tyranny of a majority over a minority—just as easily as the postulation of unresolvable differences can justify the suppression of common interests. Consequently, Habermas argues that rational debate should be aimed, not at discovering some preexisting General Will, but at determining whether common interests can be brought about by *transforming current* needs which frustrate the attainment of long-term happiness for all. Democracy should not merely register areas of agreement and disagreement that can be *passively represented* in elected bodies; it should also serve the *active* goal of *critical enlightenment*.

Habermas's discourse ethic is best understood, then, as a deep justification for grass-roots democracy. Rather than advance a concrete conception of the good, it encourages the proliferation of political discourses in local and small-scale associations. It is hoped that such discourses will generate an autonomous and critical public opinion aimed at radicalizing discussion regarding generalizable interests at the party-politics level.

In a recent essay, "Justice and Solidarity" (hereafter *JS*), Habermas asserts that the basic intuition embodied in a discourse ethic is that, "under the moral point of view, one must be able to test whether a norm or a mode of action could be generally accepted by those affected by it, such that their acceptance would be rationally motivated and hence uncoerced."[3] Notions of autonomy and universalizability play as central a role in this ethic as they do in Kant's. Yet, it is Habermas's contention that these notions are better articulated by an ethic, which doesn't exclude substantive needs and goods as grounds of moral reasoning.

According to Kant, persons are only free when they interrupt the causal influence of particular interests and desires in the name of reason, which commands forbearance from all actions, except those which can be willed consistently as a universal law. Interests and desires no doubt shape the formulation of substantive maxims of action, but not their critical evaluation and justification. Consequently, there can be no empirical motive for acting morally in Kant's system.

Understandably, Kant's purification of the moral will was criticized by his successors as incoherent. On one hand, freedom remains an indeterminate transcendent idea. On the other hand, the real content of moral conduct—the interests and desires which motive us to act—are accepted as given, or causally predetermined.

Habermas largely accepts Hegel's critique of Kant's separation of the empirical, "needy" self from the transcendent, "free" self. It therefore comes as no surprise that his line of thought so closely parallels the Hegelian pragmatism of George Herbert Mead, who, along with Charles Peirce, pioneered the idea of an ideal community of communication as an alternative to the subject-based philosophy of Kant. Mead insisted that moral motivation resides in everyday embodied speech. Simply stated, we must tacitly adopt a moral stance whenever we seek to communicate with others, and we must communicate with others in coordinating our actions and shaping our identities. Mead observes that standards of moral reflection, like the needs, interests, and desires that comprise the motives and ends of action generally, are not innate in the individual psyche, but reflect shared interpretations. Because interpretations of needs comprise the basic standards and motives of ethical life, they, too, must be included among the candidates for rational moral deliberation, along with maxims and principles. Not only must socially interpreted needs and interests function as reasons in accepting or rejecting particular maxims, but they must enter into a process of critical evaluation. Without this *cognitivist* assumption, it would make no sense to distinguish rational interests—or interests that are universally valid—from interests that are merely privatistic, or worse, irrational. Yet, this distinction can only be made in a public conversation, in which freedom from prejudice is secured through critical questioning by others.[4]

The same considerations that lead Habermas to embrace a communicative reformulation of autonomy, also compel him to adopt a communicative conception of Kant's procedure for testing the universal validity of norms. In Kant's theory, the universalizability procedure is authorized by the pre-established harmony of isolated agents, who possess the same rational faculties. Since Kant privileges private moral conscience, he must limit practical reasoning to the *consistency testing* of substantive maxims. Basically, consistency testing rules out maxims whose universalizability, or application as a general law governing all of humanity, would be incompatible with the basic trust necessary for social cooperation of any kind. Strictly speaking, it *forbids* only the most grievous *violations of right*—murder, stealing, fraud, and so on—consonant with the equal and unconditional *protection* of each person's dignity and autonomy. It, therefore, sanctions as morally permissible arrangements which, though not in everyone's interests, are nonetheless compatible with very abstract conceptions of equal respect for all. Thus, laws against begging, loitering, and even collective bargaining would appear to be permissible on Kantian grounds.

In Habermas's opinion, Kant's bracketing of all empirical questions, concerning the consequences of norms as these bear upon the happiness of those affected, limits and distorts the procedure of universalizability. It legitimates laws and norms which may be detrimental to the interests of some persons. This defect is ostensibly remedied by a communicative ethic, in which "a well-founded consensus is made dependent on considerations of the consequences that a contested general practice might have for the satisfaction of the interests of all concerned" (*JS*:43). Thus, *rational consensus* replaces *lawful consistency* as a criterion of moral right. To paraphrase Thomas McCarthy, it shifts the emphasis from what *each* person independent of any consideration of historical interests can will to be a *general law*, to what *all*, in agreement with others on such interests, can accept as a *universally binding norm*.

Most importantly, however, a communication ethic seeks to bring social norms into harmony with *rational* interests, which may not have yet found popular acceptance. The existing consensus, regarding which needs and interests ought to be pursued, may be ideologically constrained (recall Marcuse's discussion of how the military-industrial complex colludes with the mass media and educational system in manipulating the way we think about ourselves). Consequently, a communication ethic must specify conditions under which an impartial and unconstrained consensus can come about. That means it must provide the criteria for distinguishing valid agreements from invalid ones. By the same token, it must establish criteria for distinguishing true (rational) interests from false (ideological) interests.

The ultimate aim of a communication ethic, then, is to bring about conditions of rational participatory democracy, in which existing needs can be critically assessed and transformed. For only by publicly discussing our needs can we begin to assess their impact on the lives of others. And, only by assessing their impact on the lives of others, can we determine their rationality, or compatibility with the general interest of all concerned.

People will be motivated to enter into democratic discussions such as the above because, as speakers, they are tacitly required to. Because they are accountable to others for what they say and do, they must always be prepared to justify—through the giving of reasons in argumentation—the beliefs underlying their conduct. It is Habermas's contention, however, that the very concept of argumentative justification already implies certain rights and obligations that *precede* discussion.

Habermas reconstructs this concept by appealing to both the shared—but largely implicit—intuitions of competent speakers and the theoretical hypotheses of philosophers, such as Stephen Toulmin, who appeals to a pragmatic account of argumentative validity as a more viable alternative to deductive or inductive approaches. Viewed from this perspective, conversations, or what Habermas calls "discourses," replace propositional inferences as the primary concern of logic. It is axiomatic for Habermas that discourses typically arise whenever the justice of a norm, the sincerity of an expressed intention, or the truth of a cognitive belief is disputed. Claims to justice and truth are of special interest to him, since, whenever we assert that something is true or right, we imply that all other persons should agree with us. Thus, consensus, not foundational deduction, functions as the touchstone for truth and justice in Habermas's discursive logic. And, it is consensus which bridges the gap between contingency and necessity, particularity and universality, factuality and normativity in discourse. Just as the principle of induction, applied under controlled conditions, enables scientists to agree on the factual necessity and universality of causal relations, so, too, under controlled conditions approximating complete impartiality and fairness, the *moral principle of universalizability* (*U*) enables us to agree factually on the consequences, favorable or otherwise, of norms, in a manner that is itself normatively binding.[5] In other words, we are entitled to infer an "ought" (e.g., Norm X is right) from an "is" (e.g., We agree that norm X is in our universal interests), *to the extent that the procedure used in reaching agreement is fair—guaranteeing to all the freedom and equality necessary for arriving at an impartial (just) result.*

U can bridge the gap between "is" and "ought," because, as Habermas formulates it in "Discourse Ethic: Notes to a Program of Justification" (hereafter *DE*), *U* states that a norm is justified only when "the consequences and side effects for the satisfaction of the interests of *every* individual, which are expected to result from a *general* conformity to it, can be accepted by all *without compulsion*."[6] Stated somewhat paradoxically, it is the pragmatic conditions securing the impartiality and universality of discourse which endows factual consensus with unconditional prescriptive force. Adopting the recommendation of Robert Alexy, Habermas states these conditions as follows:

1. Each and every person capable of speech and action may participate in discourses.

2.(a) Each and every person may call into question any proposal.

2.(b) Each and every person may introduce any proposal into the discourse.

2.(c) Each and every person may express his attitudes and needs.

3. No one ought to be prevented from exercising the rights listed under 1. and 2. by constraints internal or external to discourse (*DE*:99)

Taken together, the above rules define an *ideal speech situation*, which mandates equal moral autonomy for any competent speaker whatsoever. This means that, whenever anyone claims that a norm is universally binding, he or she implies three things: first, that anyone potentially affected by the adoption of a norm—a class of people whose geographical and historical boundaries remain essentially indeterminate—would agree with all others that it was in the interest of each and every one of them; second, that they would do so under argumentative conditions providing equal opportunity; and third, that they would do so freely, unobstructed by ideological prejudices, temporal limitations, and external domination—be it cultural, social, political, or economic.[7]

Before proceeding to discuss the ethical implications of the ideal speech situation, let me briefly note an important addition Habermas has recently made in it that touches upon the question of individual rights and social democracy. Habermas now claims that the justice, or equal rights, guaranteed to individuals in the ideal speech situation, cannot be conceived without *solidarity*.[8] To quote Habermas:

From the perspective of communication theory, there emerges instead a close connection between concern for the welfare of one's fellow man and interest in the general welfare: the identity of the group is reproduced through intact relationships of mutual recognition. Thus the perspective complementing that of equal treatment of individuals is not benevolence but solidarity. This principle is rooted in the realization that each person must take responsibility for the other because as consociates all must have an interest in the integrity of their shared life context in the same way. Justice conceived deontologically requires solidarity as its reverse side . . . *Justice* concerns the equal freedoms of unique and self-determining individuals, while *solidarity* concerns the welfare of consociates who are intimately linked in an intersubjectively shared form of life—and thus also to the maintenance of the integrity of this form of life itself. Moral norms cannot protect one without the other: they cannot protect the equal rights and freedoms of the individual without protecting the welfare of one's fellow man and the community to which the individuals belong (*JS*:47).

The complementary relationship between individual rights (moral autonomy) and solidarity (willingness to submit one's personal interests to public critique with the aim of reaching consensus on interests that are valid for everyone) is important to bear in mind. Individual rights without solidarity don't get us beyond current libertarian conceptions of democracy, in which private interests compete for political dominance, without the least concern being paid to the common welfare. Solidarity without individual rights, however, restricts the freedom of individuals to refuse participating in conversations which they feel are ideologically biased, unequal, or unfair.

Habermas's notion of an ideal speech situation is significant because it provides him with an example of a *formal* (procedural) model of reasoning which is moral rather than instrumental. Contrary to Weber and first-generation critical theorists, ultimate choices regarding interests, values, and ends need not be conceived as reducible to rational instrumental calculations of consequences, on one hand; or, unconditional commands stemming from some wholly transcendent, irrational faith, on the other. On the contrary, rational moral choice may be understood as a collective achievement of consensual communication and need interpretation under universally valid—and hence, purely formal—conditions. Specifically, the ideal speech situation provides a procedural interpretation of freedom, equality, and reciprocity which defines *justice* in terms of *formal rules of democratic fairplay*. Moreover, since these rules represent a bonafide type of formal rationality, their institutionalization in democratic organizations is certainly possible; and, therefore, may be compatible with the institutionalization of instrumental types of rationality in science, industry, etc.

According to Habermas, formal rules of democratic procedure are so abstract that one cannot directly infer from them any concrete prescriptions regarding the just organization of society. If one could, the organization would require such stringent conditions of freedom and equality that any humanly possible democratic institution would seem unjust by comparison. It would be absurd to condemn every democratic polity that failed to live up to counterfactual ideals of freedom and equality. For this reason, a discourse ethic cannot privilege directly over representative democracy. Such organizational questions can only be resolved in discourse, by persons faced with very specific circumstances. Even very imperfect forms of democracy may be justifiable under fairly common conditions. Habermas remarks that, in modern complex societies, conflicts of interest are unavoidable. Yet, these conflicts require highly specialized forms of legal regulation. In this instance, bureaucracy exercises a limiting influence with respect to democracy; and representative democracy exercises a limiting influence with respect to direct democracy (*JS*:52).

Of course, participatory democracy should exercise a reciprocal influence on partisan political elections and government administration. It is not unthinkable that, if persons in modern societies were to deliberate rationally about what kinds of arrangements would make them happier, they might prefer more democracy to bureaucracy—a preference that just might entail leading simpler, more egalitarian life-styles built around tightly woven communities. Yet, the main imperative which follows from a discourse ethic is nothing quite this specific. We—that is, those of us living in modern "rationalized" societies—ought to engage in, and help encourage the proliferation of, discourses in which we rationally deliberate about our needs. This imperative follows from the necessary link between the publicly acknowledged legitimacy of institutions, their instantiation of just norms satisfying the general interests of everyone affected, and the idea of democratic procedure—conceived on the model of public discourse—as the privileged means for rationally deliberating about general interests.

Therefore, the imperative is provisional. It is provisional on the existence of a necessary connection between communication and democracy: We cannot refuse to engage in communication systematically without denying ourselves the recognition from others necessary to sustain a stable, rational identity; but we cannot engage in communication without satisfying mutual expectations of rational accountability, which obligates us to justify our actions, values, and needs in public discourse. Second, it is provisional on the existence of boundary conditions that assure those participating that their rights will be protected. This is especially important to bear in mind since true equality, freedom, and solidarity are at best approximated in real life. It cannot always be demanded of the oppressed that they foresake the security of weapons for the insecurity of consensus oriented negotiations with their oppressors!

If Habermas's discourse ethic did nothing else but show that we are provisionally obligated to engage in, and encourage the proliferation of, democratic discourses, that in itself would be a considerable achievement. Yet, for many persons, it might not be enough. For that reason alone, it is important that we bear in mind some other ethical implications that Habermas's discourse ethic has. Three come to mind: First, the discourse ethic can function as a "regulative" idea guiding the economic, political, social, and cultural reform of society. Second, it can serve to establish a very general warrant for adopting a "moral point of view," which in turn warrants the recognition of basic rights and obligations. Finally, it can provide both a warrant and a procedure for ideology critique.

As a regulative idea, the discourse ethic seems to imply a non-specific goal to be achieved. The goal—the establishment of a just society—cannot be defined in advance of actual historical struggles revolving around the reform of specific institutions. Yet, it does seem to suggest that the general direction of reform—the democratization of society—would, perhaps, require greater equality in the distribution of resources, skills, and opportunities necessary for including everyone as full, equal participants in democratic discourses. This goal may not be as specific as even Marx's vague idea of a communist society. It may even be less utopian, in that it may not necessarily require the abolition of all classes, the passing away of the state bureaucracy, or the implementation of a particular distribution of wealth. Still, it does capture the idea of social justice and solidarity, which Marx's ideal was aiming toward.

Habermas's discourse ethic is also intended as a deep justification and interpretation of the moral point of view. That is to say, it shows why we ought to regard the interests of others as possessing a weight equal to our own; and it shows how this equal consideration of interests is best captured by democratic procedures ensuring justice and solidarity. This use of the discourse ethic is important because Habermas wants to stake out a sphere of individual rights and obligations that is less immune to acceptance or rejection based on contingent consequences. If basic rights and obligations were contingent on actual agreements regarding shifting constellations of "need interpretation," they would forfeit their universality and unconditionality.

Following this line of reasoning, the weight of a discourse ethic falls less on the side of consensus—or what persons might happen to agree were basic rights and duties—than on the side of procedure: what everyone must recognize as a basic right or duty simply in order to engage in discourse at all. The idea behind this shift in emphasis seems sensible enough: certain basic rights and duties, such as the granting of symmetrical opportunities to speak, cannot be critically rejected by participants in discourse without committing a "performative contradiction." For, it is just these rights and duties that comprise the necessary rules for the possibility of conversing in such a way that only the force of the better argument—not prejudice, coercion, or special advantage—prevails.

There are, of course, certain limits to this interpretation of the discourse ethic. First, it cannot show that everyone is always and unconditionally obligated to respect the rights and duties constitutive of discourse, since there are occasions when we are permitted to exclude ourselves from discourse. Real inequalities in power may warrant the adoption of a strategic, rather than a moral attitude. Second, it would appear that whatever rights and duties are held to be constitutive of discourse must be interpreted in such a way as to avoid any concrete organizational implications. Yet, such an interpretation is problematic. If Habermas's discourse ethic doesn't pretend to prejudge the concrete needs of historical agents, how can it privilege certain individual freedoms?

Perhaps we must distinguish the *idea* of basic rights and obligations constitutive of discourse from its concrete interpretation, in the form of specific "legislative" proposals. The basic rights and obligations that flow from a communicatively grounded moral point of view are very abstract and, one might add, highly utopian. Take the principle that all persons affected by the implementation of a given policy have a right to discuss it with legislators and other citizens. The inclusion of all persons in face-to-face debates about such policies would be difficult, if not impossible, to implement in a modern complex society such as ours. Just imagine how difficult it would be for all rational adult Americans to converse with one another about a simple tax proposal!

The idea of basic rights, then, has to be understood as a regulative idea guiding democratic reform, rather than as a specific set of rights and duties. Paradoxically, this implies that we can debate about the specific interpretation and justification of this idea in discourse, even though, while doing so, we are necessarily obligated to presuppose some provisional interpretation of it as (temporarily) beyond question. As Seyla Benhabib notes, the trick is to "bracket them (the provisional rights and duties) in order to challenge them but (not to) suspend them altogether."[9] Whether this means what Benhabib thinks it does—that it is their prior implication in discourse, not their universal acceptance by all those affected, that validates them—is another question altogether. By conceding that we might, under certain circumstances, be compelled to challenge them for the sake of possibly reinterpreting them, do we not imply that their validity is contingent on consensus, after all?

Still, there is one way to understand this validating relationship without necessarily making the idea of basic rights and duties contingent on unstable agreements. Habermas's claim, that basic rights and duties in general—however we choose to interpret them—are universally valid, is to be understood as a hypothesis: If the conditions of an ideal speech situation were ever obtained, perfectly rational persons would unanimously agree that basic speech rights and duties would be in everyone's interest. Of course, these conditions will never obtain, since they would mandate the inclusion of all competent speakers—past, present, and future—as well as the achievement of perfectly transparent self-understanding, univocality of meaning, and finality of what, in principle, would be an interminable discourse.

This last observation leads directly to a consideration of the third use to which the discourse ethic might be put. Even if the designs underwriting "ideal conversations" are impossible to realize, we can still think of them as "monological" thought experiments for testing substantive proposals. For Habermas, "when it is a question of examining norms with a genuinely universal domain of validity, that is, norms in the strict sense, this idea is purely regulative," in the sense that arguments are "played out in 'the internal forum' " (*JS*:41).

Let us leave aside the fact that, by proposing a private use of the discourse ethic, Habermas has forfeited at least some, though perhaps not all, of the advantages that were to accrue to it in comparison to its Kantian counterpart. What moral guidance might a purely personal use of the ideal speech situation provide?

If we are to accept the verdict of Agnes Heller and Albrecht Wellmer, not much. Heller argues that "what we get is a *substantive limitation* placed on our intellectual intuitions: We as individuals, should only claim universal validity for those moral norms which we can assume would be accepted by everyone as valid in an ideal speech situation of symmetric reciprocity."[10] Both she and Wellmer argue that the idealistic features of the ideal speech situation render it virtually useless as a test procedure for guiding moral conduct. How can individuals, faced with moral decisions here and now, possibly calculate how an unlimited community of persons would respond to a given norm, under conditions of perfect reciprocity and freedom, unlimited by time, and with full consciousness of all consequences and side effects, as these bear upon a potentially unstable context of needs and interests? It is better, they argue, to think of the discourse ethic as a principle of political legitimation, applicable on a local basis with respect to shared but non-universalizable interests.

Indeed, Habermas explicitly conceives the ideal speech situation as providing a warrant and procedure for testing the legitimacy of specific social arrangements. Given the constraints distorting actual discourses—ideological as well as economic, social, political, and cultural—the critical theorist is entitled to question the validity of any actual set of institutions and laws. Of course, there is a danger in suspecting every shared understanding—including language—as possibly instantiating a constrained consensus or pseudo-compromise. However, in response to Gadamer's objection, that the ideal speech situation authorizes us to refuse to converse with others, Habermas points out that refusal to converse and, therewith, the right to adopt a critical posture, is only justified whenever there are good empirical reasons to suspect that a shared understanding is, in fact, ideologically constrained (e.g., in those instances where conflicts of interest appear manifest).[11] For this reason, the moral injunction to engage in ideology critique remains purely hypothetical.

From a procedural perspective, the ideal speech situation does not really specify a criterion for distinguishing illegitimate from legitimate norms, universalizable from non-universalizable interests, otherwise all existing social institutions would be condemned as unjust. Instead, it provides a procedure for hypothetically testing whether existing norms and institutions correspond to the rational needs of those affected. The question the critical theorist must then ask is

how would the members of a social system, at a given stage in the development of productive forces, have collectively and bindingly interpreted their needs (and which norms would they have accepted as justified) if they could and would have decided on an organization of social intercourse through discursive will-formation, with adequate knowledge of the limiting conditions and functional imperatives of their society?[12]

The "internal" or "monological" simulation of rational dialogue, in the manner suggested above, enables the critical theorist to hypothetically postulate which social arrangements represent true compromises (i.e., fairly established balances of power between competing private interests)—as distinct from pseudo-compromises—and which represent agreements instantiating universal interests. Whether and, to what extent, existing property relations are actually unjust, cannot be decided simply by comparing them to some ideal society, which would perfectly approximate the ideal speech situation. Persons who enter discourse are neither perfectly rational nor perfectly harmonious in their needs. Consequently, Habermas's discourse ethic is best seen as a recommendation to institute participatory democratic discourses at a grass-roots level, however imperfect they may be. Only under these conditions can people define their needs rationally, develop their reflective competencies collectively, regulate their property relations freely, and choose with full consciousness those very specific rights and duties that conform to their sense of justice, given their peculiar historical circumstances.

THE GROUNDING OF A COMMUNICATIVE ETHIC: HABERMAS'S THEORY OF SOCIAL EVOLUTION

In the conclusion of chapter six, I noted that Habermas's recent philosophy has de-emphasized the role of ideology critique in favor of a critique of social reification. Today, Habermas is less interested in criticizing the falseness of needs prevalent in modern capitalism than he is of exposing capitalism's destruction of communicative contexts necessary for fostering a democratic culture. With the withering away of traditional authority, rationalized society bestows on individuals an ever-greater responsibility in deciding for themselves what needs, interests, and values they should hold. The need to be self-determining and, therewith, the need to form democratic associations, in which the interests and values constituting one's identity are publicly formed, has become more and more integral to the modern psyche. The proper task of critical theory is, therefore, twofold: to show how a communication ethic, already deeply implicated in the rational culture of the West, designates the ultimate goal of moral evolution; and to show how tendencies inherent in modern capitalism undermine the emancipatory and communal aspects of this culture, thereby generating social crises.

This section will address the first of these tasks: the demonstration of the necessity and universality of a communication ethic as the evolutionary terminus of moral rationality. The first part of this demonstration focuses on the way in which the universalizability principle, as well as the moral ideals of freedom, equality, reciprocity, and justice, are embedded in necessary and universal structures of everyday communication.

The heart of Habermas's theory of communication is that portion which deals with the necessary connection between speech and social interaction, and what he calls "universal pragmatics." This approach signals a radical departure from the more speculative grounding of critical theory undertaken by Marcuse. For one thing, it appeals to precisely those scientific and philosophic research programs that Marcuse considered to be dangerously ideological. They are the *structural linguistics* of Noam Chomsky, which aims at reconstructing universal competencies necessary for generating grammatically well-formed sentences, and the more empirically oriented speech-act theories of John Austin and John Searle. The result is a wholly new program designed to reconstruct the *pragmatic* conditions necessary for mastering the *performative* rules of *social interaction*, especially those revolving around *speaker* and *listener* roles.

According to Habermas, everyday speech—in contradistinction to poetic and literary language—contains a performative as well as an informational component. The informational component normally consists of a factual proposition P (e.g., "It is raining outside"). The performative component consists of a first-person verb phrase (e.g., "I promise (know, assure, etc.) that P"), in which the speaker proposes to take on certain future obligations in exchange for the listener's entering into social interaction with him. A speech act consists of both components. For example, "I know that it is raining outside," succeeds when the listener voluntarily accepts its truth, appropriateness, and sincerity. In return for this acceptance, the speaker tacitly agrees to take on an obligation to show that the claim is well-warranted should the listener so request it.

Habermas's unique contribution to speech act theory consists of his novel application of the structural linguistic model to a field for which it was never originally intended, that is, everyday communicative interaction. What is original in Habermas's universal pragmatics is its discovery that every conceivable speech act raises, either implicitly or explicitly, four major (validity) claims: to truth, normative rightness, sincerity, and comprehensibility. These claims vary in emphasis, depending on the kind of speech act under consideration. A factual assertion, for example, highlights a claim to truth, whereas a moral command highlights a claim to normative rightness. However, since all four claims are raised simultaneously in any speech act, one could in principle challenge the sincerity, normative rightness, or even comprehensibility of a factual assertion. Thus, someone who claimed that the right to own private property was a "natural" right, could be challenged to justify not only the truth of this claim, but also its very meaningfulness. What could it mean to say that a freedom of this sort is natural? That it is necessary for survival? That all societies whatsoever have been observed to acknowledge it? And how can a moral prescription be inferred from some fact about self-preservation and/or human society? Perhaps the claim is not factual at all but moral, in which case its normative correctness, aside from any reference to nature, would be at issue.[13]

It is Habermas's contention that rational speakers must be prepared to justify the truth, rightness, sincerity, and comprehensibility of their communications—if so challenged. To the extent that they are *predisposed* to coordinate their actions communicatively—bearing in mind that unconstrained communication is a necessary condition for maintaining stable social and personal identity—*discourse* must always remain an immanent possibility for them. Consequently, unless circumstances warrant a departure from standard practice—the strategic use of power and manipulation are sometimes called for in adversarial relations—rational speakers will *tacitly* assume that the normative conditions specified by the ideal speech situation obtain, even if they, in fact, don't. We generally act on the assumption that people are rationally accountable for their behavior, that they are not deluded about their true interests, and that they could convince others that this is the case.

As an analysis of what rational speakers in Westernized societies tacitly assume, this conviction may not seem very controversial. However, as a claim about linguistic communication, in general, it seems obviously false. No anthropologist would entertain seriously the notion that the sorts of mythic narratives and cultic practices around which aboriginal peoples conduct their lives are structurally differentiated into distinct cognitive, normative, and expressive components (recall what we said earlier about rationalization, as a process of differentiation). Nor, for that matter, would they find any evidence of universalistic moral attitudes in aboriginal modes of ethical reasoning. To be sure, even speakers in tribal societies will treat some members of their *own* society with equal respect. Such mutual recognition among speakers, which prohibits them from making any exceptions in the way they "play" *their* language games, is a necessary condition for the possibility of communication, generally. Yet, this sort of mutual accountability is hardly capable of generating the universal rights and duties we take to be central to the moral point of view. It is only with the advent of modern society that mutual accountability has taken on truly universal (i.e., rational) dimensions. Just as the notion of "justification" has evolved from simple appeal to brute force and dogmatic authority to reflective notions of Socratic dialogue, so, too, the scope of reciprocity has progressively expanded to include virtually all of humanity.

The second part of Habermas's defense of a discourse ethic, then, rests on a demonstrable parallel between individual maturation and social evolution. Such a theory is indispensable to social critique, Habermas insists, for without an evolutionary ranking of universal types of social organization (analogous to, but more abstract, than Marx's "mode of production"), it would be impossible to identify "progressive" developments in morality and law that act as "pacesetters" for, *and* limits to, economic and administrative growth.

The fullest version of Habermas's argument is set forth in in his two-volume magnum opus, *The Theory of Communicative Action* (hereafter *TCA*), which appeared in 1981. There, he contends that individual cognitive and moral development is intimately related to acquiring communicative competence. Pragmatism, he believes, has shown that spatial perception is primarily developed through the manipulation of objects. Yet, he notes that the identification of things and their properties is linked to the propositional use of names and predicates.

The acquisition of communicative competence is also essential to moral development. Following Jean Piaget and Lawrence Kohlberg, Habermas divides moral development into three major stages: preconventional, conventional, and postconventional. Preconventional morality is primarily self-centered, and involves the moral assessment of actions solely in terms of their consequences for the judging ego. Yet, despite its egocentric focus, this stage of morality presupposes the beginning of a kind of reciprocity, which manifests itself in the form of an I'll-scratch-your-back-if-you'll-scratch-mine attitude. Reciprocity here involves a capacity to identify with two points of view: that of ego and alter. The ability to identify with the other in this way, however, is predicated on the ability to assume the reciprocal roles of speaker and listener roles.

The conventional stage of morality implicates communicative competence even more deeply. At this stage, persons learn to issue commands which claim a validity transcending the satisfaction of personal interests. In issuing moral commands, the speaker must not only identify with the second-person listener role (alter), but also must identify with the third-person standpoint of a *generalized other*, representing the interests of the community, the nation, etc. Finally, at the postconventional level of morality, persons learn to evaluate conventional norms in light of their possible universal acceptance by all rational beings, temporal and geographical boundaries notwithstanding. At this level, communication involves the freedom to propose and reject, justify and criticize, validity claims *at ascending levels of generality* (*TCA2*:27–42).

Habermas claims that changes in language also affect social evolution in a manner that parallels moral-cognitive development in the individual. Individual development involves the progressive *differentiation* of cognitive, normative, and expressive attitudes as well as the progressive *decentration* of the ego with respect to its own perspective. Something similar happens at the level of social evolution, in which (as Weber has shown) the unitary religious *worldviews* of premodern cultures are differentiated into objective, social, and subjective "worlds" and value spheres. Habermas dubs the mechanism by which this is accomplished the *linguistification of the sacred*.

The lack of cognitive and moral differentiation evident in mythic worldviews finds a correlate in ritualized modes of social interaction which permit little individual freedom. Even the metaphysical worldviews of more advanced traditional societies lack the differentiation requisite for critical reflection. Religious and metaphysical forms of speech conflate the informational, performative, and expressive uses of language so that it is difficult to determine whether an utterance is a factual assertion raising a claim to objective truth, a moral command raising a claim to intersubjective rightness, or an expression of feeling raising a claim to subjective sincerity. Again, the assertion that private property is a natural right appears to be a moral prescription masquerading as a fact about nature. (John Locke, who first defended this right on the grounds that it was natural, also understood this to mean that it was divinely preordained, as evidenced by passages in the Bible which he assumed to be sincere expressions of God's will.) The confusion of validity claims immunizes ideological justifications, such as the above, against rational critique by making it difficult to determine what, if anything, the assertion (moral prescription or subjective expression) is claiming.

The possibility for *rational critique* and *progressive learning* first arises when communication evolves to the point of *grammatically differentiated speech*, in which cognitive assertions, normative prescriptions, and subjective expressions are clearly distinguished from one another in accordance with the structural components of speech action. A higher stage is achieved when specialized domains of *discourse* (science, law, morality, and art) branch off from everyday communicative action (*TCA2*:77–118).

Habermas follows Weber in describing social evolution as a process of *cultural* and *social rationalization*. From the standpoint of the participants engaged in modern life, the process appears as a rationalization of a communicatively integrated *lifeworld*. Rationalization here refers to the establishment of formally consistent modes of behavior incorporating an efficient calculation of means and ends (what Weber calls *purposive rational action*) in accordance with universal norms. It, too, is characterized by structural differentiation: learning processes centered around the cultural value spheres of truth, rightness, and aesthetic value are institutionalized in science, jurisprudence, and art. Nature is divested of its teleological meaning. Religious sentiments find secular embodiment in universal ethical and legal institutions (civil and democratic rights). The latter, in turn, permits individuals greater freedom to pursue private interests and criticize authority (*TCA1*:157–58).

To sum up: the process of social rationalization enables individuals to become increasingly autonomous with respect to culture and society. *Concrete contents* of life experience are gradually distinguished from *formal-universal* cognitive structures, normative principles, and personal competencies; and levels of *critical reflection* are progressively deepened (*TCA2*:140–52). This results in increased individual responsibility for bestowing meaning and value on the world one inhabits and *increased demand for democratic participation as a condition for bestowing legitimacy on social norms and institutions*.

COMMUNICATIVE LIFEWORLD VERSUS FUNCTIONAL SYSTEM. CRISIS TENDENCIES IN LATE CAPITALISM AND THE POSSIBILITY OF MORAL RENEWAL

So far, we have seen how a communicative ethic might serve to facilitate ideology critique and promote the spread of participatory democracy. In the preceding section, I briefly sketched Habermas's argument in support of this ethic. The demands imposed on us by a communicative ethic are not external. On the contrary, they are built right into universal conditions of communicative competence. Consequently, they are integral to our very identity as responsible speakers and actors, and therefore cannot be denied without self-contradiction.

In this section, I will outline Habermas's diagnosis of modern society. Although he has commented on problems facing bureaucratic socialist societies, most of his remarks have been directed toward explaining crisis tendencies in the capitalist democracies of the West. These remarks strike at the heart of his disagreement with his predecessors, especially Adorno and Horkheimer. Unlike them, Habermas does not think that enlightenment per se produces alienation and reification. Instead, these symptoms of social disintegration, he contends, are to be attributed to the external effects of capitalism.

Habermas's first attempt at explaining the chronic identity crisis facing modern capitalism was developed in *Legitimation Crisis* (1973).[14] There, he argued that the welfare state manages economic contradictions at the expense of incurring "rationality deficits." Torn between contradictory demands—the allocation of revenues for sustaining economic growth and the compensation of the victims of such growth—the welfare state must suppress debate regarding its own foundation in a system of private property. And it must do so in order to procure the loyalty of its citizens.

Contrary to the view held by his predecessors, Habermas does not think that the analysis of state capitalism propounded by Pollock accurately captures the internal complexities of the modern welfare state. The state is torn between too many factions to serve as an efficient, rational manager of the economy. Far from being the linchpin of a totalitarian system of domination, it is neither a simple tool for implementing the united interests of the capitalist class nor a politically neutral mechanism for adjudicating conflicting economic interests. It is premised on the existence of private property, but sometimes defends the interests of those who are victimized by it.

Ideally, the state could resolve its rationality crisis if it could manage the economy without being held publicly accountable for its decisions. Demands for public accountability are indeed weakened by a political system that encourages the apathy of voters and the "depoliticization" of the public generally. But, despite the apathy of "happy consumers," such demands have not abated, since increased state intervention in education, health, and welfare tends to repoliticize the public. Moreover, if Habermas's own grounding of a communicative ethic is any indication of the intransigence of political self-determination as an abiding need of rational persons, then the demand for democratic participation is, if anything, likely to increase.

Thus, chronic *legitimation crises* appear unavoidable—a condition that is further compounded, Habermas believes, by the erosion of consumer and achievement ideologies. According to Habermas, the erosion of consumerism and competitive striving for upward mobility gives rise to a chronic "motivation crisis." Students, blue-collar workers, and the chronically under-employed are less motivated than before to compete for the scarce rewards offered by the system. But, legitimation and motivation crises are not the only cultural crises advanced capitalism must confront. These other crisis tendencies, which center around the *impoverishment of culture*, the *fetishism of commodities*, and the *bureaucratization of everyday life*, are perhaps even more serious.

Impoverishment of culture manifests itself in a deterioration of aptitudes necessary for critically analyzing and synthesizing experience. Commodity fetishism and bureaucratization involve, respectively, the excessive growth of consumer attitudes, which assimilate all relationships to the buying and selling of commodities, and the substitution of legally organized spheres of economic-administrative activity for communicative interaction. Together these syndromes conspire to undermine the communicative conditions for transmitting culture, coordinating action, and fostering personal identity freely and rationally. The result is fragmentation and objectification of life. Such a dehumanized life is experienced as a fate over which one has no control. Not surprisingly, Habermas finds this destruction of moral autonomy to be most prevalent among welfare clients. Lacking the economic, social, and political bases for equal empowerment and dignity, these victims of capitalist growth can be compensated for their misery only through cash payments that reinforce their sense of dependency and lack of self-respect.

Habermas contends that the loss of freedom, meaning, and identity plaguing modern society is caused by two parallel processes: the *splitting off of elite (specialized) subcultures* and the *inner colonization of a communicatively structured lifeworld by economic and political systems*. By encouraging passive acceptance of one overriding goal—managed economic growth—the welfare state fosters an equally passive acquiescence in the authority of administrative elites claiming technological expertise. To a certain extent, of course, the institutionalization of specialized fields of knowledge permits a more rational resolution of technical problems. However, the welfare state encourages the reduction of all political problems to the single technical problem of maintaining stable economic growth. Confronted with the technical intricacies of economic management, citizens are more than willing to let specialists do the thinking for them. Yet, the cost is high. Citizens cease to regard themselves as guardians of moral ideals to which administrative elites must be held accountable. Consequently, they abdicate responsibility for critically generating an informed public opinion with regard to their own common good.

The inner colonization of a communicatively structured lifeworld by economy and bureaucratic state is chiefly responsible for the predominance of instrumental, or strategic, modes of interaction in everyday life. Persons acting strategically are inclined to view others as mere obstacles and/or means to the realization of their own personal good, with minimal regard for the moral rightness of their actions. This neglect of the common good, typified by a failure to act communicatively with respect to the claims of others less fortunate, is also encouraged by the *internal dynamics* of capitalist growth. Paradoxically, it is the rationalization of the lifeworld which first makes possible the normative conditions permitting this state of affairs.

According to Habermas, the process of rationalization involves an "uncoupling of lifeworld and system." Marx, he notes, was correct in holding that contradictions (or crises) in the economic and political system provide the stimulus for evolutionary advances. However, Weber was justified in arguing against Marx that evolutionary advances in the economic and political system presuppose the attainment of moral and cognitive competencies at the level of culture requisite for implementing economic and political changes.

In Habermas's opinion, the rationalization of the lifeworld makes possible the expansion of civil law in the private sector and constitutional law in the public sector. This legal formalization of communicative interaction serves as the normative, legitimating basis for market economy and bureaucratic state, respectively. Family and public realm (the "critical public" constituted by mass media, cultural exhibits, political gatherings, etc.) are primarily located in the *lifeworld*, where individuals *intentionally* coordinate their actions through norms agreed upon in communication. State and economy, by contrast, are located in self-regulating *systems* which are *functionally* integrated by wholly impersonal and anonymous *exchange relationships*. These relationships are mediated by *money* and *power*. Unlike mass-communication media, money and power enable persons to coordinate their activities strategically and monologically, through a purely instrumental calculation of rewards and punishments.

From the standpoint of the lifeworld, actors may be said to intend (in a purposive-rational sense) the strategic goals they pursue. The same, however, cannot be said of the *aggregate effects* of their actions, as reflected in the often unpredictable vicissitudes of the market. Such vicissitudes are not any less comprehensible than intentional actions, but their significance (or "rationality") can be *objectively explained* only by an *observer* on the *outside looking in*, namely, as lawful fluctuations of an adaptive *system* (*TCA*:153–97). Thus, the distinction between lifeworld and system roughly corresponds to the methodological distinction between subjective (interpretative) and objective (causal-explanatory) approaches to reconstructing social behavior.

Habermas maintains that the distinction between lifeworld and system is essential to understanding the sorts of social pathologies which figure predominantly in current debates about modernity. At first glance, it does indeed appear as if the rationalization of the lifeworld is paradoxical: the formalization of communicative rationality through the medium of civil and constitutional law makes possible the growth of economic and administrative subsystems that threaten to turn back and "devour" the very lifeworld which lends them legitimacy. Administrative regulations threaten to strangle democratic initiative and create bureaucratic dependency, while moral incentives get eclipsed by the unbridled pursuit of power, pleasure, and wealth.

Habermas has serious reservations about the unchecked growth of the system. Like Marx, he diagnoses the problem in terms of the *objective lawfulness* of forces, which have escaped the rational control of social agents, and now confront them with a *natural fate* to which they must submit. Although he thinks that some uncoupling of lifeworld and system is rational—he doesn't place much credence in a perfectly transparent, stateless community of the sort envisaged by Marx—he feels that it has gone too far. The system must be made accountable to a democratized lifeworld. Nothing less than the ecological and geopolitical survival of the planet depends on it. Indeed, the very identity of persons—as free, morally accountable agents—hangs in the balance as well. For this, too, depends on the cultivation of critical public opinion in associations permitting free and open debate.

Are there any social trends that resist social reification and thereby confirm Habermas's hypothesis regarding the inherent need for grass-roots democracy? He himself has pointed out that the decline of patriarchal authority in the nuclear family as a result of the women's movement has made possible a less repressive, and more egalitarian, form of socialization. While his predecessors looked to the Freudian model of moral development, with its emphasis on internalizing patriarchal authority, he has sought inspiration from interactive theories based on communication. Consequently, he does not regard the passing away of patriarchal authority as an obstacle to achieving moral autonomy. Nor does he feel that moral autonomy need be purchased at the expense of instinctual repression. For, contrary to Marcuse and the others, he believes that needs are determined by culture and social interaction, not by fixed, biological instincts.

Again, Habermas is less pessimistic than his predecessors regarding the critical potential of popular culture and mass media. Although popular culture and mass media are powerful tools for reinforcing ideology, they are far from being the homogeneous purveyors of mass culture implicit in the pejorative notion of the "culture industry." Popular culture often conveys critical messages, TV networks and their programs often reflect opposing values, interests, and cultural life-styles, and even ideological messages are liable to produce unintended reactions in an audience that undermines their force. Habermas even detects the rudiments of a television democracy in a recent upsurge of "video-pluralism."

Most importantly, Habermas does not consider the decline of proletarian militancy as signaling the end of radical resistance. New political movements have arisen that have taken the place of the older ones (the civil rights and women's movements are cases in point). Other political movements have emerged that focus on a different set of issues pertaining to the "grammar of lifeworlds" rather than to questions of economic and political justice. Composed of predominantly young, middle-class, college-educated people, these movements seek to wrest control, over local habitats and other resources bearing on the quality of life, from corporations and government bureaucracies. By doing so, they have let it be known that peace and ecology are issues of common concern that need to be decided on by everyone. Indeed, Habermas himself observes that the extension of democracy envisioned by these movements is already taking hold in economic cooperatives and grass-roots participatory associations of a sort not dissimilar to that found among members of the Green party in Germany.

It would be mistaken to think that Habermas is more optimistic than his predecessors regarding the prospects for social change. On the contrary, he is well aware of forces in the system that might suffocate the few vestiges of democratic resistance yet remaining. At the same time, however, he has a greater appreciation of the trenchancy of this resistance. It is not necessary that the rational need for freedom and communal solidarity find refuge in unconscious instinct and its aesthetic embodiment. If it were marginalized in this way, figuring solely as the mute voice of feeling inhabiting an underground artistic counterculture, it would indeed be as susceptible to totalitarian annihilation by a one-sided technological reason, as first-generation critical theorists believed it was. However, the rational need for freedom and solidarity is not censored from public life in the way this marginalization suggests. For it inhabits the very conditions under which persons communicate and reason. These needs, therefore, possess a greater necessity and universality than one might otherwise suspect.

CONCLUDING REMARKS

We began this chapter by noting that Habermas's theory of communicative action is designed to overcome some of the difficulties that have traditionally attended critical theory's attempt to resolve the theory/practice problem. Habermas's reconceptualization, of transcendental philosophy as rational reconstruction, circumvents the overly speculative side of his earlier theory of cognitive interests by acknowledging the close collaborative effort linking philosophy as a "place holder" for moral speculation with empirical science, interpretative science, and the everyday common sense of competent moral agents. The extent to which theoretical hypotheses cohere with one another across disciplines, and cohere with the common sense of competent speakers across cultures, suggests a model by which "facts" and "values" might mediate one another. This mediation is further clarified by Habermas's model of practical discourse, which shows that moral prescriptions follow from factual agreements to the degree that the latter approximate ideal standards of rationality. Finally, Habermas's reinterpretation of social and cultural rationalization shows that the heritage of the Enlightenment need not be as dialectically self-destructive as Weber and first-generation critical theorists were inclined to think. The development of science and technology need not come at the expense of moral rationality. And true democracy need not install a tyranny of the majority opposed to the needs and rights of the minority.

Yet, some problems still remain. The most important concern the grounding of the discourse ethic. Habermas's argument in support of the necessity of those moral rights and obligations underwriting the possibility of discourse is divided into three parts. The first part shows that communication—or shared understanding of meaning—presupposes commonly recognized, mutual expectations, which are grounded in speaker-listener roles. The rules governing "language games" specify norms which cannot be violated without loss of communication. Some of these concern obligations of accountability. We discussed this part of Habermas's argument when we mentioned how speakers of any language must recognize the rights of other speakers to challenge claims and request justifications. However, we noted that, at this level, what counts as justification, and who is entitled to demand it, can be quite vague. In some aboriginal societies, justification may involve appeal to force, and those entitled to demand it may be limited to a select few.

The second part of Habermas's argument attempts to show that "post-conventional" stages of ontogenetic and phylogenetic development presuppose modes of communication—and justification—that are logically superior to their preconventional and conventional counterparts. Not only are these modes of communication and justification more rational—at this stage speakers must appeal to universal standards in convincing virtually anyone of the rightness of their actions. But, such justification itself appeals to the "unforced force" of the better argument. The third part of Habermas's argument consists in showing that the "unforced force" of the better argument implies an ideal speech situation whose very possibility depends on the recognition of basic rights and duties.

The first part of the argument seems basically correct, but is too weak to provide a basis for universal rights and democratic solidarity. However, the second and third parts are more problematic. Take the second. By far and away the most important research program for Habermas's defense of the logical superiority of postconventional moral competencies has been the developmental psychology of Jean Piaget and Lawrence Kohlberg. Yet, there is now a substantial body of literature devoted to the formidable *conceptual* difficulties attending such a program: Is it possible to defend a structural parallelism between social evolution and individual development? Can one abstract a universal typology of moral dilemmas, which can be translated from the sociolinguistic context of one culture into that of another? If not, how can the universality of the theory be cross-culturally established? Does it make sense, in general, to talk about increased problem-solving capacity *in general*, rather than increased problem-solving relative to some culture-specific, context-bound set of problems? In any case, can we assume that cognitive and moral capacities develop at the same rate in different cultures? Might the peculiar problems facing distinct cultures not lead them to develop specific moral and cognitive competencies at different rates?

Habermas is aware of the magnitude of these difficulties, but he has yet to concede that they are insuperable.[15] By the same token, the lack of strong

evidence confirming Kohlberg's sixth (and highest) stage of moral development (roughly corresponding to the theory of universal rights found in the
writings of such thinkers as Kant and John Rawls) does not, he insists, count
against the logical superiority of universalistic moral theories generally.[16] Nor,
he believes, does the incidence of moral regression and relativism among test
subjects. Ultimately, he thinks that these difficulties can be explained away
in terms of a disjunction between levels of attained moral consciousness and
levels of motivation, or between levels of justification and levels of application.[17] Still, even he concedes that the ranking of various postconventional
theories (his own included) must await the outcome of future dialogue among
rational speakers.

I shall return to these problems in the postscript, where I take up certain
feminist objections to privileging universal rights-based theories as developmentally normative. For the present, however, let us continue examining the
remainder of Habermas's argument. The third part of Habermas's argument
purports to show that certain rights and duties are implicit in postconventional
forms of argumentation. In "Discourse Ethic. Notes to a Program of Justification" (1983), Habermas himself tried to ground these rights and duties in
two conditions. These were (a) "the universal and necessary presuppositions
of communicative speech" and (b) "knowledge of what it means to justify a
norm of action."[18] This strategy owes a great deal to Karl-Otto Apel's observation that the relationship that obtains between these conditions and basic
rights is neither deductive nor inductive, but cogent in a manner that can best
be captured by the idea of a *performative contradiction*. Using an argument
first articulated by Jaako Hintikka, who noted that utterances such as "I
doubt that I exist" involve a *performative* contradiction between a speech act
and its pragmatic presupposition, Apel maintained that the skeptic's refusal
to acknowledge the claim to universal validity inherent in his factual utterances
and moral assertions, as well as his refusal to acknowledge basic speech rights,
is belied by his attempt to persuade others rationally. Therefore, basic concepts of universal validity as well as basic notions of freedom and equality
are not ideas, which participants in discourse (practical *or* theoretical) *could*
elect to reject, without contradicting the pragmatic presuppositions of their
own behavior.

In Apel's opinion, this demonstration proves that these ideas belong "to
those transcendental-pragmatic presuppositions of argumentation that one
must always (already) have been accepted, if the language game of argumentation is to be meaningful."[19] Habermas eschews this strong transcendental characterization in favor of a weaker one. What the demonstration
provides is not some ultimate, or foundational justification, that can be con-

firmed by anyone in transcendental reflection, but fallibilistic evidence in support of the contingent universality of certain norms for persons who have attained a postconventional stage of reasoning.[20]

Despite his qualifications regarding the weak "transcendental" import of his argument, Habermas has not really shown that the *specific* rights and duties associated with the ideal speech situation really follow from "the force of the better argument." As I remarked above, the universalist injunction against considering natural and cultural differences in specifying who is permitted to participate in discourse is not a performative presupposition of Socratic dialogue, as is evidenced, e.g., by the ethnocentrism of certain Greek philosophers.[21] Habermas concedes as much when he claims that "*of themselves* these normative obligations do not extend beyond the boundaries of a concrete lifeworld of family, tribe, city, or nation." Such boundaries, he adds, "can be broken through only in discourse, to the extent that the latter is institutionalized in modern societies" (*JS*:48).

Nor does "knowledge of what it means to justify a norm of action" obviously entail taking into account the satisfaction of *each* individual's interest as against the collective interest of the majority. Habermas concedes this point when he observes that utilitarian as well as Kantian, contractarian, and communicative moral schemas represent interpretations that are compatible with a postconventional universalistic level of reflection.[22] Utilitarian moral schemas advocate maximizing the greatest happiness for most (but not necessarily all) people. Social contractarian and Kantian schemas establish equal rights for all, but in a way that still permits laws and norms which favor the interests of some and not others. In short, the rights implicit in the ideal speech situation are not necessary presuppositions of argumentation per se. Rather, they follow from additional assumptions about the peculiar needs and expectations of persons living in modern societies.

I would like to conclude this section by turning to another difficulty that pertains to Habermas's discourse ethic. Seyla Benhabib has recently remarked that Habermas's own understanding of what a discourse ethic is supposed to accomplish seems torn between two goals—the liberal defense of individual freedom and the radical defense of democracy.[23] Habermas's uncertainty, as to the ranking of these goals, is reflected in his concern about the "totalitarian" dangers of sacrificing individual freedom to pure democratic solidarity, on one hand, and the "ideological" dangers of securing personal rights prior to, and independent of, democratic discourse regarding collective needs and goods. This uncertainty is also reflected in his distinction between *practical* and *aesthetic* discourse. Ideally, *practical* discourses encompass all rational speakers, temporal and geographical boundaries notwithstanding. Since agreement in these instances necessarily excludes all but the most universal of goods, such discourses appear to be limited to resolving only the most abstract questions of right. Aesthetic discourses, by contrast, are devoted to the *evaluation* and *discovery* of concrete conceptions of the good. Conflicts over substantive conceptions of the good are resolved only when parties reach a shared, but nongeneralizable, consensus with respect to their peculiar social needs (*TCA1:16*).

The problem with the distinction between practical and aesthetic discourse becomes apparent once we examine the abstractness of those idealizations which Habermas builds into his notion of practical discourse. Some critics, such as Albrecht Wellmer, observe that the presumption of transparent self-understanding, temporally and geographically unlimited conversation, and linguistic univocality obtaining in Habermas's notion of practical discourse effectively rules out any disagreement that might occasion dialogue. The system of inalienable moral rights, stipulated by the discourse ethic, would then be understood as the result of single rational choice, or as a logical implication of rationality itself.[24] In effect, the discourse ethic would be indistinguishable from ahistorical "deductive" theories of natural law—that end up legitimating certain individual rights as unconditional and inalienable. Resisting any mediation with real practice, these theories are ideological in more than just one sense of the term.

In order to avoid any semblance of a deductive theory of natural right, Habermas's discourse ethic must be understood as subordinating ideal discourses to actual discourses, and practical discourses to aesthetic discourses. At the same time, however, ideal practical discourses must retain a certain theoretical priority, if only to retain the critical focus proper to a discourse ethic. However, the mediation of aesthetic and practical discourse would then complicate the problem of mediating individual freedom and democratic self-determination that Habermas inherits from the Enlightenment. The idea that individuals ought to possess rights would be guaranteed by the ideal speech situation, conceived as the outcome of an ideal, practical discourse. However, specific individual rights—be they negative property rights or positive rights to resources and opportunities to self-determination—would no longer be inviolable. Their scope would be dependent on the outcome of real, historical discourses. But, in that case, there would be no guarantee that specific societies wouldn't choose to define the scope of individual liberty in a manner that might appear to some, at any rate, as highly illiberal.

As we shall see in the concluding chapter, there may well be other limits to the critical use of a communicative ethic than those mentioned above. The introduction of aesthetic critique as implicit within moral discourse already suggests that the aesthetic imagination, with its claim to a more global, pre-discursive rationality, might yet be indispensable to critical theory, after all. If so, the debate between Habermas and his predecessors would have to be resolved rather differently from the manner suggested here.

NOTES

1. J. Habermas, *Communication and the Evolution of Society*, trans. T. McCarthy (Boston: Beacon Press, 1979), pp. 8–20.

2. J. Habermas, *Legitimation Crisis*, trans. Thomas McCarthy (Boston: Beacon Press, 1975), pp. 123–24. See the selection reprinted in *Critical Theory: The Essential Readings (CTER)*.

3. J. Habermas, "Justice and Solidarity: On the Discussion Concerning 'Stage 6' " in *The Philosophical Forum*, vol. XXI, nos. 1–2 (Fall-Winter 1989–90), p. 36. Here-after *JS*.

4. Cf. G. H. Mead, "Fragments on Ethics" in *Mind, Self, and Society*, ed. C. Morris (Chicago: University of Chicago Press, 1962), pp. 379–89; and J. Habermas, *The Theory of Communicative Action. Volume Two. Lifeworld and System: A Critique of Functionalist Reason*, trans. T. McCarthy (Boston: Beacon, 1987), pp. 94–96. Here-after *TCA2*.

5. Following the example set forth in Toulmin's *The Uses of Argument*, Habermas analyzes the structure of justification into four main components: (a) a *conclusion C* (e.g., a validity claim in need of justification); (b) a *ground D* (the reasons justifying the conclusion); (c) a *warrant W* (a rule of inference, principle, or law which grounds the justification); and a *backing B* (the evidence in support of the warrant). The transition from *B* to *W* is *cogent*, but non-deductive. Habermas illustrates this point in the following example:

—Recommendation C in need of justification: "You ought to give A fifty dollars by the end of the week."
—Justification D: "A had lent you that money for a period of four weeks."
—Grounding (of D) through a norm of action W (a corresponding norm, e.g.): "Loans ought to be paid back within the specified period."
—Casuistical evidence B for the backing of the norm (a series of references to the consequences and side-consequences of the application of the norm for the ful-fillment of accepted needs, e.g.): "Loans make possible the flexible use of scarce resources."

In the above example, the general *normative* principle W, "Loans ought to be paid back within the specified period," would be justified by the *fact* B that all rational parties to the discourse: (a) agree on the consequences of everyone's accepting the norm (e.g., that "loans make possible the flexible use of scarce resources"), (b) agree that these consequences satisfy the needs of each and everyone, and (c) agree that these needs are true needs (i.e., are needs which could be justified as rational, or compatible with the common interest of all). Thus, there is a non-deductive relationship of support linking what *is* the case (rational agreement that a given norm is in everybody's true interests) with what *ought to be* the case (the state of affairs enjoined by the norm). See J. Habermas, "Wahrheitstheorien" in *Vorstudien und Ergänzungen zur Theorie des kommunikativen Handelns* (Frankfurt a.M: Suhrkamp, 1984), p. 165.

6. J. Habermas, "Diskursethik. Notizen zu einem Begründungsprogramm," in *Moralbewusstsein und kommunikatives Handeln* (Frankfurt: Suhrkamp, 1983), p. 103. English translation in *The Communicative Ethics Controversy*, Seyla Benhabib and Fred Dallmayr, eds. (Cambridge, Mass.: MIT Press, forthcoming). Hereafter *DE*.

7. "Wahrheitstheorien," p. 178.

8. This addition seems to have been motivated by Carol Gilligan's critique of Lawrence Kohlberg, especially her juxtaposition of an ethics of care to an ethics of justice. Kohlberg responded to this critique by attempting to show that both justice (the principle of equal treatment for all) and benevolence (the principle of doing good and avoiding harm) were derived from equal respect for persons, conceived either in general or in particular. In effect, he conceded that equal respect for the dignity and integrity of individuals as concrete particulars implies furthering the conditions of their self-realization and welfare.

Habermas's appreciation of Kohlberg's concession is typically coupled with a critique of bourgeois moral theories whose communicative insights are concealed behind the ideological facade of possessive individualism. Because the principle of benevolence implies duties only with reference to particular individuals, it cannot possibly ground a larger "concern for the common welfare"—a weakness reflected in Kohlberg's monological conception of "ideal role taking" as a kind of empathy (*DE*:45–6). See below for Habermas's critical appropriation of Kohlberg's developmental psychology. I discuss Gilligan's critique of rights-oriented ethical theories of the sort defended by Kohlberg and Habermas in the postscript. Cf. Carol Gilligan, *In A Different Voice: Psychological Theory and Women's Development*. Cambridge, Mass.: Harvard University Press, 1982); and Lawrence Kohlberg, Dwight Boyd, and Charles Levine, "Stage 6 Revisited" in *From the Moral Domain* (Cambridge, Mass.: MIT Press, forthcoming).

9. S. Benhabib, "In the Shadow of Aristotle and Hegel: Communicative Ethics and Current Controversies in Practical Philosophy," in *The Philosophical Forum* (loc. cit.), pp. 8–9.

10. A. Heller, "The Discourse Ethics of Habermas: Critique and Appraisal," in *Thesis Eleven*, x–xi (1984–85), p. 7.

11. In an earlier essay ("Der Universalitätsanspruch der Hermeneutik") Habermas seemed to imply that refusal to participate in any language game might be justifiable. The inconsistency between this view and Habermas's own communication ethic was pointed out to him by Gadamer in his "Replik." The essay and Gadamer's response were published in *Hermeneutik und Ideologiekritik*, ed. K.-O. Apel (Frankfurt a.M.: Suhrkamp, 1971). For a discussion of this debate see my "Habermas, Gadamer, and Bourdieu on Discourse: A Communication Ethic Reconsidered" in *Man and World* 15 (1982), pp. 149–61.

12. *Legitimation Crisis*, p. 113. This passage is reprinted in *CTER*.

13. The details of Habermas's universal pragmatics are worked out in "What is Universal Pragmatics?," included in *Communication and the Evolution of Society*; "Towards a Theory of Communicative Competence," in *Inquiry* 13 (1970), pp. 360–75; in *TCA*:273–337; and "An Alternative Way Out of the Philosophy of the Subject: Communicative Versus Subject-Centered Reason," reprinted in *CTER*.

14. The argument of *Legitimation Crisis* is summarized in "What Does a Legitimation Crisis Mean Today? Legitimation Problems in Late Capitalism," reprinted in *CTER*.

15. See, for example, Habermas's own discussion of the translation problem in *Moralbewusstsein und kommunikatives Handeln* (loc. cit.) pp. 49–50, and my discussion of related difficulties in David Ingram, *Habermas and the Dialectic of Reason* (New Haven: Yale University Press, 1987), pp. 132–34.

16. Habermas introduces his own discourse ethic as a seventh, and more radical, stage of postconventional morality. Unlike the deontological morality represented in Kohlberg's sixth stage, the discourse ethic advocates the insertion of personal needs in a collective formation of the will. See L. Kohlberg, "From Is to Ought," in T. Mischel, ed. *Cognitive Development and Epistemology* (New York, 1971), pp. 151–236.

17. *Moralbewusstsein und kommunikatives Handeln*, pp. 183–200.

18. *DE*, pp. 75–76, & 97.

19. K.-O. Apel, "The Problem of Philosophical Fundamental Grounding in Light of a Transcendental Pragmatics of Language," in K. Baynes, J. Bohman, and T. McCarthy, eds., *After Philosophy* (Cambridge: MIT Press, 1987), p. 277.

20. "What is Universal Pragmatics?" pp. 22–25.

21. This and the following criticism are developed by Seyla Benhabib in *Critique, Norm, and Utopia. A Study of the Foundations of Critical Theory* (New York: Columbia University Press, 1986), pp. 302–09.

22. J. Habermas, "A Reply to My Critics" in *Habermas: Critical Debates*, eds. J. B. Thompson and D. Held (Cambridge Mass.: MIT Press, 1982), p. 260.

23. *Critique, Norm, and Utopia*, pp. 310–16.

24. See A. Wellmer, *Ethik und Dialog: Elemente des moralische Urteils bei Kant und in der Diskursethik* (Frankfurt a.M.: Suhrkamp Verlag, 1986), pp. 54–112.

SELECTED BIBLIOGRAPHY

J. Habermas. *Communication and the Evolution of Society*. Trans. T. McCarthy. Boston: Beacon Press, 1979.

————*Legitimation Crisis*. Trans. T. McCarthy. Boston: Beacon Press, 1975.

————*The Theory of Communicative Action. Volume One. Reason and the Rationalization of Society*. Trans. Thomas McCarthy. Boston: Beacon Press, 1984.

————*The Theory of Communicative Action. Volume Two. Lifeworld and System: A Critique of Functionalist Reason*. Trans. T. McCarthy. Boston: Beacon Press, 1987.

Commentaries: The reader should consult McCarthy (1978) for detailed treatments of Habermas's philosophy of language and his communicative ethic. For works dealing with *The Theory of Communicative Action* see David Ingram, *Habermas and the Dialectic of Reason* (New Haven: Yale University Press, 1987); Stephen White, *The Recent Work of Jürgen Habermas. Reason, Justice, and Modernity* (Cambridge: Cambridge University Press, 1988); Rick Roderick, *Habermas and the Foundations of Critical Theory* (London: MacMillan, 1986); and Richard Bernstein (ed.), *Habermas and Modernity* (Cambridge, Mass.: MIT Press, 1985).

EIGHT

THE FUTURE OF CRITICAL THEORY

Much of Habermas's work over the past two decades can be seen as a response to his predecessors' failure to address adequately the theory/ practice problem. One aspect of this problem concerns the relationship between happiness, on one side, and freedom and justice on the other. First-generation critical theorists did not naively assume that a free and just society would necessarily be the happiest. In fact, they noted tensions between modern moral conceptions of right and the desire for happiness. However, they never abandoned the idea that autonomy and communal justice were necessary (if not sufficient) for true (as opposed to illusory) happiness.

Habermas has also stated his belief that the moral and cognitive development undergone by the species does not necessarily result in greater overall happiness. As rational achievements, individual freedom and social justice are part of a general process of demythologization and disenchantment, in which the existential consolations provided by religion and spiritualized nature no longer obtain. Rational society is not as well equiped as traditional society to deal with problems of death, meaning, and alienation (fragmentation). Its compensation for this loss, however, is considerable. Moreover, it may well be that modern forms of art and moral orientations, based upon a communication ethic, can provide rational substitutes for existential meaning, communal solidarity, and integral identity.

More recently, Habermas appears to have acknowledged the one-sidedness of a critical theory that focuses exclusively on questions of freedom and justice. These are undoubtedly the most important questions that critical theory raises, but they cannot be considered in total abstraction from considerations of happiness, either. That is to say, the injustice or lack of freedom characteristic of any given society will undoubtedly have a bearing on the happiness of that society, but there are other considerations which also have a bearing, such as material prosperity, and these may compensate for the injustice and lack of freedom.

In acknowledging the one-sidedness of a critical theory that focuses exclusively on questions of individual freedom and social justice, Habermas has begun to take seriously the idea of a happy society in which moral considerations, such as individual freedom and social justice, are "balanced" in a noncompromised way with the desire for material prosperity and its presupposition: the existence of a relatively complex—and that means differentiated and stratified—set of social, economic, cultural, and political institutions. Since happiness is related to the aesthetic notions of balance, harmony, and integrity, it is not surprising that Habermas has recently expressed interest in the way in which aesthetic experiences, especially those involving works of art, might provide enlightenment regarding the proper balance obtaining with respect to the satisfaction of moral and material needs. Aesthetic experience might furnish, however indirectly, some intuitive understanding regarding the proper balance that should be obtained between our desire for democracy and freedom, on one hand, and our desire for material prosperity, on the other. This intuitive understanding can then be made more or less explicit in aesthetic and practical discourse.

The best way to approach the problem of happiness is by recalling Habermas's defense of the Enlightenment's faith in reason as a basis for moral and cognitive progress. The reader will especially recall some of the important differences between Habermas's diagnosis of modern society and that of his predecessors. Habermas's diagnosis seems more optimistic, if only because he locates emancipatory needs in communicative structures that shape individual consciousness and public life. Enlightenment is not inherently dialectical, or self-contradictory, since instrumental and communicative types of rationality designate complementary, not opposed, attributes of reason. It is appropriate that instrumental reason prevail in science, economy, and administration. Likewise, it is appropriate that communicative rationality prevail in spheres of moral life—family, education, health and, of course, politics. Yet, there is an overlapping of both types of reason in each of these spheres as well. The problem is to ensure that each type of rationality is sufficiently cultivated in all spheres of activity, so that neither eclipses the other.

By privileging private ownership over the basic means of production, and by encouraging the growth of its economy and bureaucracy, capitalism upsets the balance of instrumental and communicative reason requisite for a free and happy life. The family, for example, is destabilized due to increased economic pressures requiring greater job mobility and more work. Such stress is exacerbated for lower-income families, but even affluent families have to confront the erosion of moral values fostered by consumerism and competition. Education, too, is increasingly oriented toward vocational training rather than critical thinking. Here again, the "virtues" of competition and deference to authority outweigh the achievement of moral insight and independence gained through the appreciation of literature, history, art, and philosophy. True individualism founded on moral autonomy is submerged in the abstract materialistic individualism of self-preservation.

Last, but not least, politics has become the exclusive preserve of lawyers, business administrators, economists, and other technically trained specialists. Apathy, deference to authority, and narrowmindedness conspire to dilute the democratic process. Rational discussion of issues is all but obliterated in the mindless spectacle of the campaign. Those who vote—about 50 percent of the American electorate during presidential campaigns—are comprised largely of those who have a financial stake in the outcome, which excludes the poor. However, the possibility of casting a meaningful ballot is undermined by the narrow range of candidates and options, and by the manipulative irrationality of campaign advertisements and beauty-contest debates. Given the role that special interests play in determining the outcome of elections, it is not surprising that many political scientists have come to interpret politics along economic lines, as a market system designed to balance competing sources of effective demand (power).

In Habermas's opinion, critical theory should be more concerned—about these imbalances in social rationalization—than about ideology. This is not to deny the importance of ideology critique. However, it is his belief that ideology would naturally diminish if communicative rationality were cultivated to the greatest extent possible. The question therefore arises: How can a discourse ethic and its ideal of pure, rational communication be put to use in criticizing the colonization of the lifeworld and the impoverishment of culture caused by the splitting off of specialized discourses?

I shall argue below that a discourse ethic designates certain democratizing tendencies in Western culture which, in turn, circumscribe limits to economic and administrative growth. However, whether (and to what extent) a given society violates these limits, cannot be determined by appeal to ideal standards of rational communication alone. The ideal speech situation designates purely formal procedures for ensuring justice and freedom; these can only be approximated. Moreover, any attempt to give them concrete institutional shape will, at best, reflect the needs and interests of persons inhabiting very specific societies and possessing imperfect competencies for rational reflection.

But this is not all. Pure democracy runs up against a process of rationalization that necessarily issues in specialization and uncoupling of system from lifeworld. Condemnation of this process is both romantic and reactionary, Habermas claims, since there exists no alternative other than regression to a simpler form of life. Therefore, a discourse ethic—at most—enables the critical theorist to pinpoint realistic potentials for democratization that specialization and uncoupling tendentially undermine. These potentials cannot be determined abstractly. In some sense, they refer to the very concrete needs of subjects who must decide, in light of their own imperfect knowledge and reason, how their own well-being is best served. The critic of ideology may simulate a conversation in which hypothetically reconstructed interest positions yields an intelligent guess as to how these subjects would collectively organize their life if they were in a position to do so freely and rationally. But the well-being of a society cannot, in any case, be reduced to questions of justice and freedom.

Something else besides knowledge of existing injustice and lack of freedom is needed to provide insight into preferred states of social democratization. In the final analysis, the critical theorist is called upon to determine whether a given society's mode of rationalization selectively encourages the growth of technological modes of behavior at the expense of democracy. In doing so she/he must be guided by some concrete notion of a healthy life, of a happy balance of rationality complexes which conduces to the fulfillment of persons as integral moral beings.

It was first-generation critical theorists who were preoccupied with human happiness. For them, art was the last vestige of utopian redemption and fulfillment. Art embodied in its very form the kind of peak, fulfilling experience which ought to be realized in all spheres of social activity. Formal symmetries and tensions enliven all faculties and senses, help to synthesize what are otherwise disparate experiences, and set up a kind of communication between reason and the senses. It is this communication which sensitizes the individual with respect to others, and holds open the promise of communal reconciliation.

I will argue below that the task which Habermas sets for critical theory cannot succeed without the help of aesthetic imagination. Aesthetic imagination does not replace the kind of critical enlightenment achieved in actual discourse. Nor does it replace the critical enlightenment afforded by an ideology critique based upon simulated discourses. Yet aesthetic imagination—and exposure to art and other forms of aesthetic experience—may be instrumental in both instances. The utopian anticipation of reconciled life embodied in authentic works of art provides a standard, however imprecise, for judging the lack of integral moral fulfillment experienced in alienated society. This intuitive understanding, of course, should not remain inarticulate and imprecise. It should be articulated in discourse, both aesthetic and practical. But even here one should not discount the importance of works of art—or more precisely, exemplary aesthetic experiences—as reasons (arguments) that might serve to enlighten others. Before I make this argument, however, I would like to address some residual problems besetting the notion of ideology critique, since these ultimately bear upon the issue of happiness as well. This discussion will then be followed by a more detailed analysis of some difficulties with Habermas's resolution of the dialectic of enlightenment.

CAN THERE BE TRUE INTERESTS?
IDEOLOGY CRITIQUE RECONSIDERED

Habermas, you will recall, originally agreed with his predecessors that the proper task of critical theory was ideology critique. Not just any false belief counts as an ideology. In order for a belief to be ideological, it must satisfy three conditions. First, it must falsely assert that certain needs and desires are in the real (rational and true) interests of those agents who act upon it. Second, it must *function* to maintain social institutions permitting surplus repression. Finally, it must have its *origin* in such repressive institutions.

What does it mean to talk about an agent's real (true) interests? When we say that it is in the best interest of an alcoholic to stop drinking we do not imply that he himself actually knows this to be so. Even if he knows this to be so he may not desire it. Thus, an agent's real interests are just those dispositions which foster a rational integration of possible needs and desires conducive to leading a healthy and happy life, in the long run.

At this juncture, it might be helpful to distinguish ways in which a set of desires (needs) might be said to be in someone's real interest. A certain set of desires might be said to be in someone's best interest, *given their actual circumstances*. Thus, it might well be in the best interest of someone, living in conditions of abject poverty and cutthroat competition, to behave selfishly. However, the rational needs of someone under these circumstances would not necessarily be those of someone living in a society in which all are equal and prosperous. Since rational persons would not prefer conditions of life requiring greater sacrifice and repression, they would not prefer the sorts of needs that it might be rational to have under these conditions. Therefore, we can say that the sorts of desires—that would be in someone's best interest, *ideally speaking*—are those that he or she would have in a nonrepressive society. Once again, such a society would be composed of relatively equal, sufficiently affluent and educated persons capable of collectively choosing their needs, in light of perfect knowledge regarding their own circumstances and other possible social arrangements.

The distinction between true and false interests (needs) is closely related to the functional and genetic properties of ideology mentioned above. From a genetic point of view, we may say that false consciousness regarding one's true interests arises from ignorance about the motives underlying one's acceptance of them. Agents suffering from ideological delusion believe that their preferences are the result of free, rational deliberation when, in fact, they are not. If they knew that the conditions, in which they deliberated about their needs, demanded *surplus* repression in ways that severely violated the norms underlying the ideal speech situation, they would no longer continue to believe that their preferences were rational. But preferences, known to be irrational in this respect, would be rejected as false (i.e., as not conducive to the truly happy life that would obtain under truly emancipated social conditions).

Finally, ideologies arise not only from ignorance of the institutionalized forms of social domination that unfreely motivate their acceptance; they also function to legitimate, and thereby perpetuate, these very forms of domination. This leads to an obvious question: Does one establish the falsity of an ideological belief by appeal to its genesis and function, or vice versa? It would seem that one must first establish the truth or falsity of certain needs before explaining their genesis and function. In order to criticize a belief on the grounds that it legitimates surplus repression, one would first have to establish the degree of repression necessary for the society in question, given its economic development. Repression is relative to scarcity. But, we cannot determine the extent of socially *un*necessary repression without some notion of what needs ought to be fulfilled, *if possible*. The determination of needs that ought to be fulfilled is problematic, since the potential for human fulfillment exceeds the satisfaction of biological desires.

Thus, the major task of ideology critique consists in establishing the true interests of social agents. Once that is accomplished, the social critic can show how existing needs are false. And she/he can do so in ways that reveal their ideological cast. That is, she/he could show how, for such and such a group of persons, satisfaction of false needs seemed to allow for the development and expression of their basic humanity because their capacity for rational reflection was stultified by repressive social conditions. In turn, stultification of reflective aptitudes could be shown to be functionally supportive of modes of thinking and behaving—which perpetuate these very same conditions.

An ambiguity arises at this stage. Are needs false just because they are not ones which persons in an ideal speech situation would choose? Persons in an ideal speech situation would inhabit a perfect, emancipated society. They would doubtless possess needs that cannot yet be fulfilled, given current conditions of scarcity. But, surely, it cannot be held against a society that it has not yet solved all problems of scarcity. Therefore, needs are not false simply because they fail to correspond to the needs of persons inhabiting an ideal speech situation. Rather, they are false because they do not permit the fullest happy life possible, given existing conditions of scarcity.

Nevertheless, we can show this only by appealing to what persons, possessing full knowledge of the limits and possibilities of their society, would choose as their needs, if they could do so under conditions of ideal communication. We hypothetically reconstruct the needs that perfectly rational agents inhabiting a perfect society would have, and then we ask ourselves how far these needs can be realized, given the level of scarcity necessitated by the size of the population and the current state of science and technology. Notice, too, that the level of scarcity necessitated by the size of the population and the current state of technological development need not be identical to existing levels of scarcity. The latter are determined by economic and social institutions which may deploy technological capacities in ways that are inefficient, wasteful, and disadvantageous to segments of the population.

There are, however, several difficulties which attend the concept of critical theory as it has been elaborated above. First-generation critical theorists, like their positivist opponents, assume that any talk about the rationality of needs and interests is meaningless unless it is capable of being certified as true or false. That is, they believe that the rationality of a preference would have to be a function of its confirmed truth. Of course, since positivists hold that only statements about observable states of affairs are capable of being confirmed as true or false, they naturally conclude that preferences, being a species of value judgment, are noncognitive and, thus, irrational. Critical theorists, by contrast, maintain that the truth of value judgments like these can be confirmed in reflection.

To say that a given need is true (or false) implies that its rationality is not one of degree. It also implies that there is only one set of needs that is rational. But clearly this is false. Our discussion of how ideology critique works shows that the rationality of a need is relative to current levels of necessary repression as well as to hypothetically reconstructable ideals. A need that is rational for persons living in advanced Western societies (e.g., the need for freedom, equality and democracy), may not be rational for primitive cave dwellers living in conditions of great scarcity. Ideological delusion is, therefore, not false consciousness. It is, however, a state of mind in which persons mistake irrational needs for rational.

Habermas, curiously enough, avoids this problem. Although he, too, sometimes speaks of practical and aesthetic enlightenment regarding needs as a kind of knowledge, he leaves no doubt that the kind of knowledge presupposed here is ill suited to strong, cognitive conceptions of truth. To begin with, he prefers to speak of "need interpretations," rather than of "needs." According to Habermas, even biological needs are shaped by social conditioning. Part of this conditioning involves processes of linguistic naming and description in which needs are interpreted. In any case, we have access only to needs that are socially conditioned and linguistically "interpreted."

Habermas, then, never succumbs to the temptation that leads Marcuse to speak (however inconsistently with his own historicist interpretation of psychoanalysis) of true or authentic needs which preexist society and its false, cultural need interpretations. Since Habermas talks only about the aesthetic "correctness" of needs, relative to a given culture's commonly shared assumptions or, more importantly, relative to a given society's shared cultural ideals, he can easily accomodate the possibility of there being a plurality of valid need interpretations with respect to societies in general (or with respect to any society in particular). Such a plurality of valid need interpretations, however, is perfectly compatible with the idea that some need interpretations are aesthetically "incorrect." Just as some interpretations of a text are wrong, because they fail to take into consideration or otherwise misread certain portions of it so, too, some need interpretations are false, that fail to live up to the cultural ideals (or real possibilities of fulfillment as expressed in some avant-garde works of art), which inform a given society's collective understanding of itself.

The above analysis of needs and their validity is borne out in the very way in which ideology critique seeks confirmation of its own "truth." As Habermas points out, the ascription of real interests to actual social agents is capable of being confirmed, only to the extent that they act on these interests by changing their society in appropriate ways. If persons acted on the advice of the social critic in the way predicted by her/him that would tend to confirm the theory. However, if they didn't, then what?

The worst-case scenario, envisaged by Marcuse, is a society in which persons feel perfectly satisfied with their shallow lives. They are not aware of any unfulfilled desires, and are likely to resist the "enlightenment" proffered by the critical theorist. How can they be convinced that cultivation of intellect, moral autonomy, and democratic association is more fulfilling than reaping the material benefits of a high-stress job? Are they not likely to regard the critical theorist as a kind of cultural elitist?

Rebuffed by her/his clients, the critical "therapist" knows that her/his theory has, at least, not been disconfirmed. For popular rejection of the theory would count only as disconfirming evidence if it were based on rational grounds. But these grounds are not likely to obtain in any case. Collective choices regarding needs and interests can be rationally made (in the fullest sense possible) only in an emancipated society. *Absolute* confirmation, or disconfirmation, of the theory would have to await the coming of utopia.

But this is surely paradoxical. The capacity of critical theory to enlighten is relative to the current state of emancipation. Yet, emancipation is dependent on enlightenment. The same circularity obtains with respect to confirmation: the "truth" of the theory is relative to the current state of reflective insight—and vice versa.

The above circularity need not render ideology critique a totally futile endeavor. For one thing, it is unlikely that the one-dimensionality, described by Marcuse, is as pervasive as he thinks it is. Most persons reflect on the meaningfulness of their lives and so might be susceptible to some enlightenment. Second, the circularity involved in confirmation would be damaging to critical theory, only if the theory claimed that its insights were true or rational in some absolute sense. Since its degree of insight is relative to current levels of emancipation, there is no question of its being absolutely true or false. At most, it is more or less reasonable, to the extent confirmed by social agents who are themselves more or less reasonable.

As I have said on more than one occasion in discussing Habermas's notion of ideology critique, it is never a question of condemning as ideological all factual agreements that fail to live up to the counterfactual expectations of the ideal speech situation. All such agreements, of course, may be suspected of being potentially ideological. However, if the actual agreement arose under conditions in which only *necessary* forms of repression served to distort communication, it might not be ideological. That is to say, it might be judged rational on the grounds that existing inequalities in opportunities to participate fully and freely in discussion where unavoidable (and therefore "rational" in a qualified sense), given the necessary restrictions that attach to a society having reached that stage of development.

Of course, distinguishing necessary from surplus forms of repression may already presuppose a critique of ideology. As opposed to surplus forms of repression, necessary forms of repression would be those which ultimately, given a particular stage of technological and moral development, were in the best interests of all concerned. In that case, however, we would be moving in a circle. Ideological would be those agreements that we knew were constrained by forms of surplus repression, yet surplus forms of repression would be precisely those that we knew were legitimated by ideological agreements (i.e., agreements that were not in the best interests of those concerned).

Is this circle a vicious one? Not if we bear in mind that ideology critique can never entirely transcend the nexus of real practice which serves to disconfirm or confirm it. Such confirmation or disconfirmation will never be absolute, because the criteria of rationality, in light of which needs and levels of repression are evaluated, are not those which would absolutely obtain in the ideal speech situation. Ultimately, ideology critique, no less than practical discourse, is drawn into real conversations with historical agents, whose needs are as historically specific as the peculiar circumstances in which they find themselves. It is their concrete aspirations for happiness that are in question here. However indicative an ideal speech situation might be for pinpointing the role that freedom and justice play in happiness, it cannot itself provide concrete examples which enlighten us as to the particular balance of freedom, justice, material prosperity, *and* aesthetic integrity that ought to obtain in any given social nexus. For this we need aesthetic enlightenment.

HABERMAS AND THE DIALECTIC OF REASON RECONSIDERED

I indicated earlier that Habermas no longer regards ideology critique as the principal task of critical theory. This is not because ideology has disappeared, but because the most effective way of enlightening people about it involves helping them develop a greater aptitude for critical reflection. Yet, they are unlikely to develop this aptitude so long as communicative rationality remains uncultivated in the public sphere. The failure of communicative rationality to take root in the public sphere, however, is due to the impoverishment of culture, caused by the splitting off of specialized discourses, and the colonization of the lifeworld, caused by the hyperextension of the economic and administrative system. Therefore, it is these tendencies, inherent in modern capitalism, which must be combatted.

Nevertheless, it remains unclear whether the cultivation of rational speech alone is sufficient to establish a happy and meaningful life. As Habermas asks:

Is it possible that one day an emancipated human race could encounter itself within an expanded space of discursive formation of will and yet be robbed of the light in which it is capable of interpreting its life as something good? The revenge of a culture exploited over millennia for the legitimation of domination would then take this form: right at the moment of overcoming age-old repressions it would harbor no violence, but it would have no content either.[1]

The problem raised in the above passage harks back to the purely formal, or procedural, notion of emancipation contained in Habermas's ideal speech situation. This notion is capable of stipulating rights pertaining to free speech and democratic justice. However, it is not capable of fleshing out a concrete notion of a fulfilling life. According to Habermas, if "we do not wish to relinquish altogether standards by which a form of life might be judged to be more or less failed, deformed, unhappy, or alienated, we can look if need be to the model of sickness and health" (*TCA1*:73–74). Yet the "balance among non-self-sufficient moments, an equilibriated interplay of the cognitive with the moral and aesthetic-practical" implied in the model of sickness and health cannot be derived from "the formal concept of freedom which modernity's decentered understanding of the world has left us." Hence the importance of cultural tradition in providing particular values and meanings, specific to a given society's unique vision of itself, that articulate a model of global well-being.

Habermas is concerned that a purely emancipated society may not be fully rational, after all. Paradoxically stated, if rationality boils down to acting in accordance with rules of free and fair speech, then with the destruction and or withering away of tradition, there would be no values and meanings worth talking about! Therefore, rationality *must* imply more than emancipated communication. It must imply a global vision of health that is intimately linked to the specific prescriptive contents of tradition. In other words, if reason is conceived *purely formally*, in terms of *specific* types of argumentation, which are restricted to thematizing just *one* type of validity claim—truth, moral rightness, aesthetic correctness (or expressive sincerity)—how do we rationally determine what conduces to global happiness? Without some rational enlightenment regarding the felicitous balancing of moral freedom and justice, material prosperity, and aesthetic integrity—in short, without some nonformally specialized discourse (or experience) in which all validity claims are simultaneously thematized—we do indeed run into the paradox of rationality—the dialectic of enlightenment—encountered by Weber and first-generation critical theorists. For a society can be rational only when all these aspects are reconciled in some felicitous balance.

Let us briefly recapitulate Habermas's attempt to avoid this dialectic. The reader will recall that this dialectic draws much of its inspiration from Weber's paradox, which is itself fueled by a narrow conception of rationality. What is rational, Weber believed, is formalizable, or reducible to abstract procedure. In his judgment, only the calculation of efficient means fits this description. Commitment to an aesthetic or moral value for its own sake implies, so he argued, a commitment to a specific meaning or goal which cannot be captured in terms of general procedure. Therefore, he concluded that reasoning about the highest values was ultimately a matter of subjective preference. Lacking an objective basis for moral reasoning, persons cease thinking of themselves as moral agents, and all values—even truth itself— become meaningless.

The loss of freedom and meaning that Weber attributes to rational society is further compounded by the fact that the various orders of life, which gravitate around the distinct value spheres of truth, justice, and aesthetic pleasure, come into conflict with each other. Since no formalizable conception of rationality exists that can unify these *specific* orientations (other than the purposive rational pursuit of success), he concluded that this struggle must issue in a polarization of life into purely hedonistic orientations on one side and purely ascetic orientations on the other. Lacking any grounding in pleasure or reason, higher moral and aesthetic values, such as justice and the supreme good, simply wither away.

Habermas is inclined to agree that the loss of freedom, meaning, and identity are indeed prevalent features of modern society, as Weber describes it. However, instead of attributing these symptoms to an internal logic underlying cultural and societal rationalization (as Weber does), he attributes them to the inner dynamics of capitalism. Capitalism, Habermas notes, compels the expansion of economy and state into areas of everyday life—family, school, culture, and so on—that are not inherently disposed toward profit maximization and efficient administration. These areas of life are responsible for socialization and the coordination of activities around shared norms. Such functions, however, are fulfilled only in *communicative* interactions in which persons try to achieve *mutual understanding*, free from sanctions and selfish inducements. Economy and state, by contrast, designate systems of strategic, success-oriented action in which persons confront one another as obstacles or mere means. Value-rational commitments to justice and truthfulness, reciprocity and freedom, structure a lifeworld constituted by communication; purposive-rational orientations, toward profitability and status (domination), drive a system mediated by money and power.

Weber misdiagnosed the real causes underlying social reification because, Habermas argues, he confused the *universal* developmental logic underlying *cultural* rationalization with its contingent and historically specific embodiment in social institutions. This confusion, in turn, was facilitated by Weber's narrow identification of reason with instrumental rationality.

Weber's identification of reason and instrumental rationality is precipitous, however. Habermas's theory of communicative action shows that there exists a necessary and universal grounding of certain value *forms*, if not, to be sure, specific value *contents*. If Habermas is right, speakers are committed to at least three values—truth, rightness, and truthfulness (or authenticity)

—whenever they try to reach mutual understanding. Moreover, potential for dispute implies commitment to rational dialogue, whose *formal* characteristics appear to be common to learning processes in all disciplines. Since these characteristics, in turn, imply normative commitments to freedom, equality, and justice, Habermas can conclude (contra Weber) that rational persons are inherently oriented toward something like an unconstrained democratic community.

But does this solve the problem of conflicting spheres of rationality? Weber noted that when conflicting spheres of rationality collide in the same domain of life (e.g., science and morality in the fields of medicine, government administration, or law), one domain—usually the scientific—is likely to eclipse the other. Habermas cites this as an example of what he calls *selective rationalization*. Habermas claims that selective rationalization occurs when

(at least) one of the three constitutive components of cultural tradition is not systematically cultivated (*bearbeitet*) or when (at least) one cultural value sphere is insufficiently institutionalized without a structure-building effect for the whole society or when (at least) one sphere of life prevails so far that it subordinates other orders of life under its alien form of rationality. (*TCA1*:240)

A society would not be fully rational if it allowed scientific and technological values to occlude or otherwise prevent moral and aesthetic values from having a structure-building effect for *society as a whole*; nor would it be fully rational if the economy and state absorbed communicative lifeworld. Of course, persons are free to adopt, say, either a scientific or a moral point of view in their dealings with society. For Habermas this means that conflicts between overlapping "rationality complexes" are unavoidable. There is no easy way, for example, to resolve the dispute between behavioral science and interpretative sociology, except perhaps to insist upon the limited (if not exactly equal) rights of both.

Fortunately, conflicts between rationality complexes are limited by the fact that not all points of view are susceptible of being converted over into rational learning processes furthering the progressive accumulation of knowledge. Habermas does not think that a scientific orientation toward the subjective world of desire (a hedonistic calculus) can succeed as a rationalizable endeavor. The same, he feels, applies to moral and aesthetic orientations toward nature and society respectively.

What is important here is the *exclusion* of a domain of aesthetic "learning," by which societies might evolve more sophisticated, or "enhanced," visions of their own collective good, health, and happiness. Habermas asserts that, "expressively determined forms of interaction" (e.g., countercultural forms of life) "do not form structures that are rationalizable in and of themselves." This view, which seems at odds with the tradition of critical theory from Adorno to Marcuse, deprives society of perhaps the only medium capable of communicating aesthetic discoveries, gained in rational discourse, to social agents engaged in everyday moral conversation. It sanctions, in other words, a kind of selective rationalization. For the balanced interplay of value spheres, rationalization complexes, and life-styles which would instantiate a collective vision of global well-being—and which might help resolve conflicts between aesthetic form and systemic function that arise, say, in urban planning—becomes the exclusive property of a community of artists *cut off* from public intercourse.

In more recent writings, Habermas has sought to redress this problem by appeal to the power of a work of art to illuminate the *totality* of our experience. Articulating a *global* conception of individual and social well-being, art provides an insight that has hitherto been characterized by Habermas as metaphysical and speculative—in short, prerational. Recently, however, Habermas has suggested that the *poetic* disclosure of a utopian world implicated in a work of art makes possible a kind of rational learning that is not specialized with respect to one single type of value (or validity claim). More specifically, "as soon as such an experience is used to illuminate a life-historical situation and is related to life problems, it . . . not only renews the interpretation of our needs in whose light we perceive the world," but it also "permeates as well our cognitive significations and our normative expectations and changes the manner in which all these moments refer to one another."[2]

Previously, Habermas had agreed with Weber that rationalization involves the differentiation of cognitive, moral-practical, and aesthetic-expressive experience under distinct types of claims: to truth, moral rightness, and expressive authenticity (sincerity). Once differentiated, problems regarding knowledge, morality and law, and aesthetics could be dealt with efficiently by trained specialists, according to different standards of rationality. However, the sort of rational "problem solving" engaged in by artists and professional critics regarding technique, formal unity, expressivity, and so on seems far removed from the day-to-day concerns of the average citizen. How can this highly specialized and esoteric knowledge be of use in enlightening us about the imbalances (or *dis*integrity) of an alienated and unhappy life? It would seem that, in order for the enlightenment to complete itself and thus avoid the dialectic of specialized trivialization and fragmentation, it would have to somehow reverse itself. That is, rationalization would have to compensate for its own fragmenting tendencies by generating tendencies toward reunification and popularization.

Habermas observes one such tendency in the popular reception of an authentic work of art:

The aesthetic "validity" or "unity" that we attribute to a work of art refers to its singularly illuminating power to open our eyes to what is seemingly familiar, to disclose anew an apparently familiar reality. This validity claim admittedly stands for a *potential* for "truth" that can be released only in the whole complexity of life-experience; therefore this "truth-potential" may not be connected to (or even identified with) one of the three validity-claims constitutive for communicative action, as I have previously [been] inclined to maintain.

The one-to-one relationship which exists between the prescriptive validity of a norm and the normative validity claims raised in speech acts is not a proper model for the relation between the potential for truth of works of art and the transformed relations between self and world stipulated by aesthetic experience.[3]

The introduction of the poetic function of art to illuminate our lifeworld creates new difficulties for Habermas's account of aesthetic rationalization. Originally this notion was tied to the emergence of *a discourse specialized with respect to pragmatic expressive claims to authenticity*. Now it appears to be related to a claim to "truth," which, if it is not to be regarded as irrational, must imply a *totally different conception of reason*. For this claim arises in and through the reception of the work of art (i.e., in *experience*). Hence, it implies a notion of rationality that is in some sense intuitive—compelling in a metaphoric-rhetorical, rather than discursive, way. Thus, Habermas approvingly cites Wellmer's claim that

Neither *truth* nor *truthfulness* may be attributed unmetaphorically to works of art, if one understands "truth" and truthfulness in the sense of a pragmatically differentiated everyday concept of truth. We can explain the way in which truth and truthfulness— and even normative correctness—are *metaphorically* interlaced in works of art only by appealing to the fact that the work of art, as a symbolic formation with an aesthetic validity claim, *is at the same time an object of the lifeworld experience, in which the three validity domains are unmetaphorically intermeshed* (*QC*:237–38—emphasis added).[4]

The importance of this new conception of aesthetic rationality for Habermas's critical project as a whole should not be overlooked. Habermas had been inclined to regard his predecessors retreat into the murky regions of aesthetic imagination as symptomatic of their failure to locate the *public* ground of practical and aesthetic rationality in communication. This failure was attributed to their adherence to a Weberian reading of formal rationality. Since they identify formal and instrumental rationality, they could retrieve only the emancipatory and reconciliatory moments of a *substantive, utopian* reason by privatizing them in the aesthetic *unconscious*.

Habermas's discovery, that a purely formal conception of communicative rationality could provide a publicly accessible norm capable of grounding our desire for freedom and justice, marked an important advance over his predecessors. Clearly, aesthetic experience was too vague a notion in which to ground these ideals. However, once we understand that even a critique of ideology touches upon aesthetic considerations pertaining to happiness and the validity of concrete needs, it becomes apparent that aesthetic experience— and not just aesthetic discourse (critique)—is a necessary condition for social critique. Aesthetic experience is no substitute for aesthetic and practical discourse. But in order to reflect about the harmonization of distinct cognitive, moral, and aesthetic needs in discourse, one must first be presented with aesthetic experience. More importantly, the varieties and qualities of aesthetic experiences that one has had will influence (along with whatever arguments might be marshalled) what sorts of needs competent speakers would rationally prefer and in what configuration.

So long as reason is dispersed over disparate regions of value, validity, and discursive problem-solving, it cannot provide the ground for a global critique of unhealthy imbalances that obtain among separate rationalization complexes and needs. I have already suggested that the distinction between practical and aesthetic discourses must be relativized, in order for Habermas's discourse ethic to avoid the stigma attached to purely transcendental thinking. Now, I am suggesting that an important presupposition of practical discourse are aesthetic experiences, whose global harmonization of cognitive, practical, and aesthetic needs should be susceptible of rational evaluation as well, though not in a manner that is restricted to just one formal value.[5]

Sometimes Habermas himself seems to acknowledge the importance (if not rationality) of such global experiences, as when he points out that late capitalist societies have "found some functional equivalent for ideology formation," which consists in "preventing holistic interpretations from coming into existence." Such interpretations involve critically evaluating "totalities, forms of life and cultures, and life contexts" *as a whole*. Yet, Habermas also says that, despite the critical importance of global interpretations, engaging in them is something which a critical theory, restricted to formal criteria of morality (or justice), "must refrain" from doing (*TCA2*:383).

Why does Habermas say this, if elsewhere he acknowledges the importance of holistic interpretations for evaluating the happiness of societies? There appear to be two reasons why. First, Habermas notes that happiness is not a formal value that can be rationally grounded in the way that truth, moral rightness, and expressive sincerity can be. Not only are the guiding values underlying holistic critique, health and happiness, not intrinsic to the necessary pragmatic conditions underlying rational communication, but such values are inherently substantive and, therefore, refer to contents (need interpretations) that are essentially contingent and nonuniversal. Of course, neither of these reasons would speak against the rationality of need interpretations as such. Habermas himself argues that need interpretations can be rationally evaluated in terms of their conformity to the shared expressive values of particular societies, so their nonuniversality wouldn't necessarily count against their rationality.

However, he does not seem to think that need interpretations can be evaluated in terms of the way they fit together to form a total package of goodness and happiness. In this reading, questions of happiness must be sharply distinguished from questions of morality and expressivity. However, if practical discourses inevitably incorporate aesthetic discussions regarding needs, and if discussions regarding the rationality of needs inevitably touch upon their global harmonization, it would seem that this sharp distinction can no longer be rigorously maintained.

I would like to argue that the redirection of Habermas's thought away from matters pertaining to ideology, toward matters pertaining to social imbalances, is incompatible with his refusal to countenance holistic critique grounded in substantive values of health and happiness. Moreover, if I am not mistaken, these substantive values refer back to the aesthetic concerns of first-generation critical theorists. Health and happiness imply a well-balanced, integrated life in which creativity, spontaneity, receptivity—in short, openness with respect to the "other"—are each allowed free play.

Perhaps it is the implication of aesthetic values in holistic criticism which has recently led Habermas to appreciate the "utopian" significance of poetic world-disclosure. Such disclosure, Habermas now claims, is related to a *substantive* vision of a *reconciled* form of life, in which *formally differentiated* value spheres and rationality complexes interpenetrate in a healthy and harmonious equilibrium. The recovery of the "utopian" dimension in Habermas's aesthetics certainly casts a different light on his previous attempts to distance himself from the aestheticism of first-generation critical theorists. Art, he now claims, reaches into our cognitive interpretations and normative expectations and transforms the *totality* in which these moments are related to one another. In this respect, modern art harbors a utopia that becomes a reality to the degree that the *mimetic powers* sublimated in the work of art find resonance in the *mimetic relations of a balanced and undistorted intersubjectivity of everyday life* (*QC*:237—emphasis added).

How reminiscent this passage is of Adorno's discussion of the mimetic "communication" between self and other that obtains in the work of art! It is also reminiscent of Marcuse's discussion of the link between *eros*, imagination, and play. Like Marcuse, Habermas appeals to the aesthetics of Schiller to capture the integrated and harmonious play of *subjective* faculties and *objective* social institutions (rationalization complexes) definitive of utopia:

For Schiller an aestheticization of the lifeworld is legitimate only in the sense that art operates as a catalyst, as a form of communication, as a medium within which separated moments are rejoined into an uncoerced totality. The social character of the beautiful and of taste are to be confirmed solely by the fact that art "leads" everything dissociated in modernity—the system of unleashed needs, the bureaucratized state, the abstractions of rational morality and science for experts—"out under the open sky of common sense."[6]

It is precisely at this juncture, where Habermas's aesthetics joins up with Adorno's and Marcuse's, that the concept of communicative rationality returns to the poetic and metaphorical. The attempt to ground communicative rationality in pragmatic conditions of speech succeeded in establishing a scientifically confirmable basis for critical theory, but at the expense of depriving it of critical content. The recovery of critical content by way of appropriating cultural tradition—and not by critically transcending it—once again opens up a utopian dimension that had hitherto been lacking in Habermas's thought.

Of course, the rationality of a communicative equilibrium, between distinct but interpenetrating rationalization complexes, can no more be rigorously grounded in formal criteria than can the rationality of basic needs and interests. But that is just to say that critical reason is just as essentially contextual as it is transcendental. To return to our original formulation of the theory/practice problem, social critique presupposes some rational basis that must transcend, in however limited a manner, the specific need interpretations that are publicly sanctioned and encouraged. The ideal speech situation contained in Habermas's discourse ethic does just that. At the same time, the critique of ideology as well as the critique of reification must forever remain relative to the level of enlightenment achieved by more or less reasonable persons, whose "common sense" is nourished on prediscursive aesthetic experiences and prerational traditions.

Perhaps Adorno's idea of a negatively conceived dialectic which occupies a no-man's-land (utopia), of a reflection which never completely returns to itself, best captures the strange constellation of formal competencies and substantive intuitions that constitutes the force-field of practical reason. Recoiling from both sides of the theory/practice, discourse/lived experience, idea/reality, universal/particular, form/content, transcendental/contextual dichotomies, practical reason is as much second nature as it is transcendent freedom. This is to say that we move within an implicit understanding of, and habitualized response to, a global situation (or social nexus), whose rational integrity is as much a function of the affective needs and aesthetic experiences we have (or have had), as it is of any discursive reasoning. Put simply, to speak of the rationality of needs and interests is to speak as much about their content and harmony as about their form of collective articulation.

NOTES

1. J. Habermas, *Philosophical-Political Profile*, trans. F. Lawrence (Cambridge, Mass.: MIT Press, 1984), p. 158.

2. J. Habermas, "Modernity versus Post-Modernity," *New German Critique* 22 (1981), p. 12. The complete and revised translation of this essay appears in *Critical Theory: The Essential Readings* under the title "Modernity: An Unfinished Project."

3. J. Habermas, "Questions and Counter-Questions," *Praxis International* 4, no. 3 (1984), p. 237. Hereafter abbreviated *QC*.

4. Albrecht Wellmer, "Truth, Semblance and Reconciliation," *Telos* 62 (1984)/ 85):89–115.

5. Habermas notes that "a work validated through aesthetic experience can . . . take the place of an argument and promote the acceptance of precisely those standards according to which it counts as an authentic work. In practical discourse, reasons or grounds are meant to show that a norm recommended for acceptance expresses a generalizable interest; in aesthetic criticism, grounds or reasons serve to guide perception and to make the authenticity of a work of art so evident that this aesthetic experience can itself become a rational motive for accepting the corresponding standards of value" (*TCA1:20*). In a note to the above passage, Habermas suggests that what guides perception in these instances is the *perlocutionary*—or implicit and prediscursive—effect attached to what are otherwise simple, descriptive statements such as, "The drawing X is particularly balanced." A perfectly appropriate aesthetic reason might consist of silence or just emphatic pointing accompanied by perlocutionary inducements of the form, "Just see here!" or "Just feels (imagine) it!."

6. J. Habermas, *The Philosophical Discourse of Modernity. Twelve Lectures*, trans. F. Lawrence (Cambridge, Mass.: MIT Press, 1987), p. 50; and F. Schiller, *On the Aesthetic Education of Man in a Series of Letters* (New Haven, 1984):139.

SELECTED BIBLIOGRAPHY

J. Habermas. "Questions and Counter-Questions." *Praxis International* 4, no. 3 (1984): 229–50.

―――"Modernity: An Unfinished Project." *Critical Theory: The Essential Readings* (New York: Paragon House, 1991). Versus Postmodernity." *New German Critique* 22 (1981): 49–69.

―――*The Philosophical Discourse of Modernity*. Trans. F. Lawrence. Cambridge, Mass.: MIT Press, 1987.

Commentaries: The best analytic treatment of conceptual difficulties attending ideology critique is Raymond Geuss's *The Idea of Critical Theory* (Cambridge: Cambridge University Press, 1981). For a more detailed discussion of the role of aesthetics in Habermas's recent social philosophy and its relationship to first generation critical theorists see Ingram (1987) and his essay "Completing the Project of Enlightenment: Habermas on Aesthetic Rationality," in *The Aesthetics of the Critical Theorists*, ed. R. Roblin (Lewiston, N.Y.: Edwin Mellen Press, 1990).

POSTSCRIPT: CRITICAL THEORY AND CONTEMPORARY TRENDS IN SOCIAL PHILOSOPHY

No discussion of the future of critical theory would be complete without addressing three trends in recent social philosophy that at once complement and challenge its idealistic heritage. These trends are poststructuralism, postmodernism, and feminism. Together they constitute a formidable critique of existing forms of domination based on race, gender, class, and technical expertise. At the same time, they challenge some of the more cherished assumptions underlying critical theory's approach to the theory/practice problem, the most important being its faith in the emancipatory potential of universal reason.

What follows is a thumbnail sketch of these trends showing their relationship to critical theory. I shall argue that the dialectic of enlightenment elaborated by first-generation critical theorists has much in common with some of the positions articulated by poststructuralists and postmodernists. Not surprisingly, this kinship has provoked a sharp response from Habermas, who rejects any wholesale critique of reason. The intersection of critical theory and feminist theory is more complicated. The main question we will be concerned to answer is whether or not there exists a male bias in critical theory. For brevity's sake, I shall limit my examination of this issue to possible gender biases in Habermas's program in particular.

THE CHALLENGE OF POSTSTRUCTURALISM AND POSTMODERNISM: CAN THERE BE A UNIVERSAL EMANCIPATORY REASON?

Poststructuralism and postmodernism designate distinct but overlapping tendencies. Poststructuralism, as the name implies, grew out of structuralism, a predominantly French movement that established itself in linguistics and anthropology during the fifties and sixties. The single most striking feature about structuralism is its critique of subjectivism, or the view that language and society are products of conscious, intentional action. Structuralists, such as anthropologist Claude Lévi-Strauss, sought to show that conscious behavior was largely predetermined by impersonal objective structures governing the selection of words and the patterning of social interaction. For Lévi-Strauss, these structures were embedded in the brain and, hence, were universally binding for all persons. Indeed, structuralism can best be understood as an attempt to found linguistics and sociology on an objective, scientific, basis.

Poststructuralists share the structuralist critique of subjectivism. However, they do not share its goal of founding the human sciences on universal structures. Indeed, they tend to take a dim view of the rationalist pretensions of such sciences and, in some cases, even contend that this rationalism has led to their transformation into technologies of domination.

To begin with, poststructuralists argue that the basic rules, norms, and structures governing linguistic and cultural practices are not rigidly fixed, but undergo constant mutation. Consequently, they emphasize the contextuality and relativity of all structures, including those governing so-called rational behavior. Yet poststructuralists are also inclined to interpret this feature of rationality politically. Like critical theorists, they are opposed to the over-extension of bureaucratic domination, the totalitarian subordination of dissident subcultures to the dominant scientific culture, and the marginalization of the ethical and the aesthetic. They are also inclined to blame these tendencies on the rational demand for systematic unity, purity, and universality.

Postmodernism also dates back to the fifties, where it began as a literary movement. By the seventies, it had become a catchword for stylistic trends in architecture, painting, film, music, dance and theater. Basically, the postmodern movement rebelled against the formal purity of modernist works of art, which were cut off from everyday mass culture. Its impact has been most apparent in architecture. As against the cold, functionally efficient, standardized cell-block construction typical of monumentally sculpted high-rises, postmodern architecture seeks to foster a more humane, environmentally balanced living space by blending old and new styles in often striking ways.

Poststructuralists and postmodernists share a strong antipathy toward a modern culture dominated by technological rationality. Their emphasis, on the rich contextuality of life and language, is as much directed against the transcendental universalism of formal rationality as it is against its lack of spontaneity, irony, and heterogeneity. Therefore, it is not surprising that they turn to Nietzsche, the great advocate of artistic and expressive liberation, for help in debunking the emancipatory claims of pure reason.

We briefly alluded to the importance of Nietzsche for Weber and first-generation critical theorists. Nietzsche sought to show that the highest moral and cognitive ideals of Western culture were the product of a power struggle in which the weak, resentful masses imposed their will on noble individuals possessing superior power, intelligence, and virtue. Although the asceticism demanded of such ideals led to higher forms of self-mastery, it also functioned to suppress the natural, biological drives furthering life. In Nietzsche's opinion, the most basic of these is the Will to Power. Nietzsche maintained that the empty abstraction and generality of universal moral ideas such as Kant's categorical imperative were so transcendent of the real natural and historical forces governing life's struggles that they showed themselves to be purely nugatory. Anyone attempting to live up to them would be required to deny life itself. Despite the negative implications of this nihilism, Nietzsche believed that those who understood its full implication—the negation of transcendence, the "death of God"—might actually affirm life to the fullest by assuming absolute responsibility for their actions. Those who overcame dependence on transcendent (and transcendental) illusions could create new standards of value and meaning by which to "interpret" the world. These interpretations would be beyond "good" and "evil," "true and false." Although Nietzsche held that there could be no rational evaluation of them, he suggested that they might be ranked in accordance with their maximization of the Will to Power, or their affirmation of life's creative forces.

It is unclear what, if any, political consequences follow from Nietzsche's teachings. First-generation critical theorists took note of the antidemocratic and antiegalitarian (even racist) spirit of Nietzsche's thought. Clearly, the Will-to-Power doctrine could be, and indeed was, enlisted in the service of fascism (despite Nietzsche's explicit disdain for anti-Semitism). However, there also appears to be a strong anarchistic flavor to Nietzsche's "aesthetic" doctrine of continual, creative self-overcoming, which appeals to many poststructuralists and postmodernists. Despite the critical implications of Nietzsche's philosophy with respect to the universalistic humanism of the Enlightenment, his own suspicion of criticism as a purely negative form of revenge seeking refuge in transcendental ideals, and his own emphasis on the positive affirmation of biological drives, renders his thought highly unsuitable for the kind of ideology critique undertaken by the Frankfurt School. It is, therefore, hardly surprising that poststructuralists such as Derrida, Foucault, Deleuze, Guattari, Baudrilland, and Lyotard have at various times pointed out the difference between their deconstructive, genealogical, and/or libidinal approaches from ideology critique proper. It also raises serious questions about the extent to which their theories can even be characterized as political as opposed to "anti-political."

There is no denying that a certain "anti-politics" can be detected in the writings of many poststructuralists and postmodernists. This position often takes the form of a refusal to engage in the sort of *normative* or *prescriptive* philosophizing, whose underlying rationalism is believed to lend itself all too easily to ideological manipulation in the service of "totalitarian" social engineering. Nevertheless, I shall argue below that poststructuralist and postmodernist theories possess a political character, if not an explicitly prescriptive political philosophy. For the sake of convenience, I shall treat postmodernism and poststructuralism as two distinct, but kindred movements. However, because postmodernism *as a social and political philosophy* has largely evolved in response to poststructuralism, I shall treat the latter first.

The two most influential poststructuralist thinkers of the past decade have been Jacques Derrida and Michel Foucault. With the exception of his very recent work, Derrida's research has focused primarily on texts drawn from the tradition of metaphysics, rather than on social and political thought. Yet, he himself has recently stressed the political character of his work.[1] His brand of literary criticism, what he calls *deconstruction*, attempts to show that the traditional binary oppositions and hierarchies permeating rational discourse break down when scrutinized against the backdrop of textual signifiers, which lend them meaning. This activity is political because such oppositions as male/female, reason/emotion, identity/difference, end up privileging one side of the opposition (e.g., the rational/male/identity side), in ways that dominate our entire way of thinking and acting. Thus, some followers of Derrida have been quick to point out the metaphysical connection between, say, scientific rationalism and sex discrimination or between scientific rationalism and totalitarian conformism.

The main opposition that Derrida seeks to reverse is that between speech and writing.[2] It is the privileging of speech (*phonocentrism*), as the preferred model of signification, that is most deeply implicated in the privileging of transcendental reason (*logocentrism*). The simultaneous presence of an objective state of affairs referred to by speakers and their own speech creates the illusion that language is a transparent medium of meaning and reference. In speaking about some object in the presence of that object, it seems as if the object itself provides a univocal, certain ground for establishing the meaning of the name by which it is referred. It is because meaning seems so clearly grounded in pure immediate perceptual experience, experience unadulterated by parochial culture-bound accretions, that we think a universally valid (i.e., rational) system of signifiers is possible.

Derrida's strategy in dispelling this illusion is to show how writing, not speech, is a better model for understanding the relationship between reference and meaning. Because writing is normally detached from any specific context of reception, it lacks conditions of immediate objective reference that might establish univocality of meaning. A text can be interpreted differently depending on when, where, and by whom it is read. Since neither the author nor the object of reference is immediately present, the reader must rely on his own context to fill in the meaning. Given the indefinitely numerous contexts in which a text might be read, the task of interpretation can never be finished. As Derrida puts it, textual meaning differs, or loses its identity, from one moment to the next. Thus, its meaning is also deferred, remaining forever incomplete and indeterminate.

Relying on Ferdinand de Saussure's structural linguistics, Derrida argues that not just writing, but all language, including speech, is contextual in ways that frustrate closure and univocality of meaning. Meaning is essentially contextual. A signifier such as "black" gets its meaning from the system of terms that both resemble it and differ from it—phonetically, graphically, and semantically. Moreover, signifiers also acquire their meaning, with respect to the specific sentence, paragraph, speech act, etc. in which they appear. "Black," for example, can be used literally (as in "The cat is black") or figuratively (as in "Her finances are in the black"). This dual contextuality with respect to an implicit system of signifiers and an intertextual field of sentences, utterances, and other background determinants, is itself open-ended. For the implicit system of signifiers changes with respect to mutations in the field of discourse.[3]

Basically, Derrida's discussion of meaning recalls the part/whole circle of textual interpretation discussed by Dilthey and Gadamer. But here, the accent is on the inescapable open-endedness and mutability of (con)text. Such mutability constantly shifts and destabilizes the meaning of signifiers, thereby rendering even a highly historicist and dialectical notion of "universal truth" of the sort defended by Gadamer all but impossible.

The indeterminancy and reversibility of meanings—highlighted by deconstruction—has much in common with Hegel's theory that identity is dialectically constituted through difference. Reality is unstable because the basic concepts in terms of which it seems to acquire a fixed and stable, meaningful identity—being/becoming, quantity/quality, essence/appearance—incorporate within themselves their opposite signification. Given this deconstructive feature of language, it is easy to see that absolute binary oppositions, such as reason/unreason, freedom/domination, and so on, necessarily break down. A similar deconstruction of meaning may be found in Adorno's critique of the totalitarian implications of rational identity and transcendence in *Negative Dialectics*.[4]

Derrida's deconstructive method has become a powerful weapon in the arsenal of contemporary radical social criticism, including feminist criticism of male domination in Western culture and society. Equally influential, in this regard, has been the work of Michel Foucault. Like Derrida, Foucault is highly suspicious of the universalist emancipatory claims made on behalf of Western rationalism. He continually emphasizes the discontinuities and ruptures in social and cultural practices that render ideas of historical progress and universal reason highly problematic. Aside from this radical relativism, he is also critical of the ideal of self-determining subjectivity informing the critical tradition. In this respect, both he and Derrida are more radical in their deconstruction of the emancipatory ideals of the Enlightenment than either Adorno, Horkheimer, or Marcuse.

Nevertheless, as Habermas himself has pointed out, there is much in Foucault's critique of Western rationalism that draws him especially close to the Frankfurt School.[5] First of all, Foucault was trained in clinical psychology and, therefore, undertook a critique of rationalism from an empirical, sociological perspective. He was less interested in unraveling the internal inconsistencies of textual meaning, than in exposing external relations of power that constitute the practices and discourses of the human sciences. Consequently, his "materialist" approach to social critique has a lot in common with the kind of ideology critique advanced by Marx and other critical theorists, even if it remains ungrounded in universal reason.[6] Moreover, his analysis of the ways in which psychology, sociology, economics, and political science contribute to sustaining the "disciplinary" practices of a well-administered society directly harks back to the critique of technology and science, inaugurated by Weber and continued by Kirchheimer, Marcuse, and Habermas.[7]

Foucault's method of critique continues the kind of *genealogical* criticism made famous by Nietzsche. It traces the "noble" ideals of reason—individuality, liberty, justice, truth, and logic–back to systems of thought serving the interests of social and political domination.[8] To begin with, Foucault undertakes a structuralist bracketing of subjectivity. The humanist ideal of self-determining subjectivity is meaningless, Foucault argues, since it embodies an untenable contradiction: the individual as cause (producer) of itself. On Foucault's reading, the subject is but the intersection of objective patterns of speech and behavior governed by impersonal rules, which possess but a historically accidental and geographically localized force.[9]

According to Foucault, what counts as a true, meaningful statement is likewise a function of impersonal rules. These impose order by excluding certain types of statements from the realm of permissible discourse. In turn, these rules acquire their normative force with respect to actual practices that are themselves governed by power relations. Since such relations arise out of social conflict, their "validity"—and therewith the truth and meaningfulness of permissible statements—is ultimately a function of arbitrary violence. Thus, the rational discourse of science constrains us whether we freely assent to it or not. For it is that discourse which, owing to its elaboration of technologies and hierarchies of control functional for maintaining a system of domination, has installed itself above all others.[10]

In Habermas's opinion, Foucault's main contribution to critical theory consists in showing how modern disciplinary practices, aided by the development of medicine, psychology, social statistics (demography), and behavioral science (criminology and pedagogical-administrative technology), have transformed overt violence and domination into subtle forms of self-discipline. Individuals are more or less passively constituted as compliant subjects through forms of bodily training and conditioning that produce both pleasure and knowledge. This way of interpreting domination, it should be noted, resonates nicely with Marcuse's theory of repressive desublimation.[11]

Foucault's analysis of power eschews global theories of economic and class domination in favor of empirical functionalist analyses which show how power is unintentionally and anonymously insinuated into bodily habits and micro-technologies of a local nature, such as the religious confessional, the clinical examination, and the military exercise. The overlapping and cross-fertilization of these techniques in conjunction with the rise of the human sciences during the nineteenth century gave rise to new forms of detention, surveillance, behavioral conditioning, statistical measurement, classification, and therapy associated with modern "carceral" society. This concentrated form of "bio-power" drew upon the objectifying techniques of normalizing judgment, hierarchical observation and examination that had already been deployed in hospitals, monastaries, and military barracks to impose discipline within schools, factories, and households.[12]

Psychoanalysis is also implicated in the techniques of domination. Early in his career, Foucault had argued that the rational suppression of madness as a disease requiring treatment and therapeutic confinement, that first occurred in the seventeenth century, foreshadowed later techniques of social control. In his last writings, he noted that the conceptualization of sexuality, as a dangerous, potentially destructive, antisocial force, that arose in the nineteenth century, played a decisive role in this regard. The Victorian preoccupation with hysteria, masturbation, proper breeding, race, and homosexuality found expression in new laws restricting abortion and prohibiting prostitution, homosexuality and other "perversions." These normalizing tendencies also found expression in psychotherapy, which furthered the idea that persons possessed hidden drives requiring disclosure, interpretation, and control.[13]

Among critical theorists, only Adorno ever adopted such a negative assessment of Freud's theory (Marcuse and Habermas, by contrast, had a much higher estimation of its value). Yet, it is also safe to say that the ambivalence of psychoanalysis was not lost on any of them. In practice, psychoanalysis often reinforces conformity to repressive norms. In theory, however, it sets forth a model of individual health and integrity that is critical of existing social repression. Nevertheless, it is just this ideal of radical "autonomy" that poststructuralists criticize as "repressive."

No one has been more critical of this notion than Jean-François Lyotard. As the major exponent of postmodernism today, Lyotard's political thought has occupied a nebulous terrain intersected by what appear to be radically opposed tendencies: the modern tendency toward indefinite novelty and self-transcendence and the more traditional tendency toward parochial particularism (contextualism). If he is right, this schizophrenic mixing of different voices, styles, and philosophies is emblematic of the postmodern condition in which we live. This is a condition radically subversive of the sort of stability, unity, and identity attributed by rationalism to the autonomous subject.[14]

Rejecting the totalitarian tendencies of universal reason, Lyotard has made it clear that it is Adorno's, not Habermas's critical theory he prefers.[15] Yet, despite sharing Adorno's faith in modern art as a bastion of resistance, Lyotard's use of linguistic philosophy to justify his position has much in common with Habermas's.

Lyotard nowhere provides a neat definition of postmodernism. Basically, the term is used by him to denote the radical undermining of what he calls "grand narratives," those rational doctrines of universal humanity and progress that arose during the Enlightenment. The two narratives that prevail today correspond to two models of political legitimation. One model states that technological efficiency is the sole criteria for evaluating the performance of the state. As a self-regulating system, the state adapts itself to changes in domestic and world economies by absorbing and processing information. Its legitimation is procured by sustaining economic growth and maintaining law and order.

The freedom of the government to make technical decisions without fear of public reprisal ultimately requires manipulating democratic input from above, if not scaling it back altogether. This aspect of the political system is opposed by the second model of legitimation, which justifies political decisions on the basis of their universal, rational acceptance. Lyotard explicitly equates the second model of legitimation with that proposed by Habermas, in which unconstrained consensus provides a touchstone for truth and justice.

According to Lyotard, neither the first nor the second model of legitimation is compatible with the radical heterogeneity and undecidability of scientific, moral, and political "reason." Take, for example, the first model of legitimation. The rise of multinational corporations, which outstrip government capabilities in data processing, severely challenges the state's capacity to globally manage its economic environment. The state is no longer in control of the technical apparatus necessary to guarantee efficient administration and economic growth. And, it is not just because the data banks are in the hands of hostile corporations. On the contrary, the absorption of greater amounts of highly complex information itself proves disfunctional when it outstrips the capacity of the system to process data and make simple decisions.

This indecidability penetrates to the heart of modern science itself. Paradoxes revolving around, say, Heisenberg's Principle of Indeterminacy, which states that it is impossible to determine both the location and velocity of subatomic particles simultaneously, introduces an element of subjective decision and imprecision into scientific measurement and prediction. Most importantly, however, the impurity of scientific observation as a composite of subjective and objective elements bears witness to the instability, indeterminacy, and ungroundedness of social life itself.

This feature of social life is at the root of Lyotard's repudiation of the second model of legitimation, the consensus model put forward by Habermas. Lyotard rejects Habermas's claim that there are universally binding validity claims and consensual norms underwriting communication. Communication is essentially fragmented into radically distinct "language games," whose rules are absolutely irreducible to one another. Appealing to the very speech act theories cited by Habermas, Lyotard emphasizes the essentially local and contextual nature of all language games. At the same time, however, he acknowledges their basic impurity and instability. Even language games are not closed systems. Participants in a given language game contest and thereby alter the meaning of rules, which are supposed to govern their production of meaningful statements. And different language games can overlap one another to create "a monster formed by the interweaving of heteromorphous classes of utterances." Recall, for example, the hybrid, descriptive and prescriptive nature of a scientific discourse.

The indeterminacy of meaning continually frustrates the formation of a unitary political culture based on principles of rational consistency and personal sovereignty. Summoning the spector of deconstruction, Lyotard writes, "the social subject itself seems to dissolve in this dissemination of language games. The social bond . . . is not woven with a single thread, (but) by the intersection of at least two (and in reality an indeterminate number of) language games obeying different rules."[16] For this reason, he concludes that the democratic demand, that social practices conform to a universally binding consensus as a condition of their legitimation, cannot but have totalitarian implications.

The only notion of legitimation which is compatible with the postmodern condition is "legitimation by paralogy." Above all, what is legitimate is the innovative and unconventional shattering of established hierarchies of thought, disciplinary boundaries, and canonical forms into new configurations of discourse. Such transgression operates in accordance with established criteria, the rules of the game, even while working "at the limits of what the rules tolerate in order to invent new moves, perhaps new rules and thus new games." In doing so, it counteracts the totalitarian impulse toward stability and homogeneity. Paralogical activity, then, is at once aesthetic (innovative) and ethical, protecting the plurality of political, ethical, and expressive language games from the tyranny of the cognitive, scientific, and technological.

In the all too brief and oversimplified summary of poststructuralism and postmodernism I sought to show some of the ways in which their social criticism and that of first-generation critical theorists intersect. However, it is Habermas and his followers who have directly responded to the challenge posed by these movements. Their reaction has ranged from mildly sympathetic (as in the case of Foucault) to extremely hostile. Habermas himself has contributed somewhat to this tension by characterizing those who follow Foucault and Derrida as "young conservatives."[17]

This is a strange label to pin on poststructuralists and postmodernists, given their awareness of the role played by capitalism in maintaining various forms of domination. Their suspicion of Marxism and bureaucratic socialism notwithstanding, these movements possess a profile that is anything but conservative. Habermas knows this, but nonetheless finds conservative *implications* in their rejection of universal reason. In his opinion, the worst of these implications is their rejection of freedom, individuality, communal solidarity, and democratic self-determination. For him, these are the very values underwriting opposition to totalitarianism.

Of course, poststructuralists and postmodernists reject such rational values on the grounds that they tacitly support totalitarian tendencies. In Habermas's opinion, this diagnosis reflects a narrow conception of reason restricted to instrumental domination. By failing to attend to the nonobjectifying emancipatory rationality inherent in communication, they end up opposing tolerance of plurality and difference to reason in general. In doing so they repeat the same mistake committed by first-generation critical theorists.

By neglecting the complementary relationship between difference and identity, respect for the other and orientation toward agreement inherent in communication, poststructuralists and postmodernists, Habermas contends, are forced to accept the anarchic consequences of a one-sided pluralism. But this fragmentation of social bond undercuts their own political stance. The poststructuralist dissolution of the acting subject into a plurality of language games (Lyotard), a force-field of power relations (Foucault), or an open system of linguistic signifiers (Derrida) relativizes all rational distinctions and identities to the point where political resistance becomes meaningless. Why be political if there is no ideal to be fought over, no subject to be emancipated?

At stake in this debate is the extent to which reason itself is contextual. Poststructuralists and postmodernists maintain that reason is nothing apart from the existing institutions and language games in which it is embodied. These institutions and language games are relative to Western culture. More importantly, they have actually functioned to sustain domination. One can, of course, talk about the emancipatory ideals which purportedly legitimate these institutions and language games. But as Hegel pointed out, whatever definite meaning such ideals possess is relative to these very same institutions and practices. Even their normative validity (i.e., their "rational" power to morally obligate and constrain), is at least partially a function of actual linguistic exclusions and corporeal habits that remain below the threshold of explicit consciousness. Thus, it is futile to argue, as Habermas does, that rationalization, enlightenment—in short, reason—can be neatly distinguished from capitalism and its pathological side effects.

Habermas, of course, acknowledges that capitalism and rationalization have exercised a mutual and profound impact on one another. For that very reason, he cannot but be sensitive to the interlacing of power and knowledge described by Foucault.[18] Likewise, he can hardly deny the rhetorical and poetic aspect of discourse alluded to by Derrida.[19] In actual conversations, rational assent is procured through figures of speech which often have a covert impact on the emotions of the listener. This transgression of the rational boundaries separating cognitive, prescriptive, and expressive language resonates with Lyotard's view that everyday speech is largely impure and non-consensual in nature. Yet, despite the rootedness of thought and action in parochial contexts of language and speech, there is, he maintains, a universal core of validity claims and expectations that point beyond actual practices. Transcending the pressures, distortions, and social inequalities of everyday speech, these expectations imply an ideal speech situation which resists all forms of social domination.[20]

Habermas's defense of the transcendent power of reason with respect to actual speech largely appeals to the pragmatic contradictions that attend a pure contextualism. A purely contextualist theory could not assert its own truth or validity without implying the possibility of universal assent. If it did not claim to be valid at all, then no one would take it seriously. If it claimed to be valid only for persons whose prejudices happened to be shaped by the same sorts of parochial values and habits it articulates, then only those persons would take it seriously. It would not have any power to persuade others, who share a different set of cultural assumptions. Only if the theory claimed to be true (universally binding for all), would it possess a critical scope that all would have to take seriously.

By attacking weaknesses in contextualism, Habermas hopes to secure the validity of his own position. However, it is not obvious that this strategy succeeds. The contextualist, after all, need not feel compelled to defend her/his peculiar way of talking to outsiders. She/He may not think it important to reach agreement with others sharing different worldviews.

Where does this leave us? Lacking positive evidence to support the transcendentalist position, the contextualist remains undaunted in her/his belief that it is faith in reason, not its denial, that is chiefly responsible for ethnocentric intolerance of non-European culture. At best, preoccupation with rational grounding of the sort undertaken by Habermas distracts the critical theorist from her/his true vocation, which is the exposure of ideologies hiding behind the veneer of universal reason. Of course, if Habermas is right that the heritage of the Enlightenment presents us with the best guarantee against intolerance, then preoccupation with rational grounding seems altogether understandable. But such grounding requires positive support. In order to provide it, Habermas has appealed to anthropological, sociological, and psychological studies, which reinforce the idea that rational moral ideas are the culmination of a long process of social evolution. These studies, however, are admittedly problematic. Many critics have argued that they are ethnocentric. Others, including some feminists, claim that they reflect a male bias. The concluding section will examine this latter criticism, as well as others made by feminists who, in most other respects, might be sympathetic to Habermas's program.

FEMINISM AND RECENT CRITICAL THEORY

The relationship between critical theory and feminist social theory is complicated. To begin with, there are important differences between French and Anglo-American varieties of feminist theory. French feminists such as Hélène

Cixous, Luce Iraguray, and Catherine Clément focus their attention on gender biases in psychoanalysis. To the extent that they undertake to develop a notion of the feminine, they are more likely to appeal to the linguistic interpretation of psychoanalysis proferred by Jacques Lacan than to the writings of Freud or, for that matter, poststructuralists. However, like poststructuralists, many French feminists criticize Western rationalism as inherently masculine and antifeminine.

No doubt, French feminists would have important things to say to critical theorists. However, the vocabulary in which they develop their theories is so far removed from that of critical theory—indeed, they seldom if ever mention critical theory in their writings—that it would be very difficult to discuss their relationship to critical theory in the short space remaining. Since this is not the case with Anglo-American feminism, which is more influenced by empirical sociology (especially Marxism), it will be more fruitful for our purposes to confine our discussion to that tradition.

Influenced by Freudian theory, first-generation critical theorists necessarily touched on issues concerning the role of women in modern and, above all, capitalist society. In general, however, they seldom spoke about the peculiar oppression of women in modern society. This may be due to the fact that most of their important work predated the Women's Liberation movement of the late sixties. Marcuse, who died in 1978, was a notable exception. In his last interviews and lectures, he voiced strong support for the goals of the women's movement. Habermas, of course, has singled out the women's movement as one of the most important, if not *the* most important emancipatory movement to surface in the past two decades. Yet he, too, has had little to say about the peculiar oppression of women in modern society (he favorably notes, however, recent changes in the family and the work force toward greater equality). Nevertheless, this neglect has not prevented feminist philosophers, sympathetic with his program, from pointing out gender biases in his research.

One important line of feminist criticism is directed against Habermas's reliance on Kohlbergian developmental psychology. Seyla Benhabib cites the empirical research of psychologist Carol Gilligan in arguing that Habermas's discourse ethic, like other formalistic, universalist moral theories, only accomodates the moral perspective of the "generalized other":[21]

The standpoint of the "generalized other" requires us to view each and every individual as a rational being entitled to the same rights and duties we would want to ascribe to ourselves. In assuming this perspective we abstract from the individuality and concrete identity of the other. We assume that . . . what constitutes his or her moral dignity is not what differentiates us from each other, but rather what we have in common. Our relationship to the other is governed by the norm of *formal reciprocity*: each is entitled to expect from us what we can expect and assume from him or her.[22]

As Benhabib points out, the moral categories that correspond to interacting with others in accordance with generalizable expectations are those of right, obligation, and entitlement. The standpoint of the "concrete other," by contrast

requires us to view each and every rational being as an individual with a concrete history, identity, and affective-emotional constitution. In assuming this standpoint, we . . . seek to understand the distinctiveness of the other. We seek to comprehend the needs of the other, their motivations, what they search for, and what they desire.

Our relation to the other is governed by the norm of *complementary reciprocity*: each is entitled to expect and to assume from the other forms of behavior through which the other feels recognized and confirmed as a concrete, individual being with specific needs, talents, and capacities.

The moral categories that accompany our treatment of others as possessors of unique attributes are those of responsibility, bonding, and sharing. Love, care, sympathy, and solidarity—not duty—are the feelings appropriate to this moral attitude.

Benhabib observes that the modern tradition of moral and political thought has tended to subordinate the standpoint of the concrete other, which it consigns to the private sphere of the family, to the standpoint of the generalized other, which is legally institutionalized in the public sphere. One of the factors motivating this subordination has been the dichotomy between reason and desire, reason and feeling. Since Kant, theories of justice have tended to emphasize the subrationality of concrete needs and have cautioned against letting particular feelings and desires figure in impartial moral deliberation. By contrast, Habermas's discourse ethic, as we have seen, is critical of Kant on just this point. For it stresses the importance of discussing the universal validity of individual needs in determining the justice of norms.

Nevertheless, as we have seen—and as Benhabib correctly points out—Habermas's discourse ethic is unclear about its own identity. On one hand, it is supposed to ground universal communication rights which transcend particular needs. These rights, which reflect the standpoint of the generalized other, are ostensibly immune from democratic discussion and recall. On the other hand, the discourse ethic is supposed to ground a democratic community in which persons care about whether their particular needs and interests are compatible with the well-being of all. Rights should flow from communal interests, not vice versa. In this respect, the discourse ethic presupposes feelings of solidarity that reflect the standpoint of the concrete other.[23]

According to Benhabib, Habermas's insistence that only the standpoint of the generalized other represents the moral point of view, ends up relegating the standpoint of the concrete other to the aesthetic sphere of feeling and desire. In turn, this exclusion of the standpoint of the concrete other, reflects a certain gender bias. Appealing to research by Gilligan and others, Benhabib argues that the standpoint of the concrete other is the one normally assumed by women in our society.

Although neither Gilligan nor Benhabib want to limit the capacity to assume this standpoint to women, they both agree with Nancy Chodorow in concluding that women are more prone to this standpoint, "because of patterns of personality formation and activities confined to nurturance, love, and care."[24] In particular, Chodorow argues that because female infants identify more closely with their mothers and vice versa, their moral development proceeds along a path which emphasizes relational bonding and contextual problem-solving. Males, by contrast, develop along a moral path which emphasizes rational differentiation and distantiation. Consequently, they are prone to develop needs for independence and competition and, thus, are more likely to develop capacities of rational abstraction, necessary for agreeing on impartial procedures of justice.

The accusation of gender bias in Habermas's discourse ethic is still problematic, however. Habermas contends, and Benhabib concurs, that the distinction between an ethics of (general) principle and an ethics of (concrete) care does not so much designate a distinction between different types of ethics, as it does a distinction between different aspects of one and the same ethics. According to Habermas, one must appeal to general ethical principles in resolving questions of justice impartially. One assumes that particular actions can be justified as permissible, on the grounds that they conform to valid norms. But the very notion of validity, Habermas claims, implies a relationship to universal interests. So generalizability of interests seems to be an essential feature of any rationally accountable moral behavior. Nevertheless, Habermas also recognizes that rational accountability is only one aspect of ethical behavior. Not only are we required to justify our actions with respect to general principles if challenged to do so, but we are also required to apply them in a manner which yields the best (happiest) results.[25]

The application of principles involves different competencies from those requisite for rational justification. It sometimes happens that several valid moral principles apply to a given situation, but in ways that yield contradictory results. Suppose I am the physician of a person who has just been diagnosed as having a serious brain disease. I have an obligation to tell the patient the truth about his condition. At the same time, I'm afraid that doing so will violate my obligation to relieve his suffering as much as possible. Indeed, it may even be the case that the patient's resolve to fight the disease might be enhanced if he didn't know the truth. What should I do?

There's no easy answer to this question. For what's at issue here is not the validity of general principles, but their relative priority in resolving a particular, *concrete* dilemma. Should I act so as to relieve suffering or preserve trust? Only the specific circumstances, or *context*, in which the dilemma arises can provide guidance here. In this instance, I must adopt the attitude of the concrete other. My caring for the patient, in particular, my solicitude with respect to the unique person he is, will help me to decide which course of treatment to pursue.

Although Habermas wants to give equal weight to both aspects of ethical conduct—the principled attitude of the generalized other, requisite for rational accountability, and the caring attitude of the concrete other, requisite for concrete application—he designates only the principled attitude as the truly rational. For only the discursive justification of ethical conduct can be captured in terms of universal procedures of fairness. Yet, this distinction seems highly questionable. If, as Habermas claims, general principles are justified in terms of their consequences for all concerned, then surely this is a function of their applicability. Habermas himself concedes as much in some of his recent remarks. Yet, he still thinks that problems of application can be resolved outside of particular contexts of action, in discourse.

But is it not the case that the meaning and validity of norms is as much a function of their applicability to particular contexts, and that such applicability is itself relative to those who possess sufficient insight? In the English common law tradition, for example, it is recognized that particular cases constitute a loose, but nonetheless coherent, legal precedent. Just how new cases supplement and modify the existing legal tradition is a matter of interpretation, not simply a matter of formal procedure. Interpretation presupposes experience, creativity, a well-formed character, and above all, a certain intuitive insight. Its not being a matter of formal, universal procedure doesn't mean that interpretation is merely subjective, or beyond the scope of rational evaluation. What it does mean, however, is that there are rational aptitudes which are also contextual.

If Gilligan and others are right, that contextual moral judgment is an aptitude that is more developed in women than in men, then Habermas's refusal to accord it the title of reasoning does indeed reflect a certain gender bias. This is none other than the masculine tendency to equate the rational with what is capable of being publicly (discursively) agreed upon by all, regardless of context. It is no wonder, then, that many feminists have been attracted to poststructuralism's critique of rationality.

Before concluding, I would like to raise one final question about gender bias in Habermas's distinction between public and private realms. Nancy Fraser has recently argued that Habermas's tendency to classify the family, as an institution within the lifeworld that is primarily responsible for the symbolic, or communicative "reproduction" of society, ignores the extent to which it contributes to the material, or economic reproduction of society, which is primarily a function of the system. By neglecting this aspect of the family, Habermas overlooks the extent to which the labor of the homemaker is unremunerated.[26]

Furthermore, Habermas's diagnosis of modern social pathology stresses the debilitating impact of the economic and administrative system on the family and public sphere. Yet, according to Fraser, the principal form of alienation encountered by women arises from the debilitating impact of the family sphere on the economic and administrative system. For it is the norm of patriarchal domination, first generated in the family, that later insinuates itself throughout society as a whole.

According to Fraser, Habermas's diagnosis yields two consequences which impact adversely on the feminist critique of male domination. First, this diagnosis compels him to view any subsumption of the lifeworld under the system as inherently pathological. It would follow, as a matter of course, that any attempt to restructure the family along the lines of an economic wage relationship would disrupt the socialization process. However, not only is there no evidence that this has happened, but the emancipation of home-makers would rather seem to require such a restructuration in any case.

Second, Habermas's diagnosis of social pathology neglects the extent to which institutionalized roles of worker, consumer, and client are themselves gendered. Habermas observes that the client-provider relationship, that obtains between welfare recipients and the state, undermines the freedom and dignity of the clients. However, he nowhere provides an adequate explanation of this phenomenon in terms of institutionalized gender roles. Not only do women constitute the vast majority of welfare clients, but it is men, not women, who experience this dependency most acutely. This is because the role of worker, *as it has been institutionalized in our society*, is primarily masculine. Men are raised to be independent, self-sufficient "bread winners." Women, by contrast, are marginalized in "helping" professions, in which they utilize their nurturing and caring skills, or in part-time, low-paying, unskilled jobs. Whether they are homemakers or workers who supplement their husband's incomes, women are not taught to think of themselves as fully independent, self-sufficient "bread winners." Consequently, welfare dependence is experienced differently by them. For them, it is but a paternalistic extension of the patriarchal domination they have suffered under during their entire lives.

Last, but not least, the role of consumer in capitalist society is primarily structured along feminine lines. Women are still the primary targets of advertising. It is they who have been trained to be the passive purveyors of desire. And it is they who have been charged with the responsibility for purchasing the goods necessary for household maintenance.

In the final analysis, it is a one-sided ethic of care, which conspires with desire, in reinforcing consumerism and dependency. Conversely, it is a one-sided ethic of principles, which conspires with individualism, in reinforcing fragmentation and isolationism. A truly emancipated society would encourage moral development along both paths, so that dependence and social fragmentation are avoided. Rational moral agents would possess the autonomy that comes from being discursively accountable for their behavior. But, they would also possess the concrete needs requisite for rational community: caring *for* others and judging contextually, in solidarity *with* others. This would necessitate a radical transformation of gender roles in which both men and women learn to realize themselves as independent beings, while remaining receptive to the needs of others.

NOTES

1. See the interviews with Derrida in *Positions* (London, 1981); and Michael Ryan, *Marxism and Deconstruction: A Critical Articulation* (Baltimore: Johns Hopkins University Press, 1982), for a discussion of the political significance of Derrida's deconstructive method. For a radical revision of the Marxist tradition, which resonates with ideas drawn from both Derrida and Foucault, see Ernesto Laclau and Chantal Mouffe, *Hegemony and Strategy: Towards a Radical Democratic Politics* (London: Verso, 1985).

2. See J. Derrida, *Writing and Difference*, trans. Alan Bass (Chicago: University of Chicago Press, 1978), and *Of Grammatology*, trans. Gayatri Chakravorty Spivak (Baltimore: Johns Hopkins University Press, 1978).

3. Think of how the traditional opposition between "black" and "white" has taken on moral, political, and racial overtones in European history. This opposition, however, shifts depending on historical and cultural circumstances. In some cases, white is neutral with respect to all colors. In other cases black is. Sometimes the opposition

is not between black and white, but between, say, red and white. I have in mind the war between the Red (Bolshevik) and White (anti-Bolshevik) armies following the Bolshevik Revolution.

4. As Ryan points out, both Derrida and Adorno undermine rational discourse from within, showing how the universal and the identical necessarily implicate the particular. See Ryan, pp. 73–81.

5. See J. Habermas, *The Philosophical Discourse of Modernity*, pp. 238–93. An overview of the central themes of Foucault's work is contained in his essay, "The Subject and Power" reprinted in *Critical Theory: The Essential Readings (CTER)*.

6. For further details regarding the philosophical similarities and differences between Foucault's social critique and that of other critical theorists, see my article "Foucault and the Frankfurt School: A Discourse on Nietzsche, Power and Knowledge," in *Praxis International*, vol. 6, no. 3 (Fall 1986), pp. 311–27.

7. Foucault's remarks about first-generation critical theorists are few and unilluminating. This is not the case with his debate with Habermas. See "What is Enlightenment" in *The Foucault Reader*, ed. P. Rabinow (New York: Pantheon, 1984), and "Subject and Power."

8. See M. Foucault, "Nietzsche, Genealogy, History," in *Language, Counter-Memory, Practice: Selected Essays and Interviews by Michel Foucault*, ed. D. Bouchard (Ithaca: Cornell University Press, 1977).

9. See M. Foucault, *The Order of Things* (New York: Random House, 1973). In Foucault's last work on human sexuality, this view is modified to allow for the subject's self-constituting activity.

10. M. Foucault, *The Archaeology of Knowledge*, trans. A. M. Sheridan Smith (New York: Pantheon, 1972).

11. See M. Foucault, *Discipline and Punish: The Birth of the Prison*, trans. A. Sheridan (New York: Pantheon, 1979). Unlike Marcuse, who primarily stresses the repressive nature of power, Foucault follows Nietzsche in also emphasizing its "positive" and "productive" nature (e.g., in the form of enabling structures, know-how, technologies of discipline and self-control).

12. M. Foucault, *Knowledge/Power: Selected Interviews and Other Writings by Michel Foucault, 1972–1977*, ed. Colin Gordin (New York: Pantheon, 1980).

13. M. Foucault, *The History of Human Sexuality, Volume I: An Introduction*, trans. R. Hurley (New York: Pantheon, 1979).

14. See J.-F. Lyotard, *The Postmodern Condition: A Report on Knowledge*, trans. G. Bennington and B. Massumi (Minneapolis: University of Minnesota Press, 1984). Portions of this book have been reprinted in *CTER*.

15. I have dealt more extensively with Lyotard's political philosophy and its relationship to critical theory (especially Habermas) in "Legitimacy and the Postmodern Condition: The Political Thought of Jean-François Lyotard," *Praxis International*, vol 7, nos. 3, 4 (Winter 1987–88), pp. 284–304.

16. *Ibid.*, p. 40.

17. J. Habermas, "Modernity: An Unfinished Project," reprinted in *CTER*.

18. One of Habermas's major objections to Foucault's genealogical enterprise is its tendency to vacillate between two senses of power. Like Nietzsche, Foucault hopes to show that, by uncovering the hidden context of power relations underlying normative institutions, one destroys their claim to rational, universal validity. At the same time, however, he treats power as if it were a universal force underlying the constitution of all knowledge and discourse. In that case, however, he would not be able to defend the rational validity of his own critique. See *The Philosophical Discourse of Modernity*.

19. Habermas acknowledges that philosophical discourse must possess figurative (metaphoric) devices for mediating between the technical language of science and everyday speech. However, he criticizes Derrida's deconstruction of the philosophy (reason)/literature (rhetoric) distinction for two reasons. First, it reduces philosophical truth claims to rhetorical figures possessing at most a kind of aesthetic conviction. Second, it transforms philosophy from an enterprise in which claims are resolved through rational argument to a kind of expressive, poetic literature. Deprived of its argumentative structure, philosophy ceases to function as a problem-solving guide for science, while also ceasing to communicate the insights of science to average persons. See *The Philosophical Discourse of Modernity*.

20. Habermas's critique of Foucault brings to bear distinctions between different kinds of normative force. As Nancy Fraser points out, Foucault comes very close to conceiving power relations as a quasi-transcendental universal in the same manner that Nietzsche conceived the Will-to-Power. This metaphysical tendency in Foucault's thought not only runs counter to his own historicism, but it indirectly undercuts his genealogical method of criticism. That method ostensibly criticizes rationalist discourses by showing that their claim to universal validity as essentially emancipatory and/or egalitarian is contradicted by their rootedness in historically specific power relations. However, if all discourse whatsoever is rooted in historically specific power relations, then the worst that can be said about these discourses is their ideological misrepresentation of their own origin. One could not criticize them *because* they are grounded in power relations that are normatively illegitimate or unjust. Habermas's approach, on the contrary, does not deny the ubiquity of power relations—even the unconstrained force of the better argument, which his ideal speech situation is intended to capture, implies some kind of normative "force" or constraint. However, it distinguishes those power relations, that are generated through legitimate means of rational discourse, from those that aren't. Moreover, its "genealogy" of rational structures not only attempts to show the necessity and universality of such structures with respect

to speech action, but it also points out how such structures are themselves legitimate—that is, how they enable greater freedom and justice, *if developed in a nonselective manner*.

21. See Gilligan's *In a Different Voice: Psychological Theory and Women's Development* (Cambridge, Mass.: Harvard University Press, 1982).

22. S. Benhabib, *Critique, Norm, and Utopia: A Study of the Foundations of Critical Theory* (New York: Columbia University Press, 1986), p. 340. Benhabib's argument is summarized in "The Utopian Dimension in Communicative Ethics," reprinted in *CTER*.

23. Habermas has recently stressed the importance of solidarity as a precondition of discourse. See "Justice and Solidarity," (*Loc. cit.*) reprinted in *The Moral Domain: The Ongoing Conversation Between Philosophy and the Social Sciences*, ed. Thomas Wren (Cambridge, Mass.: MIT Press, 1990).

24. *Ibid.*, p. 409, n. 124. See Nancy Chodorow, *The Reproduction of Mothering* (Berkeley: University of California Press, 1978).

25. See J. Habermas, "Questions and Counter-Questions," *Praxis International* vol. 4, no. 3 (1984), pp. 229–50.

26. N. Fraser, "What's Critical About Critical Theory?: The Case of Habermas and Gender," in *CTER*.

BIOGRAPHICAL PROFILES OF IMPORTANT CRITICAL THEORISTS

THEODOR WIESENGRUND ADORNO

Adorno was born in Frankfurt am Main, Germany in 1903 (he took the maiden name of his non-Jewish Italian mother, Maria Calvelli-Adorno della Piana, who was a singer). He studied musicology, philosophy, sociology, and psychology at Frankfurt University, where he met Max Horkheimer, his lifelong friend. After finishing his Ph.D. in 1924 he studied composition with Alban Berg, one of the leading exponents of the Vienna School of modern music. Following four years of editing a Viennese journal of music criticism, Adorno completed a study on Kierkegaard's aesthetic theories, which led to his association with the Frankfurt School. When Hitler assumed power, he fled first to Oxford and then, in 1938, to New York City. From 1941–49, he lived with Horkheimer in Los Angeles, California. Upon his return to Frankfurt, Adorno was made professor of philosophy and sociology at the Johann Wolfgang von Goethe University. From 1956, until his death in 1969, he was director of the reorganized Frankfurt Institute for Social Research. English translations of his major works include *Minima Moralia, Dialectic of Enlightenment, Prisms, Negative Dialectics, Philosophy of Modern Music, The Jargon of Authenticity, Against Epistemology, Introduction to the Sociology of Music*, and *Aesthetic Theory*.

JÜRGEN HABERMAS

Born in Düsseldorf (1929), Habermas spent his early youth in Gummersbach, Germany, where, at the age of fifteen, he was recruited into the army. From 1949–54, he studied philosophy, history, economics, psychology, and German literature at the University of Göttingen, Bonn, and Zürich. During his tenure as Adorno's assistant (1956–59), Habermas came across the *Journal for Social Research* published by the Frankfurt Institute in the thirties and forties, and fell under the influence of Marcuse's Freudian studies. In 1961, he was awarded a professorship at Heidelberg, and then assumed Horkheimer's Chair of Philosophy and Sociology at Frankfurt, where he eventually became involved in radical student politics. He later took over the directorship of the Max Planck Institute (1971–83). Today he is professor of philosophy at the University of Frankfurt. English translations of his major works include *Toward a Rational Society, Knowledge and Human Interests, Theory and Practice, Legitimation Crisis, Communication and the Evolution of Society, The Theory of Communicative Action* (2 vols.), *The Philosophical Discourse of Modernity, The Structural Transformation of the Public Sphere, The Logic of the Social Sciences*, and *Moral Consciousness and Communicative Action*.

MAX HORKHEIMER

Born in 1895 to an upper middle-class German-Jewish family, Horkheimer studied with the neo-Kantian philosopher Hans Cornelius in Munich and later with Edmund Husserl and Martin Heidegger in Freiburg, before receiving his Ph.D. in 1922. He officially assumed the directorship of the Frankfurt Institute in 1931 (the Institute was founded in 1923 under the original leadership of Carl Grünberg, a Marxist economist, who then relinquished control of the institute to Pollock in 1928). After his exile in America during the Nazi years, he returned to Frankfurt to reestablish the institute, of which he was director from 1951 to 1956. He died in 1971. English translations of his major works include *Critical Theory, Eclipse of Reason, Dialectic of Enlightenment*, and *Critique of Instrumental Reason*.

HERBERT MARCUSE

Born in Berlin in 1898, Marcuse became interested in left-wing politics during the Bavarian Revolt of 1919 (he had been a corporal in the army during the war). After studying with Husserl and Heidegger he joined the Frankfurt Institute in 1933. He later emigrated to New York and worked for the OSS during World War II translating documents and compiling a list of German industrialists who collaborated with the Nazis. After the war he taught at Columbia and Brandeis university. He was among the leading spokesmen for the New Left during the sixties and achieved wide popularity among students in France, Germany, and the United States. In 1964, he accepted an appointment as professor of philosophy at the University of California at San Diego. His students there included black activist Angela Davis and Erica Sherover, his wife at the time of his death in 1978. English translations of Marcuse's major works include *Hegel's Ontology, Negations, Reason and Revolution, Studies in Critical Philosophy, Eros and Civilization, Soviet Marxism, One-Dimensional Man, Five Lectures, An Essay on Liberation, Counterrevolution and Revolt*, and *The Aesthetic Dimension*.

GLOSSARY

Absolute Idea An expression used by Hegel to designate the fully realized and comprehended unity of the knowing subject and the known object (the totality of essential relations).

Abstract A term used by Hegel to designate a relationship, condition, or state of knowledge that is one-sided, partial, and separated from the total context of relations that essentially define (determine) it. The opposite of abstract is *concrete*.

Abstract labor time A concept used by Marx to denote the basic measure of a commodity's exchange value. It refers to the amount of time invested in the production of a commodity, including the amount of basic labor that is required to sustain and produce skilled labor.

Analytic-empirical science Those branches of natural and behavioral social science which deploy statistical (stochastic) or nomothetic (lawlike) generalizations for purposes of causal explanation and prediction. See *historical-hermeneutical science*.

Anthropocentric A term meaning "human centered."

Appearance A term which designates an accidental, superficial, or secondary level of existence (as opposed to what is *necessary*, truly real, primary and *essential*).

Biologism The view which holds that all behavior can be explained in terms of fixed biological drives.

Bureaucratic Socialism A system in which economic and political life is centrally administered by the state. In Communist regimes patterned after Marxist-Leninist ideology, the state is controlled by bureaucratic elites drawn exclusively from one party. See *Socialism*.

Categorical Imperative A term used by Kant to designate the unconditional nature of moral duty. There are two important meanings attached to it by Kant. First, we ought to always treat other persons as ends and never merely as means. Second, we ought to act in accordance with only those maxims of conduct that can be prescribed universally and consistently for all persons.

Class Consciousness The awareness that a group has of its own collective economic interests, as against the interests of other economic classes.

Colonization of the lifeworld An expression used by Habermas to refer to the way in which economic and administrative systems take over areas of familial and public life organized by communicative action. Because of colonization, interaction ceases to be regulated "democratically" by means of discussion regarding the validity of norms. Instead, it is regulated strategically, by persons interested in maximizing their own personal gain vis-à-vis money and power. The net result is commodification (the reduction of persons and things to commodities, or monetary exchange values) and bureaucratization (the subsumption of everyday life under greater administrative control).

Commodity Fetishism A term used by Marx to describe the manner in which the products of labor under capitalism take on a life of their own. The deification of the laws of the market coincides with the dehumanization of the producers, who lose control over their lives.

Communism For Marx, the highest stage of social development, characterized by the disappearance of the state as an instrument of political domination and the full emancipation and development of humanity. Today, communism has become synonymous with bureaucratic socialism. See *Socialism*.

Cultural impoverishment The inability of cultural traditions to provide meaningful values. Such impoverishment has several causes: the colonization of the lifeworld and the splitting off of elite subcultures, which prevent persons from developing the sorts of critical aptitudes requisite for analyzing and synthesizing tradition, and the ideological manipulation and devaluation of tradition to the status of meaningless habit, slogan, etc.

Cultural value spheres Weber's expression for those spheres of activity—science, law/ethics, and art/erotic life—which revolve around the three principal loci of value: the true (knowledge), the good (just norms), and the beautiful (aesthetic values).

Death instinct (thanatos) Freud's term for the natural tendency of complex unities to dissolve into their original atomic elements. Ultimately, it seeks release from tension (pain). See *life instinct*.

Dialectic Any relationship or process that contains contradictory or opposing aspects working toward resolution.

Discourse A technical term used by Habermas to refer to pure communication freed from the pressures, constraints, and inequalities in power and ability that normally accompany communicative action. See *ideal speech situation*.

Economic Determinism The notion that all social, political, and cultural changes are caused by economic changes. When applied to so-called "vulgar" Marxism, economic determinism is often understood to imply an irreversible, lawlike succession of modes of production, culminating in the inevitable downfall of capitalism and ascension of socialism. According to this view, the role of free, enlightened political action in determining the course of history is minimized.

Elective affinity Weber's expression for the correspondence, or psychological affinity, linking ideas and material interests.

Empiricism The doctrine that states that all knowledge comes from sense experience.

Essence The opposite of appearance (see above).

Ethnocentrism The tendency to view people of other ethnic (national, cultural, and racial) identities from the prejudiced perspective of one's own ethnic identity.

Existentialism A philosophical movement, inspired by the writings of Søren Kierkegaard (1813–1855) and Friedrich Nietzsche (1844–1900), which emphasizes the moral importance of individual responsibility and free choice in a world without rationally demonstrable absolutes. Its main exponents in the twentieth century were Jean-Paul Sartre, Albert Camus, and (more ambivalently) Martin Heidegger.

Explanatory understanding A term used by Weber to denote the method of sociological explanation. According to Weber, sociological explanations must refer to the *intentions, motives*, or *purposes* of agents as causal factors underlying action. Explanation thus presupposes an interpretative understanding of the *subjective meaning* of action. Conversely, understanding itself is guided by *ideal types*, or general models, of types of action which refer to statistically confirmable behavioral laws.

Fallibilism As opposed to foundationalism, the notion that knowledge is subject to future revision. Contrary to relativism, fallibilism states that persons are allowed to make assertions which claim to be provisionally true or universally valid.

Fascism A term used to designate modern political movements which seek to retain traditional forms of authority and class domination within the framework of a totalitarian state. Fascism found penultimate expression in Italy (1922–1945) and in Germany (1933–1945), where racist and anti-Semitic ideologies colluded with a virulent nationalism in fueling expansionist political aims.

Formal reason Weber's expression referring to very general *procedures* for reaching *valid* decisions. These procedures would include logical rules of deductive inference as well as scientific methods geared toward the calculation of consequences. Opposed to the contingent (situationally relative) calculation of formal rationality is *substantive rationality*, which principally consists of unconditional commands (e.g., "Don't lie!") whose validity is ostensibly rooted in some metaphysical absolute (e.g., God, nature, etc.). See *purposive rationality*.

Hermeneutics The science of textual interpretation (named after the Greek messenger-God Hermes). In contrast to the specific methodological concerns of hermeneutics, *philosophical hermeneutics* (a term coined by Gadamer) designates that type of philosophical reflection which uncovers the communicative and interpretative structure underlying all forms of experience whatsoever.

Historical-hermeneutic science Those branches of historical and cultural science (history, cultural anthropology/sociology, existential and phenomenological psychology, literary criticism, philology, and philosophy) which seek to understand and interpret symbolic expressions embedded in actions, texts, and cultural artifacts.

Ideal speech situation Habermas's expression denoting conditions of absolute freedom and equality which would have to be obtained in order for participants in discourse to reach rational agreement and thereby achieve a true (universally binding) consensus. See *discourse*.

Idealism The doctrine that states that the essence of reality is mind, or thought. The opposite of idealism is *materialism*.

Ideology As defined by Marx, any doctrine or belief which purports to justify material (economic) domination and inequality by appeal to illusions (e.g., God, the People, the State, Human nature, etc.) that have no basis in real historical life. Such abstract ideas appeal to false (because ahistorical) notions of *universal* and/or otherwise *unchanging* and *eternal* relationships.

Immanent critique A form of critique whose standards are derived from the subject-matter criticized, usually some historically specific cultural ideal. *External* critique derives its standards from more universal (transhistorical and transcultural) conditions underlying speech, knowledge, and action generally.

Legitimation crisis A crisis which results when the state is no longer able to procure the voluntary loyalty of its citizens. This occurs, for example, when citizens no longer feel that the laws of the state are morally just or have been enacted in a manner that is fair, impartial, and democratic.

Life instinct (eros) Freud's term for the natural tendency of simple, atomic elements to join together in forming more complex unities. See *death instinct*.

Lifeworld A technical term referring to the way in which persons subjectively experience, understand, and interpret their world. For Habermas, it consists of those implicit cultural-linguistic assumptions, norms, and habits which form the shared background of action and thought. The lifeworld is primarily constituted through the medium of communicative action, which is itself largely responsible for the organization of family and public sphere, the two principal domains shaping life experience. It is complementary to the *system*.

Marxist-Leninism The variant of Marxism associated with the thought of V. I. Lenin. Among its chief precepts is the idea that the masses must be led by a select cadre of highly disciplined revolutionaries (the Communist party as vanguard).

Materialism The doctrine that states that the essence of reality is matter. Materialism as it is here defined must be distinguished from *historical materialism*, which does not purport to reduce mind to matter. The latter says only that physical labor (economic productivity) is the basis on which all other aspects of human life depend.

Mediation A term used by Hegel to designate a dialectical unity between mutually interdependent, opposed terms.

Neo-Freudian revisionism As used by Marcuse, a term referring to those Freudians who de-emphasize biological determination in favor of social conditioning.

Nihilism A term denoting the destruction of, or disbelief in, metaphysical and moral absolutes.

Objectification A term used by Hegel and Marx to designate the expression of inner subjectivity in an outer object through, for example, artistic and literary production, productive labor, etc.

Objectivism The view which holds that the mind passively mirrors a prior (pregiven) object.

Oedipal Phase Freud's expression referring to a necessary stage of psychosexual development in which the male child experiences desire for the mother and hostility toward the father. According to Greek mythology, Oedipus, the king of Thebes, married his mother and killed his father.

Ontogenesis In Freudian terminology, the stages or logic underlying the psychic (instinctual) maturation of the individual from infant to adult. See *Phylogenesis*.

Performance Principle A term used by Marcuse to refer to an instinctual economy geared toward competitive achievement and acquisitiveness. See *Reality* and *Pleasure Principles*.

Phylogenesis In Freudian terminology, the stages or logic underlying the psychic (instinctual) evolution of the human species. See *ontogenesis*.

Pleasure Principle Freud's term referring to an instinctual economy geared toward the immediate satisfaction of need (pleasure). See *Performance* and *Reality Principles*.

Polymorphous sexuality For Freud, that state of infantile sexuality characterized by the diffusion of erotic energy throughout the entire body. As distinct from genital sexuality geared toward reproduction, polymorphous sexuality transforms all bodily regions into zones of pleasure.

Positivism The doctrine, first introduced by the founder of sociology, August Comte (1798–1857), which states that science must consist of factually confirmable causal regularities.

Pragmatism The philosophical movement founded by Charles Peirce, which defines the truth of any belief in terms of its usefulness.

Primal Horde Hypothesis Freud's suggestion that some feelings of guilt are an archaic remnant, buried in the collective unconscious (or memory) of the species, of an ancient patricide (the killing of the ancestral patriarch). The sons who killed the patriarch were envious of his monopoly over sexual relations with his wives and daughters, but later felt remorse for their act.

Primary narcissism The term used by Freud to capture the "oceanic" stage of psychic development prior to the differentiation of *ego* and *id*, subject and object. This stage is narcissistic in a figurative sense only: since the "oceanic" self experiences reality as an extension of its own being, it is necessarily absorbed in itself. In Greek mythology, Narcissus was so absorbed in staring at his reflection in a pond that he threw himself into the water, whence he was transformed into the flower that bears his name.

Projection The projecting outward of one's own insecurities, fantasies, and emotions onto the real world. Example: you detest your own inferiority, but repress this uncomfortable thought by regarding others as inferior, or by claiming that it is they who detest you for being inferior.

Purposive rationality Weber's expression referring to the methodical calculation of efficient *means* in pursuing one's aims or purposes. It is distinguished from *value rationality*, which refers to the pursuit of unconditional aims, or aims that are prescribed regardless of consequences and/or available means.

Rationalism The doctrine that states that all knowledge comes from pure reason. In Descartes, it is related to the notion that all knowledge can be logically deduced from a few "innate" ideas.

Rationalization A technical term used by Weber to refer to the dissemination of formal rationality in culture and society. It is not to be confused with Freud's use of the term, which refers to the justification of actions whose real motives may remain concealed.

Reality Principle Freud's term designating an instinctual economy of delayed gratification and sublimation, geared toward the rational attainment of long-term happiness.

Repetition compulsion For Freud, the tendency of all life forms to return to original states (also reflected in the tendency of repressed instincts to reassert themselves).

Secularization An expression referring to the transformation of transcendent, religious ideas into secular, or worldly, norms. Secularization and rationalization are sometimes used by Weber synonymously.

Skepticism The doctrine that states that nothing about the world is known to be true (i.e., valid for everyone) with certainty and that therefore no one is entitled to claim that he or she knows anything at all.

Socialism For Marx, the stage of social development preceding communism, characterized by abolition of private property and state control over the economy. Socialism may be democratic or bureaucratic. If the former, it may permit a multiparty competition for political power.

Splitting off of elite subcultures Habermas's expression for the kind of overspecialization which renders technical knowledge opaque to the average citizen. Such specialization is dangerous because it encourages passive deference to the authority of technical and managerial elites and deprives average citizens of opportunities to develop their own critical understanding of social problems.

State (Post-liberal) Capitalism As distinct from laissez-faire, a form of capitalism in which centralized state management replaces markets as the principal source of investment and/or resource allocation. Unlike socialism, state capitalism retains property structures which permit the appropriation of profits by private individuals.

Subject-object An expression designating the relationship between a knower and what is known.

Subjective Reason The expression used by critical theorists to refer to purposive rational orientations that are exclusively oriented toward the *instrumental* (means-efficient) pursuit of *self-preservation*.

Sublimation A term used by Freud to designate the rechanneling of immediate sexual desire toward substitute forms of delayed gratification which are socially beneficial. Example: the sublimation of erotic attraction in forms of friendship, familial love, patriotism, love of humanity, etc. *Repressive desublimation* is the expression coined by Marcuse to describe the release of sexual desire from inhibitions stemming from sublimation, which release is simultaneously a repression, or restriction, of pleasure to immediate gratification in consumption.

Surplus Repression: A term used by Marcuse to designate levels of social repression (denial of gratification), which extend beyond what is necessary for collective survival.

System A term designating self-contained and self-regulating processes (such as organisms) which adapt themselves to an external environment. According to Habermas, one can regard modern societies as composed of self-regulating economic and administrative systems, which react to aggregate inputs of supply and demand (as reflected in media of money and power) in a way that is largely unplanned and unintended. In contradistinction to the lifeworld, the system is chiefly responsible for sustaining the material reproduction of society. Its operation can be objectively (functionalistically and causally) explained, but not, like the lifeworld, subjectively interpreted as meaningful and purposive.

Teleological A term referring to the explanation of actions and events in terms of some purpose or end (*telos*).

Totalitarianism A type of political condition in which the state, under the exclusive control of a single party, dominates all aspects of civil life.

Transcendental A term used by Kant to designate the necessary mental preconditions for the possibility of gaining knowledge of objects outside the mind. These conditions include space and time as forms of sensory intuition as well as the categories of understanding, such as causality and substance. More generally, any condition may be said to be transcendental if it is necessary for the possibility of experience, action, or personal identity.

Truth A term used by Hegel to designate the correspondence of a reality with its idea. Hegel reverses the common sense understanding of truth as correspondence of thought (idea) with a pregiven object. On Hegel's reading, existing reality can be criticized as "untrue," or as a partial realization (appearance) of its ideal essence. For Hegel, only the totality of a fully mature historical form of spiritual life, such as that characteristic of Western civilization, can be called "true" in his sense.

Worldview An expression that denotes the system of beliefs that globally informs a given culture's outlook on life; that is, its basic way of perceiving reality and organizing society.

INDEX